D1610109

Labour Governments
and Private Industry

Labour Governments and Private Industry

The Experience of 1945–1951

edited by
H. MERCER
N. ROLLINGS
and
J. D. TOMLINSON

EDINBURGH UNIVERSITY PRESS

© Edinburgh University Press, 1992

Edinburgh University Press
22 George Square, Edinburgh

Typeset in Alphacomp English
by Pioneer Associates Ltd., Perthshire, and
printed in Great Britain by
the University Press, Cambridge

A CIP record for this book is
available from the British Library.

ISBN 0 7486 0339 5

Contents

Notes on the Contributors

MARTIN CHICK is Lecturer in Economic History, Edinburgh University
MARGUERITE DUPREE is a Research Fellow at the Wellcome Unit for
the History of Medicine, Glasgow University and Senior Research
Fellow, Wolfson College, Cambridge
DAVID EDGERTON is Lecturer at the Centre for the History of Science,
Technology and Medicine, Manchester University
LEWIS JOHNMAN is Senior Lecturer in Economic History, Thames
Polytechnic
HELEN MERCER is Lecturer in Economic and Social History, Leeds
University
NICHOLAS PRONAY is Director of the Institute of Communications
Studies, Leeds University
NEIL ROLLINGS is Lecturer in Economic History, Glasgow University
NICK TIRATSOO is Lecturer at the Centre for the Study of Social
History, Warwick University
JIM TOMLINSON is Reader in Economics, Brunel University
RICHARD WHITING is Lecturer in History, Leeds University

Preface

Most of the papers in this book were given at a conference in September 1990 held under the auspices of the LSE Business History Unit. We are grateful to the Unit, and its Director, Terry Gourvish, for his support, and to the Nuffield Foundation and Brunel University for financial assistance for the conference.

We would like to thank the other participants at the conference for their support and contributions. We would also like to thank certain people closer to these events for their views and their interest in the project: E. F. L. Brech, William Hughes and Peter Shore who attended the conference and Douglas Jay who sent written comments.

One

Introduction

HELEN MERCER, NEIL ROLLINGS and
JIM TOMLINSON

BACKGROUND

The Labour governments of 1945 to 1951 must be viewed as crucial for the British economy, laying down the lines of development from the Second World War until at least the 1970s. On short-term criteria the period saw the successful transition from a war economy to a peacetime economy centred around the need to increase exports and production. Viewing the longer term, some writers believe the Labour governments swung the economy along decisively new lines: structural re-orientation, an increase in workers' share of the national income and a government which had a clear set of objectives for reconstruction.[1] For others the Labour governments missed a unique opportunity to introduce and pursue long-term interventionist strategies of modernisation, let alone more socialist objectives of major shifts in wealth, ownership and power to the working class.[2] Conservatives and neo-liberal economists accuse the post-war Labour governments of embarking on a long – and disastrous – period of 'too much government' when planning, industrial interventionism and undue emphasis on the welfare state stifled the spirit of free enterprise.[3]

From these standpoints, policies towards and relations with private industry are central to an examination of the role of the Labour governments in tackling Britain's long-term industrial problems. It is the performance of this sector, representing 80 per cent of manufacturing output in 1950, that is of most importance for Britain's economic development. Thus Arnold Rogow's prime justification for his book with Peter Shore, *The Labour Government and British Industry 1945–51*, published in 1955, was that it was this subject that would 'throw the most light on the substantive impact of the Labour government'.[4]

Yet the subject has received scant attention from economic historians and economists. The vast majority of works on government economic policy in this period have concentrated on the macro-economic level of demand management and the 'Keynesian revolution', short-term policy objectives or on nationalisation. The focus of the major work on the economic policy of the period, Cairncross's *Years of Recovery*, is wholly macro-economic, with a relatively brief and late chapter on nationalisation and omitting 'any extended discussion of regional, commercial and industrial policy'.[5] Nationalisation set the tone for the Labour governments' relations with private industry: according to many leading industrialists of the time nationalisation immediately soured the relationship.[6] The background threat of public ownership is very important in understanding the reactions of the business community, but it is equally important to set nationalisation in the context of the much larger sphere of private ownership.

Thus two works written in the 1950s remain the most comprehensive accounts of Labour's relations with the private sector: Rogow's noted above and the less well-known *Crisis in Britain* (1950) by Robert Brady.[7] Both works pointed to the *ad hoc* nature of policy and the need for a more enduring approach. In addition the contemporary PEP study of *Government and Industry*[8] provides a useful summary of areas of government intervention and the framework of contacts between Labour and the private sector. Otherwise Labour's relationship with private industry has been subsumed under chronologically broader analyses, concerned with tracing the evolution of a new governmental framework for business operations.[9] Planning has been the focus of much of the work on the relationship between government and industry.[10] More recently a series of monographs have detailed aspects of government–industry relations in the post-war period.[11]

Studies of the Labour Party and 'Parliamentary Socialism' comment on Labour's relationship with the private sector and the historical significance of the Labour Party in government.[12] Miliband and Coates have emphasised the constraints placed by private industry on Labour's policies, Miliband castigating Labour for failing to challenge 'the power of the men who continued to control the country's economic resources'.[13] Howell believes that Labour came to view industry as a 'necessary partner' in a relationship which was 'largely on industry's own terms'.[14] From a different angle, Stephen Blank's study of the Federation of British Industry (FBI), Britain's peak industrial trade association and business lobby group, tries to clear private industry of the charge of obstructionism. He and others attribute the apparently cordial relationship between Labour and the private sector to a commendable 'moderation' on both sides.[15]

This volume seeks to correct the focus of economic historians to date and to give historical and archival perspective to these debates. Three themes are central to this: the extent to which Labour policies were socialist, or 'Labourite', the role of the Labour governments as a modernising agency in the private sector,[16] and the power of private industry to set parameters to government policies.

We therefore set out with questions not dissimilar from those posed over thirty-five years ago by Rogow and Shore:

(1) Was the 1945–51 revolution a genuine revolution; that is, was there a substantial transfer of power from the middle to the working classes? (2) To what extent did the displaced groups, primarily business or business-related, co-operate with the Labour Government and on what terms? (3) Where there was conflict between Government and industry, how did business opposition manifest itself, in general and in particular? (4) Was the Labour Government able to influence, to any considerable extent, the structure, psychology, and objectives of British industry?[17]

Of course few people now have any belief in the revolutionary intent or impact of the 1945–51 Labour governments. There was minimal shift in wealth to the working class, 'business-related' groups were not displaced from the corridors of power.[18] Keith Middlemas argues that the influence of the TUC on the formulation of Labour policy declined in this period, relative to its own wartime position and that of 'business'.[19]

This volume seeks to look again at some of these issues. It divides into two sections – one covering policies intended for and affecting all private manufacturing industry, the second covering specific sectors of private manufacturing. Banking and distribution are not covered, nor some areas of policy like company legislation. But the concentration on some key sectors of manufacturing industry and vital policy areas relates to developments which have most informed the criticisms of government economic policy from both the right and the left.

With these acknowledged limitations in the evidence provided, we turn now to some conclusions which may be drawn from the chapters in this volume, seeking to identify the objectives of Labour policy towards private industry, the instruments chosen to pursue their policies and the nature of the constraints placed upon policy by the influence of business groups and firms.

POLICY OBJECTIVES, INSTRUMENTS AND CONSTRAINTS

The chapters in this volume show that the period of the 1945 to 1951 Labour governments was crucial, not only for the British economy, but also for the development of the Labour Party and Labour economic thought. It is in their experience of dealing with the private sector that some of the most important trends in thought and policy may be traced.

The Labour government came to office in 1945 with few policies for the private sector, and with little history of consideration of the question. Prior to 1945 much of the left's political energy had been devoted to nationalisation plans, while the 'New Fabians' worked to apply Keynesianism and orthodox micro-economic analysis to clearly defined Labour aims.[20] The 1945 election manifesto, *Let Us Face the Future*, therefore had a short-term commitment to controls to ease the transition from war to peace, but in the long term its one promise was to prevent 'anti-social restrictive practices' in the private sector. There were, in this document and others, vaguer commitments to gear government departments to 'spur industry forward', to promote the application of science and research to industry, to give help to the export industries and to proceed in an atmosphere of consultation and co-operation with both sides of industry.[21] However, the nature of these aims, and the manner in which they were to be implemented were left open. In 1950, Harold Wilson prepared a paper for his colleagues in government, 'The State and Private Industry', reflecting on his time as President of the Board of Trade. He noted that, 'this problem of the relationship between Government and private industry is almost a vacuum in Socialist thought'. One failure he identified lay in the Labour Party itself: 'Little attention was paid either by the theoretical or the practical side of the movement to the problem of the role of the private sector in a socialist economy'.[22]

Instead much policy towards private industry was evolved while the government was in power. Thus Labour's 'one distinctive policy for the private sector',[23] the Working Parties and later Development Councils, was not mentioned in the 1945 manifesto, and in fact owed much to civil service wartime reconstruction discussions.[24]

As the limits on the size of the public sector grew clearer (with the consolidation of the nationalisation programme and a more explicit commitment to a 'mixed economy') the development of policy for a more-or-less permanently defined private sector became pressing. Between 1945 and 1951 the research department considered forms of intervention in privately owned industry, many of which fell only a little short of nationalisation: state wholesaling agencies with control over retailers and suppliers, state-appointed directors, public companies to compete with private firms in some industries.[25] Indeed, in 1948, when considering the content of the next election manifesto, a special sub-committee of the policy committee was devoted to privately owned industry, and was chaired by Aneurin Bevan.[26] The subcommittee on industries for nationalisation also provided a forum to discuss a range of instruments to control or direct private industry.[27]

The constant debate within the Labour movement is apparent from many of the contributions in this book. These debates within the Labour Party have continued since: the role of industrial democracy, the significance of the supposed separation of ownership and management, the balance between competition, monopoly and regulation, between planning and the price mechanism.[28] Indeed, in tracing the evolution of policies a number of tensions between very different approaches and analyses is evident.

The first tension in policy arose between Labour as a party of socialism and Labour as a government 'modernising' the existing system of private ownership of production. On one level no diversion of policy may be apparent between these two outlooks. Development Councils embodied both the 'Labourite' principle of union participation in management and schemes to make industries more efficient. Controls, declared Gaitskell, were 'the distinguishing feature of British socialist policy' and were to be used not only for budgetary purposes but also to stimulate production and productivity (Rollings, p. 22). Taxation policy aimed at both taxing that form of wealth considered to be the least legitimate – inheritance – while doing nothing to discourage enterprise (Whiting, chapter 7). Yet precisely this emphasis on fostering enterprise, apparent in policies on cartels and taxation, and on efficient management evident in productivity policy served to legitimise private capitalism through a belief in the ability of the market and the profit motive to induce reform.

The second tension in policy evident in the chapters of this book is the almost schizophrenic attitude to the role of the market, competition and free enterprise. On the one hand, the Labour government adopted a competition policy in 1948 and oversaw the removal of a wide range of controls and greater use of the price mechanism. The Ministry of Supply cited healthy competition among defence contractors as a reason for resisting Labour Party calls for nationalisation of defence production. On the other hand, Labour did not believe the market could deliver and sought to promote planned rationalisation in iron and steel, shipbuilding and cotton. It also gave covert support to the minimum-price scheme of the Yarn Spinners' Association.

A third tension, and one frequently referred to in the chapters here (Tomlinson, Edgerton, Tiratsoo, Chick and Dupree) is between Labour's short-term needs of promoting production and exports and long-term aims of industrial restructuring. The need to promote exports has been cited as a cause of the retreat from nationalisation and emphasis on co-operation with private industry.[29] In reality, the Labour government often had to adopt a pragmatic approach of trying to pick those companies with the best prospects of meeting their short-term requirements and favour them in resource allocation (Tiratsoo, Edgerton). Sometimes these companies were likely to be the most efficient and successful in the long term, sometimes they were not. None the less these concerns acted as a clear constraint on the long-term restructuring of industry. In iron and steel unwilling businessmen were able 'to exploit the inherent tension between the long-term aim of rationalisation and the immediate political concern of maximising production and minimising unemployment' (Chick, pp. 85–6). Unforeseen events presented a further constraint. The coal crisis pointed to the dangers of ignoring the short term and while Marshall Aid provided financial assistance, until the level of aid was known it was impossible to take any decisions on the future development of the economy. In similar vein Rollings comments on the irony that the need to introduce temporary controls again during the Korean War actually helped to prevent a Bill for permanent controls.

A fourth and final point of tension was in the choice of methods to be used in modernising industry – between interventionist, formal and legalistic instruments and those resting on co-operation and voluntarism. Generally, Labour's policies looked favourably on the latter approach. The 'persuasion' and 'education' of industry was a note sounded over many issues: cartels, controls and productivity. A faith in consultation is indicated in those least dirigiste of institutions, the Advisory Councils in the motor car industry, shipbuilding and engineering. Many chapters, however, record that by 1950 there was a perceptible shift in attitude and increasing flirtation with more coercive measures: in cartels a tough line on resale price maintenance, in controls a Bill to make them permanent, in shipbuilding a Development Council, in iron and steel the final nationalisation. Moreover, as chapter 3 on productivity indicates, Wilson, President of the Board of Trade since 1947, was proposing ways to increase the government's leverage at the level of the firm.

The tensions in all these areas were not resolved in any neat, clear-cut way. Policies tended to sacrifice long-term solutions to short-term needs, state planning and control to the market and industrial self-government, interventionism to voluntarism. But by 1950 the thoughts of ministers were actually tending in the opposite direction. As Rollings points out, the Labour government was neither running out of steam nor willing to compromise with industry at all costs.

Nevertheless, in this situation 'socialist' principles made little headway. But the Labour government was distinctive in its commitment to efficiency, its emphasis on science, research and technology, on better management, on rationalisation, on the gearing of industry for production and competitiveness – a package of reforms that may be subsumed under the title of modernisation. Indeed, the 1945–51 Labour governments may be seen as a high point in the Efficiency movement in Britain which originated in the period of Victorian 'failure', and which had such popularity on the Fabian wing of the Labour Party. From this standpoint it clearly seems correct to argue, as Nick Tiratsoo and Marguerite Dupree do in their chapters, that this Labour government is innocent of the accusation that it sacrificed industrial strength to building 'New Jerusalems' of the welfare state. Whiting's chapter on taxation indicates, indeed, rather the opposite: the key to taxation policy was the desire to avoid discouraging enterprise. This ranked even higher than redistributional concerns, policies for dividend restraint being designed to facilitate wage restraint.

However, many chapters cast doubt on the extent to which these policies were either new or specifically Labourite. Cripps and Wilson both emerge as important figures in the development of policy, but many Labour plans bore the imprint of Coalition discussions, of reform-minded civil servants, even of the United States of America. Trade-union ideas had little impact, except in the failed experiment with Development Councils. However, David Edgerton argues that the Ministry of Supply only became the main 'sponsoring' department of civil industries as a result of decisions by the Labour Cabinet, and this ministry is key to a study of the government's pursuit of 'developmental' and discretionary industrial policies and the continuation of the 'warfare state'.

But the organisational legacy of the wartime Coalition government is very important. Other contributions demonstrate that, given the weakness of policy instruments discussed up to 1945, the previously existing pattern of government–industry relations became crucial to understanding Labour's approach. The general context of Labour's relations with industry and with businessmen was one inherited from the war. Thus the system of contacts established remained largely untouched; even the businessmen's special committee in the Board of Trade continued. Both Rogow and Brady comment on Labour's criticism of this cosy relationship during the war but their failure to challenge it once in power.[30] The FBI was recognised as, and encouraged to be, the main spokesperson for industrial interests as a whole, with representation in ten ministries and departments, and thirty-seven committees, including the Economic Planning Board from 1947 and the National Production Advisory Council on Industry.[31] Indeed, the period of the post-war Labour governments has been identified as one where the influence of the FBI with government, in terms of constant contacts and routine consultation, reached an unprecedented and not-to-be-repeated peak.[32] It had in fact been Labour ministers under the Coalition who had contributed to the FBI's position: Dalton, as President of the Board of Trade, appointed Sir Charles Bruce-Gardner, a leading figure in the FBI as Chief Executive for Industrial Reconversion, a move criticised by contending business representatives in Whitehall.[33]

Nevertheless many of Labour's policies for the private sector may be seen as a continuing attempt to establish new agencies for modernisation aimed at re-moulding this legacy. Michael Young, who headed the Labour Party's research department at the time, put this as a primary aim of Labour's policies for private industry.[34] The most important of these were the Development Councils: the Cotton Board was to be a 'model for the post-war organisation of government relations with private industry' (Dupree, p. 153). The emphasis on tripartism is to be found also in the non-statutory Advisory Councils, while government–industry collaboration found another form in the formulation of the pre-nationalisation steel plans. A host of other agencies are catalogued in

Tomlinson's chapter and we may add to these the Monopolies and Restrictive Practices Commission. However, as Tomlinson argues and many chapters bear out, these were often dependent on pre-existing institutions, owed little to Labour thought, and were mainly *ad hoc* in their approach. The positive embracing of *ad hoc* institutions and pragmatism – Morrison's work indicates a certain pride in this position[35] – was bound to leave the Labour government wide open to a mass of influences, and to hamper the formulation of distinctively Labourite policies.

Thus the chapters in this book indicate that Labour's instruments of modernisation were weak. We have been especially concerned to analyse whether or not this failure was attributable primarily to the opposition of private industrialists themselves.

The chapters presented here indicate that private businessmen managed to establish effective limits to the Labour governments' modernising urges. At times legislation was dropped partly in anticipation of industrial hostility. In the case of monopoly policy, FBI representations moulded the form of legislation adopted. In the case of productivity the FBI co-operated only as far as they felt it was politically necessary. In the sectors studied powerful trade associations, like the Society of Motor Manufacturers and Traders (SMMT), used their pre-existing contacts to lobby the Ministry of Supply and claim media attention. In shipbuilding much evidence is cited of prejudiced hostility to Labour of a bone-headed variety. Only in defence did the Ministry of Supply override the claims of the main aircraft trade association. Dupree argues that previous industrial support for the wartime Cotton Board largely accounts for its survival as a Development Council.

But businesmen were not a united group, and where there were sufficient divergences of interest their representatives were tied. This comes out in Whiting's chapter on taxation, an area in which Labour was able to implement many of its previously developed ideas. Similarly, industrialists' need for some level of investigation into certain types of industry allowed a weak and limited anti-cartel measure. On the other hand, divisions among iron and steel producers, or between shipbuilders and shipowners do not appear to have been utilised by the Labour governments to carry through their policies. The role of the FBI deserves more attention in this context. It presented a false image of industrial unity; individual firms and trade associations may have been more willing to co-operate than the FBI allowed.

The chapters indicate various ways in which business feeling was transmitted to government. First, it came via departments and ministries, expressed either through FBI delegations, Working Parties and Development Councils, trade associations, or, as illustrated in the case of the Ministry of Supply, firms. Second, it was expressed through the

Conservative Party in the House of Commons. Third, the trade journals were a source of gauging industrial opinion. All these channels of communication have been touched on by contributors to this volume. It is also important to note that the relationship between government and private industry was not determined solely on the basis of policy formulation and implementation. Everyday and routine contact was also important (Tiratsoo, Edgerton).

Nevertheless, the strength of private industrialists cannot be viewed as an isolated feature. Some chapters – by Edgerton, Mercer and Tomlinson – draw attention to the way that Labour's own lack of focus not only increased industrial suspicions but also created a vacuum into which other actors stepped. While businessmen were one of these, other influences cannot be ignored.

The external pressures on the Labour governments, especially the need to maximise production and sustain exports, has already been discussed. Further external pressures were in defence spending, the Korean War and American political and economic pressure in the form of the Marshall Plan and the 1945 Loan. Defence spending came to dominate research and development spending, the Korean War led directly to a change of tack or a postponement of new legislation in the cases of controls and taxation. The United States figures as a direct influence on much policy, causing the government to withdraw plans to reduce British consumption of Hollywood films, to implement anti-cartel and productivity policies.

Finally civil servants emerge as a conservative influence on Labour ministers, being exceedingly cautious about disregarding what they perceived industrial feeling to be, in for instance the cotton industry, and over major policies such as cartels and controls.

These conclusions should be regarded as preliminary hypotheses which will need to be tested as more research on this vital topic is undertaken. It is hoped the chapters here will prove of relevance not only to a deeper understanding of the economic history of the post-war years and of a key 'moment' in the story of relative economic decline, but also of the evolution of government–industry relations as a factor in the weakness of modernising agencies in Britain. Finally, these essays may provide a point of historical contrast with the policy debates confronting the Labour Party today.

NOTES

The authors would like to thank the contributors to this volume for their helpful comments on an earlier draft of this introduction. Responsibility for the errors is entirely ours, however.

1. A. Cairncross *Years of Recovery* (1985) p. 509; K. O. Morgan *Labour in Power* (Oxford, 1984); S. Newton and D. Porter *Modernisation Frustrated* (1988).

2. P. A. Hall 'The State and Economic Decline' in B. Elbaum and W. Lazonick eds. *The Decline of the British Economy* (Oxford, 1986); D. N. Pritt *The Labour Government 1945–51* (1963); D. Coates *The Labour Party and the Struggle for Socialism* (Cambridge, 1975); R. Miliband *Parliamentary Socialism* (1964).
3. C. Barnett *The Audit of War* (1986); J. Jewkes *Ordeal by Planning* (1948); M. Thatcher 'What Has Gone Wrong?' D. Coates and J. Hillard eds. *The Economic Decline of Modern Britain* (Brighton, 1986) pp. 64–6.
4. A. A. Rogow and P. Shore *The Labour Government and British Industry 1945–51* (Oxford, 1955) p. 1.
5. Cairncross op. cit., p. xi.
6. Sir Norman Kipping *Summing Up* (1972) p. 16.
7. Rogow and Shore op. cit.; R. Brady *Crisis In Britain* (1950).
8. PEP *Government and Industry* (1952).
9. J. W. Grove *Government and Industry in Britain* (1962); A. Shonfield *Modern Capitalism* (Oxford, 1965); R. S. Edwards and H. Townsend *Business Enterprise* (1959); B. W. E. Alford, R. Lowe and N. Rollings eds. *Economic Planning in Britain 1943–51: A Guide to Sources in the Public Record Office* (H.M.S.O., 1992).
10. A. Robinson *Economic Planning in the United Kingdom* (1967); A. Budd *The Politics of Economic Planning* (Manchester, 1978); J. Leruez *Economic Planning and Politics in Britain* (Bath, 1975).
11. M. W. Dupree 'Struggling with Destiny: the Cotton Industry, Overseas Trade Policy and the Cotton Board, 1940–1959' *Business History* Vol. xxxii No. 4 Oct. 1990 106–28; H. Mercer 'The Labour Governments of 1945–1951 and Private Industry' in N. Tiratsoo ed. *The Attlee Years* (1991); K. Middlemas *Power, Competition and the State. Volume 1: Britain in Search of Balance 1940–61* (1986); J. Singleton 'Planning for Cotton, 1945–1951' *Economic History Review* Vol. xliii No. 1 Feb. 1990 62–78; J. Tomlinson 'The Failure of the Anglo-American Council on Productivity' *Business History* Vol. xxxiii, No. 1 Jan. 1991 82–92.
12. Miliband op. cit.; Coates op. cit.; D. Howell *British Social Democracy* (1976).
13. Miliband op. cit., p. 291.
14. Howell op. cit., p. 161.
15. S. Blank *Industry and Government in Britain* (1973); R. Streat 'Government Consultation with Industry' *Public Administration* Vol. xxxix Spring 1959; S. E. Finer 'The Political Power of Private Capital' *Sociological Review* Vol. iv No. 1 1956.
16. Concern with this is the theme of many recent works, e.g. Newton and Porter op. cit.; F. Green, *Restructuring the U.K. Economy* (1989); Elbaum and Lazonick op. cit.
17. Rogow and Shore op. cit., pp. 1–2.
18. Blank op. cit., pp. 106–10.
19. Middlemas op. cit., p. 148.
20. E. Durbin *New Jerusalems* (1985); S. Brooke 'Revisionists and Fundamentalists: the Labour Party and economic policy during the Second World War' *Historical Journal* Vol. 32 No. 1 1989 157–75.
21. F. W. S. Craig *British General Election Manifestos 1900–1974* (1975) pp. 123–31.
22. Public Record Office (hereafter PRO) CAB124/1200 Memo. by the President of the Board of Trade 'The State and Private Industry' 4/5/1950.
23. Rogow and Shore op. cit., p. 76.
24. Mercer op. cit.
25. PRO CAB124/1200 Memo. by H. Wilson op. cit.; Labour Party Archives, National Museum of Labour History, Manchester (hereafter LPA) R.D.1/ September 1945 'A Labour Policy for Privately-Owned Industry'; LPA R.D.69/October 1947 G. Miller 'Socialism and Private Enterprise'.

26. Morgan op. cit., p. 121; LPA Home Policy Committee minutes, 25/11/1947.
27. LPA R.D.129/July 1948 'Enabling Bill for Nationalisation; R.D.130/July 1948 'Industries for Nationalisation' are examples.
28. C. A. R. Crosland 'The Transition from Capitalism' in R. H. S. Crossman ed. *New Fabian Essays* (3rd edn, 1970); J. Schneer *Labour's Conscience: the Labour Left 1945–51* (1988); S. Haseler *The Gaitskellites – Revisionism in the Labour Party* (1969).
29. K. O. Morgan 'The Rise and Fall of Public Ownership in Britain' in J. M. W. Bean ed. *The Political Culture of Modern Britain* (1987) pp. 288–90.
30. Rogow and Shore op. cit., pp. 49–72; Brady op. cit.
31. Rogow and Shore op. cit., Appendices and pp. 91–3.
32. Blank op. cit.; W. Grant and D. Marsh *The Confederation of British Industry* (1977); Middlemas op. cit., pp. 143–6.
33. Dalton Diaries, London School of Economics, Box 31, 18/10/1944 and 19/10/1944.
34. M. Young *Labour's Plan for Plenty* (1946) p. 86.
35. J. Leruez op. cit., p. 62.

PART ONE

The Policies

Two

'The Reichstag method of governing'?
The Attlee governments and permanent
economic controls[1]

NEIL ROLLINGS

In the King's Speech on 31 October 1950 it was announced that the Labour government intended to introduce legislation allowing it to take on a permanent basis 'powers to regulate production, distribution and consumption and to control prices'.[2] This was by no means an uncontroversial, nor unimportant, measure.[3] Yet few seem to have heard of the proposed legislation or incorporated it into their analyses of the Labour governments. One obvious reason why this is the case is that the legislation was never brought before Parliament. However, it is still surprising that with all the interest in, and research on, the 1945–51 governments, based on the files now available in the Public Records Office, little has been made of this topic. The only references to it have been made in passing, most notably by Cairncross, Alford and Tomlinson.[4]

This chapter will attempt to remedy this situation by showing the importance which Labour ministers placed on the continuance of some controls in the long term throughout their period in power. Ignoring this, it is argued, has meant that existing perceptions of the last few years of the Labour governments, from 1949 to 1951, are to some extent misconceived and are in need of qualification. This desire to continue certain controls raises issues in a number of areas, in particular with regard to the concept of 'Butskellism' and the importance attached to budgetary policy.[5] In this chapter, however, the focus is on what this subject implies about the relationship between the Labour governments and the private sector. Obviously, the implementation of controls was a crucial aspect in determining the relationship between the government and private industry, since it was at this level that direct contact was greatest and its impact clearest. However, this chapter concentrates on the formulation of policy because this established the framework in which the implementation of controls took place. It is one thing to trace the growing ineffectiveness of particular controls, the increasing criticism of them and of those who operated them, but these all become far more significant given the context that the Labour government saw a permanent role for certain basic controls.

Existing interpretations of the Labour governments often suggest that in their last few years they ran out of steam and of ideas. Alternatively, it is seen as the period when the Labour governments openly came to accept that the basis of policy should be the amelioration of the existing economic order rather than the establishment of a new economic order. Pelling in *The Labour Governments 1945–51* has a final narrative chapter entitled, 'On the Defensive, 1950–51', and Kenneth Morgan likewise concludes *Labour in Power 1945–1951* with 'The Retreat from Jerusalem'.[6]

One aspect of this interpretation was the demise of economic planning and the growing reliance placed on indirect Keynesian demand management through budgetary policy. As part of this trend, economic controls which had been continued after the war were seen to play a declining role; each individual control being removed as and when the particular shortage was alleviated. This shift in policy has been perceived both by commentators on economic policy, like Sam Brittan, and those tracing the development of Labour Party economic thought.[7] For example, Rogow, whose study of *The Labour Government and British Industry 1945–51* was the starting point of this collection, wrote, 'Had there been no Korean War it is probable that Labour Government planning in 1951 would have been almost entirely confined to Budget policy and certain balance-of-payments controls'.[8] This view is two sided. On the one hand it charts the rise of budgetary policy and on the other, the demise of economic controls, both of which occurred under the Labour governments.

Recent research has done little to change this interpretation. There has been no change of view that decontrol was by and large inevitable as conditions returned to normal after the war and the supply and demand for individual goods came closer to balance, nor that the budget was the dominant policy tool by 1951.[9] Jim Tomlinson, in his recent work *Public Policy and the Economy since 1900*, has summed up current thinking:

> Whatever its underlying significance, the budget of November 1947 can certainly be seen as marking a shift within Labour policy from the emphasis on the use of controls to use of the budget to regulate the economy. Controls were thereafter dismantled, symbolized by Harold Wilson's 'bonfire' of controls in 1948. Planning came increasingly to mean national income planning and the use of the budget to manage demand.[10]

In other words, perceptions in this regard have changed little since Rogow.

The other aspect of existing perceptions refers to the Labour governments' relations with private industry. Controls have been seen as the mechanism by which the Labour government could have enforced structural change on private industry and ensured efficiency. Particularly important in this sense was the use of investment control, raw material allocations and price control. Thus with decontrol 'all the micro-economic decisions on the future structure of the economy . . . [were] handed back to the market'.[11] Indeed, decontrol under the Labour governments from 1948 is normally portrayed as, to a large extent, a response to mounting pressure from industry for the removal of unnecessary and bureaucratic controls.

The continued existence of the controls on the statute book by no means meant that they were rigorously enforced, since many controls were operated by businessmen. The government did refuse industry's request for self-regulation of controls, but in reality, practice, it is argued, was not vastly different.[12] However, while this may have had some impact on perceptions of the effectiveness of controls, ultimately it was the existence of legislative powers to control which was crucial. Without these, the issue of who should operate controls became redundant. The removal of controls and the growing hostility of private industry to the Labour governments, especially after 1949, are seen as illustrating the lack of an alternative basis for policy in relation to the private sector.[13] Accordingly, with decontrol a vacuum emerged in Labour's policies towards private industry, previously hidden by the use of physical controls.[14] In other words, decontrol removed an important element of both macro-economic and micro-economic policy of the Labour governments, and changed the nature of the relationship between the Labour governments and private industry.

Yet this conventional picture of the Labour governments' economic policies presents an over-simplified image of decontrol and of Labour ministers' attitudes towards controls more generally. The theoretical roots of Labour's use of economic controls lie in the 1930s literature on economic planning. Along with nationalisation, controls were to be used to implement planning. In particular this meant controls over investment and prices.[15] Given this, it is unsurprising that Labour, when elected in 1945, saw a major role in economic policy for controls.[16]

In reality, the controls which Labour governments were to use between 1945 and 1951 had little to do with the theoretical basis of economic planning and of Labour thought in the 1930s. They were tied far more closely to the realities of the aftermath of the war. Controls over prices, over manpower, allocation of raw materials, rationing, and licensing of building, production, imports and exports were all introduced during the early stages of the war. These took either the form of specific legislation, as with most price controls, or of an Order in Council issued under one of the various Emergency Powers (Defence) Acts.[17] Although reinforcing each other, each control related to a particular objective and the system as a whole was built up piecemeal. Coverage was

extensive. Price control covered about half of all consumer expenditure
at the end of the war, some of which could not sensibly be controlled or
was influenced in other ways.[18] All raw materials of any importance
were subject to allocation. Of the input into industrial production of the
fifteen main raw materials, it has been estimated that in 1946 94 per cent
by value were subject to allocation. Similarly, virtually all imports were
purchased on government account or privately under licence. The
Labour government simply continued this existing network of controls.

It is often said how lucky the Labour government was since it came to
power with the controls which it required already in place, rather than
having to introduce them rapidly. Moreover, there was general
acceptance that controls would have to continue into the transition
period after the war. This included the Conservative opposition which
desired the removal of these controls 'as quickly as the need for them
disappears', but accepted that for some time that need would continue
until the supply situation improved.[19]

Accordingly, there was little disagreement about the need for the
wartime powers of control to be continued after their expiry when the
new Labour government introduced the Supplies and Services
(Transitional Powers) Act 1945. Regulations could be used to secure
sufficient supplies essential to the well-being of the community or to
ensure their equitable distribution, to facilitate demobilisation, to assist
the readjustment of industry to peacetime requirements, to assist in
relief of other countries and to control prices. The only aspect to which
the Conservatives objected was that the powers were to be granted for
five years instead of two, which they considered sufficient. Labour
justified this on the grounds that the government could not embark on a
long-term plan with powers only for two years.

Further legislation to renew other Defence Regulations followed of
which the most noteworthy was the Supplies and Services (Extended
Purposes) Act 1947, which was introduced as a response to the
convertibility crisis. This added to the 1945 legislation three additional
purposes for which regulations could be used, and which were also to
feature prominently in the first draft of legislation for permanent
economic controls. These were:

   a) for promoting the productivity of industry, commerce, and
   agriculture;
   b) for fostering and directing exports and reducing imports, or
   imports of any classes, from all or any countries and for redressing
   the balance of trade; and
   c) generally for ensuring that the whole resources of the community
   are available for use, and are used, in a manner best calculated to
   serve the interests of the community.[20]

The Conservative Opposition objected more strongly on this occasion, in particular to purpose (c), demanding to know how the legislation was proposed to be used. Morrison could not specify but told the House that it was not a 'deep dark plot . . . to conduct a social revolution by Defence Regulations'.[21] In contrast, Churchill saw the Bill as 'a blank cheque for totalitarian government', although he did not think Labour ministers were 'likely to be second Hitlers'.[22]

This legislation extended the purposes for which controls could be used but did not extend the controls themselves. Indeed, at the same time as this legislation was being introduced in August 1947, decontrol first appears on the policy agenda. Between late July and mid-September 1947 the Board of Trade carried out an internal review of the relationship between the convertibility crisis and price controls. Its officials, including Alec Cairncross, then the Board of Trade's Economic Adviser, concluded that there should be some decontrol of prices, resulting in some rise in prices to help mop up excess purchasing power.[23]

By 1948 decontrol had started in earnest and, on the basis of existing interpretations, was to continue relentlessly thereafter, apart from the brief interruption of this trend caused by the Korean War. There was a growing awareness that some controls were no longer effective, nor enforced, such as labour controls, and there were growing demands that they should be removed. In February 1948 Harold Wilson, as President of the Board of Trade, and George Strauss, the Minister of Supply, appointed Examiners of Controls with instructions to recommend the scrapping of any controls which could safely be removed.[24] Later that year, Wilson announced the first of his famous bonfires of controls, so called because of its announcement on 5 November.

Furthermore, Wilson's Permanent Secretary, Sir John Woods, proposed in April 1948 the setting up of a high-level working party to examine the effects of government controls on preserving existing inefficiencies.[25] This issue was submitted to a new committee, the Controls and Efficiency Committee, established in June 1948, and chaired by Sir Bernard Gilbert, one of the Second Secretaries of the Treasury and a strong supporter of decontrol.[26] Andrew Chester has pointed out that the work of the committee illustrates the view prevalent amongst senior officials that 'controls clearly were an unsatisfactory hangover from wartime. [Senior officials] were looking for opportunities to re-establish the operation of market forces as far as was possible within the constraints of government policy and the economic situation'.[27]

The process of decontrol is then generally seen to continue until the Korean War, with the removal of general steel allocations in May 1950 an important stage in this development. There were minor fluctuations but the trend was clearly towards decontrol. With the Korean War, which started in June 1950, it was felt necessary to strengthen existing controls and to reintroduce some others on a variety of consumer goods. Even then, as Dow points out, this was rather belated, not imposed until July 1951 and in exceptional and temporary conditions when import prices were rising dramatically.[28] With the election in October of that year of a Conservative government committed to decontrol and with the easing of the import-price position, decontrol continued afresh in 1952 and 1953. Certainly then, there is a considerable degree of decontrol under the Labour governments which would give support to the conventional interpretation outlined.

However, even amongst those who follow this interpretation, the more sophisticated analyses do admit some problems. First, Dow, in his chapter on direct controls in *The Management of the British Economy 1945–60*, admitted that although private importers took an increasing share of imports, 'what they could import remained heavily restricted till 1953'.[29] Similarly, allocations of industrial materials 'remained of some importance till 1953 or so', and price control 'remained extensive till 1953 or so'.[30] Also, until 1954 most building work was subject to control. While there was decontrol under the Labour governments a considerable part of the economy was still controlled when it lost power in 1951.

A second qualification comes from Cairncross. In a general consideration of the purpose of controls he has written:

> At times the Labour Party had laid stress on the controls as a planning device . . . The first comment to be made is that since nearly all the controls were gradually abandoned the government cannot have held to a consistent view that they were indispensable to economic planning . . . This did not mean, however, that the controls had no place in meeting those [macro-economic] objectives. It might be a diminishing role as circumstances returned to normal and it was found possible to discontinue or relax some of the controls. But the fact that the controls lingered on into the 1950s suggests that governments, rightly or wrongly, did regard them as useful, even after the transition, in the management of the economy.[31]

Cairncross's point that governments, especially the Labour governments, found controls useful is crucial. The assumption inherent in the conventional picture that there was a natural and accepted trend towards decontrol is false and an over-simplification that views all controls in the same light. Here the consideration of permanent economic controls during 1949 to 1951 is central. Labour ministers appear to have believed that whilst unnecessary controls should be removed, some controls should be retained permanently. This is clear from both their comments and their actions.

Looking first at ministers' comments, as early as 1946, Evan Durbin believed that permanent controls over prices, building investment, imports and borrowing would be required.[32] Cripps, in June 1948, and Douglas Jay, the Economic Secretary to the Treasury, in March 1949, both voiced their concerns that decontrol was going too far.[33]

However, the three most important ministers here were Harold Wilson and Herbert Morrison, both normally portrayed as keen decontrollers, and later Hugh Gaitskell. Harold Wilson as has already been said, introduced the bonfire of controls. Yet in October 1948, the month before the first such bonfire, a Labour Party Subcommittee on Privately Owned Industry, chaired by Nye Bevan, had given Wilson the task of preparing a statement showing what powers under the Supplies and Services (Transitional Powers) Act would need to be made permanent.[34] Wilson continued to be involved in discussions within the Labour Party about the continuation of controls.

Moreover, it was Wilson who, in April 1949, made what appears to have been the first public announcement that the government intended to take action to ensure powers for permanent economic controls. He explained to the House of Commons that the government would 'maintain as a permanent part of our policy those controls . . . which are necessary to keep the economy on an even keel, and to maintain full employment'.[35]

Wilson spelt out the government's attitude in more detail during the devaluation debate in September of that year:

> Certain basic controls essential to the maintenance of full employment, to the proper location of industry, to the maintenance of our economy on an even keel – those controls will remain a permanent instrument of our national policy . . .
>
> What we want to get rid of as quickly as possible – and the right honourable Gentleman was wrong to saddle us with a desire to keep all these controls – are those controls which are a hang-over from the wartime administration, which restrict the handling or sale or manufacture of goods to specified firms engaged in their manufacture at some date in the past . . . limiting competition between those firms and preventing the entry of often enterprising, progressive, efficient firms from outside.[36]

Herbert Morrison, the Lord President of the Council, had been responsible for economic planning 1945–7, but here he approached the subject of permanent economic controls from a completely different angle, that of administration. In April 1949 he presented a memorandum to the Future Legislation Committee, which drew up the legislative programme for the following session. He pointed to the need for legislation to put 'into permanent form the wartime powers which are still required' as a replacement to the Supplies and Services (Transitional

Powers) Act which was due to expire in 1950.[37] An official committee, the Emergency Legislation Committee was then given the task of this review. From this date at least, Morrison appears to have been committed like Wilson to the retention of some permanent economic controls. In June 1949 he told the Labour Party Conference,

> The Executive and the Government have no intention that the Supplies and Services Act shall come to an end. It is an essential basis for the organisation of economic planning and control, and therefore we shall place a revised and permanent version of the Act on the Statute Book if we are returned to power.[38]

Finally, these beliefs were put into a more detailed form at the very beginning of 1950 by Hugh Gaitskell, then Minister of Fuel and Power but soon to become Minister of Economic Affairs and then Chancellor of the Exchequer. At an Economic Policy Committee meeting on 13 December 1949 he criticised a report from the official Programmes Committee, which drew up the annual import programme, for too readily assuming that reliance in the future would have to be placed on indirect means, in other words, budgetary policy, rather than direct controls.[39] As a result he and Jay drafted a paper for the Economic Policy Committee on 'Economic Planning and Liberalisation' (EPC(50)9), in which they expressed concern that the government would be drawn unconsciously to decontrol. The paper, described as 'first class' by Dalton, stressed that 'it is the use by the government of direct controls . . . which has been the distinguishing feature of British socialist policy'.[40] Moreover, controls were necessary to supplement the price mechanism in order to achieve full employment without runaway inflation and a fair distribution of income.

At the committee meeting to discuss the paper on 19 January 1950, Gaitskell, Wilson, Strachey and Bevan all favoured some permanent controls. Morrison said nothing and Cripps believed that 'there was a minimum of control beyond which they should not go'.[41] Reflecting ministers' differences with officials over the issue, one official noted that at the meeting there was 'a lot of talk about civil servants, reared in poor but honest Liberal homes, who gave misguided advice to ministers because of their background and upbringing'.[42] There is clear evidence, therefore, that many Labour ministers accepted the need for the permanent maintenance of some essential controls as a fundamental part of the government's policy. These essential controls were to be used in association with budgetary policy to ensure full employment whilst preventing an inflationary breakthrough and to ensure a fair distribution of income. Other controls, hanging over from the war, were no longer suitable, simply got in the way and should be removed.

Moreover, although ignored by most and considered only fleetingly by others, such as Cairncross and Tomlinson, action was taken by the Labour governments to implement these beliefs. First, the review of controls carried out by L. P. B. Merriam, the Board of Trade's Examiner of Controls, was not an ongoing process. Once he had completed his review, at the end of 1949, he left the Board of Trade.[43]

Second, ministers agreed at the end of May 1949 that an official committee should be established 'to make a comprehensive review of the powers and administrative machinery required in the long term for the control of capital'.[44] At the same time, following on from Morrison's paper to the Future Legislation Committee, in July 1949, the official Committee on Economic Controls was formed 'to consider what powers are likely to be required in the long term for operating economic controls on prices; production; consumption; centralised purchase; labour; and import and export licensing'.[45] Working on the assumption that policy objectives would remain in the same vein, the committee reported that, by and large, existing controls would continue to be required.[46] The price mechanism and budgetary policy were seen to play an increasing role but this would not remove the need for the powers to control continuing. The report explicitly excluded the possibility of positive powers, for example the purposive direction of industry and commerce to deal with a slump, because these would require new powers rather than simply a continuation of existing powers in the temporary legislation.

The same day as the final version of the committee's report was submitted to ministers, 27 March 1950, Morrison submitted a short paper to the Cabinet.[47] He felt that the Lord President's Committee could not consider the report and related papers without some general guidance from the Cabinet. He went on to propose the drafting of the necessary bill or bills to take permanent powers of economic control and price regulation for introduction at the beginning of the next session, hopefully before the emergency powers lapsed.[48] The Cabinet agreed to the proposals, which were to be the responsibility of the Lord President's Committee.[49]

The first draft of the Economic Powers Bill was submitted for consideration by the Lord President's Committee in July 1950.[50] The Bill covered negative powers over consumption, production and prices which could be used for four purposes (see Appendix 2.1). Both the powers and the purposes for which the powers could be used were extremely general and potentially far reaching. One official found the powers in the Bill 'so wide, and drawn in such general terms' that he could not imagine 'Parliament or public opinion standing for them in peacetime'.[51]

Yet with no apparent concern about the nature of these negative powers, the Lord President's Committee approved the Bill in principle. It was then submitted to Cabinet with the recommendation that the title of the Bill and the question of the inclusion of positive powers should be considered further, a recommendation approved by the Cabinet.[52] The issue of positive powers was submitted to Nye Bevan's Production Committee Subcommittee on Manufacture in Government-Controlled Establishments of Goods for Civilian Use.[53]

Bevan's subcommittee of ministers reported back to the Cabinet in mid-October.[54] It proposed that the government should take new powers to allow it to place orders on a continuing basis for products of all types produced by industry; to undertake the manufacture of any goods itself; and to sell any of the products obtained in either manner. Moreover, in an emergency money might be made available to private industry. These proposals caused grave concern to officials, most notably Gilbert who had chaired the Committee on Economic Controls. He believed the proposals were 'likely to cause disturbance or indeed alarm over a wide range of production'.[55]

Ministers, however, continued to believe that positive powers should play a part in the legislation but that further work was required before legislation could be introduced.[56] This was delegated to the Official Committee on the Economic Planning and Full Employment Bill. By February this committee reported with a new draft Bill now incorporating positive powers on the lines of Bevan's subcommittee's report.[57] However, the purposes for which the powers could be used and the powers themselves had now been recast to relate the powers to the policy of full employment (see Appendix 2.2).

This reflected ministerial discussions over the title of the Bill. Mirroring the move towards the inclusion of positive powers was the gradual shift in the title from one emphasising economic planning to one focusing on full employment. The Lord President's Committee when it had first considered the Economic Powers Bill had recommended further consideration of the title in order to make it more 'glamorous'.[58] When the Cabinet agreed on 23 October 1950 to the Bill's inclusion in the King's Speech it had now become the Economic Planning and Full Employment Bill.[59] It now had a preamble mentioning full employment but otherwise remained the Economic Powers Bill. However, Gaitskell believed this title verged on dishonesty and proposed at the new ministerial Committee on the Economic Planning and Full Employment Bill that full employment should form the basis of the Bill and the powers included.[60] Thereafter, until its demise, the Bill became known as the Full Employment Bill.

Clearly then, ministers in the course of 1950 invested a considerable amount of time on the appearance and contents of the draft legislation. It would seem reasonable given this to believe that Labour ministers were strongly committed to both the principle and the reality of introducing permanent economic powers, both of a negative and a positive nature. Yet on 15 February 1951 the Cabinet agreed that the Bill should not be proceeded with.[61] Instead, economic powers continued to rest on the annual renewal of the emergency powers and after the Korean War decontrol began again. As Cairncross has put it in his brief review of the subject, the Bill was dropped and none of the powers of control were ever put on the statute book.[62] The use of direct controls 'continued to rest on the emergency powers as they fell steadily into desuetude'.

Cairncross is correct in what he writes, but equally creates a false impression. Given the strong desire of Labour ministers to introduce permanent economic powers, it is obviously important to explain why the legislation was dropped in February 1951. It is only if the Bill is put into the context of the period that the reasons why Labour ministers decided not to proceed with the legislation emerge.

Eaves explains the decision as being due to two factors. He believed the government was influenced by the vehement hostility of the Opposition to the proposed legislation and by the rift within the Labour Party over the 1951 Budget.[63] However, while the former may have played some role,[64] they do not seem to offer sufficient explanation.

Two other reasons were more important. It had been intended that the Bill would be introduced before powers ran out in December 1950. However, this proved an impossible timetable and even before Cabinet had considered the Economic Powers Bill in its original form, Cabinet had agreed that emergency powers would have to be continued for a further year.[65] Without this constraint ministers wanted to make sure that they got the legislation right and in this sense it was important not to rush the Bill. As Gaitskell put it, 'The political importance of this Bill is so great that we must think out the implications very carefully before we decide what to put into it'.[66] Bevan thought likewise.[67] Permanent legislation would not be required until December 1951 after the renewal of the temporary powers for a year and could be delayed further by a second renewal of temporary powers. As it was, Labour lost power in November 1951.

However, as it stands this is only a partial explanation. It shows why no legislation was introduced but it does not explain why the Cabinet decided to take the legislation no further in February 1951. This was only the background to that decision. Here the impact of the Korean War is crucial. It was clear that further emergency powers not incorporated in the existing powers would be required for defence and rearmament purposes. The introduction of a Bill to cover permanent powers could not cover these particular needs. When the temporary legislation, the Supplies and Services (Defence Purposes) Act 1951, was introduced to Parliament the Opposition made much of the 'chaotic state' of emergency powers.[68]

If the government had introduced permanent legislation at that time, it would only have served to confuse even more both the legislative position and the general public. Ministers therefore felt obliged to accept the recommendation of the Official Committee on the Economic Planning and Full Employment Bill that the Bill could not be continued with at that time.[69]

Even more significant were the terms in which this acceptance was made. The ministerial Committee on the Economic Planning and Full Employment Bill recommended to the Cabinet that the Bill should not be introduced 'at the present time'.[70] Moreover, ministers who wished to comment on the revised draft of the Bill were invited to submit memoranda with a view to the committee undertaking a detailed scrutiny of the proposals 'in preparation for the time when it would be desirable to proceed with the Bill'. Similarly, the Cabinet agreed that it would be inappropriate to proceed with the Bill 'in present circumstances'.[71] In Attlee's brief for this Cabinet meeting, Norman Brook wrote that Morrison had accepted the conclusion that the Bill should not be introduced in the changed circumstances of rearmament, but that this had been 'with reluctance'.[72] Clearly then, the evidence would suggest that Labour ministers were still convinced of the need for permanent economic powers.

Although no further action was taken prior to the October 1951 election and the Labour Party manifesto made no reference to such a Bill, the manifesto did say that price control would be extended and strengthened and was critical of the Conservatives' desire for decontrol.[73] Moreover, at no time during the rest of the Labour administration did ministers say that the Bill had been dropped.[74] It was clear that the Bill's introduction was not imminent, but this was not surprising given the continued problems associated with the Korean War. This did not mean that the idea of permanent economic controls had been finally dropped by Labour, merely that it had had to be put on the back-burner. It was necessary to wait until peacetime economic conditions had been restored before introducing powers for those economic controls which Labour ministers regarded would be required permanently in a peacetime economy.

Indeed, there is evidence that the idea had not completely disappeared from the Labour Party's thinking on economic policy in the early 1950s. Admittedly, Tony Crosland in *The Future of Socialism* was highly critical of the use of direct controls and preferred to rely on the budget, but he had seen a role for certain controls in his contribution to *New Fabian Essays*.[75] However, many leading members of the Labour Party still saw an important and permanent role for direct controls.[76] Moreover, Hugh Gaitskell's views do not seem to have changed much from his 1950 paper 'Economic Planning and Liberalisation'. In 1953 he argued that to carry out a full employment policy the key physical controls over private industry would be foreign exchange, import and building licensing, price controls and the occasional allocation of scarce raw materials.[77] He made a similar point in moving the amendment to the Queen's Speech in December 1954, adding to the same negative controls the positive power 'to intervene at specific points to stimulate production'.[78] Further evidence of this view came in the Party's publications *Facing the Facts* and *Challenge to Britain* both of which underlined the importance of controls in the maintenance of full employment.[79]

It would certainly seem therefore not to be overstating the case in saying that instead of a trend away from controls to reliance on the budget to control the economy, controls, or rather certain controls, remained at least until 1951 a central part of the Labour governments' economic policy. Moreover, it was expected that these controls would play a long-term role in the economy. The use of the budget in this sense did not substitute the use of direct controls but was seen rather as complementary in the maintenance of full employment. It is only with the election of the Conservative government that there was a commitment to complete decontrol and reliance on indirect measures alone. Similarly, the Korean War is normally seen as a temporary break in this trend of decontrol. Ironically, the Korean War in making temporary controls necessary again, actually helped to prevent the introduction of the permanent controls.

Having recounted Labour ministers' apparent determination to have some permanent economic controls, what can be drawn out of this with regard to the relationship between the Labour governments and private industry? First, with regard to the policy itself, it is clear that certainly from 1949 there was a review of the policy tools required by a Labour government in a peacetime economy. Moreover, a wide range of ministers supported these moves. It would appear that Labour ministers did react to an awareness that the wartime controls were not necessarily the most suitable form of control once the transition to a peacetime economy had been completed. The proposed legislation goes some way to filling the vacuum in alternative policies towards the private sector once controls were removed, highlighted by Tomlinson. In the sense that ministers perceived the continuation of certain controls, there was no vacuum to be filled. This did not mean that no other measures were required, simply that they were not bereft of policy. This would suggest that the Labour government had not run out of steam by 1950–1 in all fields of policy.

Second, it is clearly wrong to refer to controls as a single homogeneous block about which perceptions were the same. Labour ministers supported decontrol for some types of control, but not for others. It is clear that control of labour was never likely, while, in contrast, restrictive controls over investment, imports and prices, together with positive controls over production, were seen as crucial in the long term. The Labour governments did not envisage complete decontrol of private industry, and hence intended to maintain some degree of direct intervention via the controls.

Third, the purpose of the controls was important. Although some still saw a micro-economic role for direct controls, the increasing focus was on the macro-economic objective of full employment. Those who did have a conscious image of their purpose, were not recommending permanent economic controls with the aim of restructuring industry. The objective was not to determine the long-term development of industry but rather to achieve short-term management of the economy. Hence, by the time it was dropped the Bill was entitled the Full Employment Bill.

All of these points give some indication of how Labour ministers viewed their relationship with the private sector, but the chapter has given little insight into the views of industry in this respect. Mention has been made of the pressure for decontrol but little else. If the Conservative Opposition can be taken as a simple guide to the views of industry, then it is clear that there was considerable opposition to the idea of permanent economic controls. On a more sophisticated level of analysis, it is hard to characterise industry's views. At the top, it is clear that the leadership of the FBI wanted decontrol.[80] However, there appears to have been little general discussion of the subject in the FBI after 1949 until the introduction of new emergency powers related to the Korean War and rearmament. More specifically, at no point does there appear to have been any discussion of the announcement of the government's intention to introduce permanent economic powers and the implications of this for private industry. Where there was any consideration of controls these tended to relate to specific aspects of policy of more immediate concern.

Below the level of the FBI leadership there was certainly a demand for the streamlining of controls but support for total decontrol was not always made clear. Many trade associations, as Merriam found out in his review of controls, were not averse to some controls.[81] Moreover, if controls were removed while the economy was still inflationary it would have to be replaced by even higher taxation to produce a larger budget surplus sufficient to control inflation. Given this, industry did not always see any real benefit in such a change. Yet with regard to the proposed permanent economic controls, the private sector would continue to be open to direct interference by government. This would not have been the case if policy were reliant solely on budgetary policy. In other words, despite a basis for common interests pushing for the removal of all controls, the sectional interest of particular trade associations in continuing some controls seems to have prevented private industry from presenting a united front on the issue of controls and their continuation.

However, to some extent the views of private industry were largely irrelevant in the formulation of the draft legislation for permanent economic powers. It would not appear that there was any formal occasion when the views of private industry on the introduction of permanent economic controls were sought during the drafting of the legislation. It was certainly never discussed at either the Economic Planning Board or the National Production Advisory Council for Industry. Similarly, there does not appear to have been any deputation from the FBI over this issue.

The Labour government does not seem to have seen the need for consultation at that level. The general policy of legislation for permanent controls was drawn up amongst ministers and officials. Moreover, consultation with industry appears to have occurred at a much lower level. Thus the FBI, the National Union of Manufacturers (NUM) and the Association of British Chambers of Commerce (ABCC) were involved in Merriam's review of controls but were not involved in policy discussions. Similarly, in 1951 when some temporary controls were reimposed, it was only after their announcement that the government conferred with industry. Even then it tended to be only with each individual industry about the operation of the particular relevant control. There was no general consultation as such. In other words, consultation was limited to the implementation of controls and occurred mainly between industries or their associations and their respective sponsoring departments.

Similarly, although officials were involved directly in the drawing up of the draft legislation, they appear to have been unable to deter ministers from this legislation. Despite concern amongst officials about the generality of the powers and the likely hostile attitude of industry which would result, there does not seem to be any evidence of ministers showing the same concern. Indeed, although officials had specifically rejected the incorporation of positive powers in the drafting of the Economic Powers Bill, ministers decided to include just such powers.

Thus, while officials had some restraining influence on the nature of the legislation, the inspiration and driving force for the legislation came solely from Labour ministers and, to a lesser extent, the Labour Party.

However, while ministers may have had a clear perception of the need for some permanent economic controls and the general purposes for which they were to be used, many obvious potential problems were not dealt with. Ministers do not appear to have considered how the controls would be implemented, how they would be made effective, nor who would operate them if industry refused to co-operate, as was quite possible in some sectors. In general, there appears to have been no thought about whether the use of permanent economic controls was realistic and likely to be effective in the long term. Whether it was or not is a separate issue; it might just have been expected that there would have been such a consideration given the long-term nature of the proposed legislation and the importance placed upon it by ministers.

Over the issue of permanent economic controls, the relationship between Labour ministers and private industry does seem to have been very much one dominated by the former. Ministers did respond to appeals for decontrol in 1948 by removing obsolete controls but this cannot be seen as a rejection of all economic controls. They seem to have been convinced of the need for the maintenance of particular controls permanently, yet were apparently unconcerned about the practicalities of implementing such a policy in the long term. Although private industry does not appear to have been so united in its condemnation of controls as is sometimes suggested, private industry's views, in any case, seem to have been irrelevant in the drafting of the legislation for permanent economic controls. In this particular case ministers did not feel it necessary to consider whether this line of policy needed moderation to ensure the appeasement of private industry.

APPENDIX 2.1

Edited version of LP(50)65, 'Permanent Economic Powers', 18 July 1950.

Draft 'Economic Powers Bill'

Clause 1

The powers conferred by the three next following sections of this Act on a competent authority to make orders and give directions shall be exercisable if and so far as it appears to the authority to be necessary or expedient for promoting all or any of the following objects, and not otherwise, –
(a) the productivity of industry, commerce and agriculture, and full employment;
(b) a sufficiency of supplies and services essential to the well-being of the community, their equitable distribution and their availability at fair prices;
(c) the balancing of overseas trade at a high level, in relation to all or any countries; and
(d) in general, the use of the resources of the community in a manner best calculated to serve the interests of the community.

Clause 2

(1) A competent authority may by order provide –

(a) for regulating the supply and acquisition of any materials or plant for industrial purposes, being materials or plant appearing to the competent authority to be scarce or likely to become scarce;

(b) for regulating or prohibiting the production or treatment of any articles or the carrying out of any building operations, or the use or consumption of any materials, or the use of any plant or process, in the production or treatment of any articles or the carrying out of any building operations;

(c) for regulating the distribution, disposal, acquisition, use or consumption –

(i) of any articles which appear to the competent authority to be suitable for export;

(ii) of any consumer goods which appear to the authority to be scarce or likely to become scarce;

(iii) of any articles, if it appears to the competent authority that such regulation is necessary or expedient for the purposes of or in connection with any arrangements for a government subsidy or a government guarantee in relation to those articles;

(d) for any incidental and supplementary matters for which the competent authority thinks it expedient for the purposes of the order to provide . . .

(7) Nothing in this section shall authorise –

(a) the imposition of any form of industrial conscription

(b) the compulsory acquisition or requisition of any property or

(c) the suppression or suspension of any newspaper, periodical, book or other publication.

Clause 3

(1) A competent authority may, if and so far as it appears to be necessary or expedient in connection with the operation of any scheme of control operated under any order made under the last preceding section, give, as respects any undertaking, directions requiring the undertakers to carry on the undertaking in accordance with the directions, and no obligation or limitation imposed on the undertakers by or by virtue of any Act or other instrument determining their functions shall prevent or excuse the undertakers from complying with the directions . . .

Clause 4

(1) A competent authority may by order provide for controlling the prices to be charged or the charges to be made –

(a) for any articles or services which appear to the authority to be scarce or likely to become scarce;

(b) for any articles or services the prices of which or the charges for which ought in the opinion of the authority to be controlled for the purpose of securing the effective control of the prices of articles or the charges of services mentioned in paragraph (a) hereof;

(c) for any articles or services the prices or charges for which appear to the competent authority to be excessive and the production or provision of which appears to the authority to be carried out in conditions which prevent or restrict competition;

(d) for any articles or services, if it appears to the competent authority that such control is necessary or expedient for the purposes of or in connection with any arrangements for a government subsidy or a government guarantee in relation to those articles;

and for any incidental or supplementary matters for which the competent authority thinks it expedient for the purposes of the order to provide . . .

Edited version of GEN343/4 'Revised draft of the Bill', 6 February 1951

Draft 'Full Employment Bill'

Introduction

Whereas it is expedient [for the purpose of making full use of the skill and energies of the people of the United Kingdom and raising their standard of life] to carry out a policy of full employment:

And whereas that policy involves, on the one hand, the maintenance of an adequate demand for goods and services and, on the other, the taking of any measures necessary to check inflation and to secure the provision of goods and services required by the community:

And whereas it is necessary, for the successful carrying out of that policy, that there should be available to His Majesty's Government, on a permanent basis but subject to Parliamentary safeguards, powers –

(a) to stimulate and facilitate the provision of capital for the financing of trade and industry,

(b) to undertake the purchase of capital goods on public account,

(c) to encourage the planning and carrying out of public works,

(d) to control prices and secure fair distribution of goods and services,

(e) to regulate production and supply so as to secure the requisite priorities for export and defence and to satisfy the needs of the community, and

(f) to regulate building operations.

Clauses of the bill

Part I (Clauses 1–5) Measures for Maintaining Demand
Part II (Clauses 6–8) Price Control
Part III (Clauses 9–12) Control of Production, Distribution and Consumption of Goods and Building Operations
Part IV (Clauses 13–32) Miscellaneous and General

More specifically this meant the introduction of
1. positive powers concerning
    a) Stimulation of investment in the private sector;
    b) Public purchase of capital goods;
    c) Stimulation of investment by public authorities and of
2. negative powers concerning
    a) price control;
    b) allocation of raw materials, and fair distribution of essential consumer goods;
    c) control of building.

Import and export licensing were not included and it was recommended that these should be covered by separate legislation (although ministers do not seem totally convinced by this). Also the powers should not include positive directions to industry.

NOTES

1. *Hansard* (Commons) 5th Series Vol. 480 Col. 174 14/11/1950, speech by R. A. Butler. The author would like to thank Sir Alec Cairncross for comments on a draft of this paper.
2. Ibid. Col. 7 31/10/1951.
3. Ibid. Col. 174, R. A. Butler.

4. A. K. Cairncross *Years of Recovery: British Economic Policy 1945–51* (1985) p. 352; B. W. E. Alford *British Economic Performance 1945–1975* (Basingstoke, 1988) p. 32 and J. Tomlinson *Employment Policy: The Crucial Years 1939–1955* (Oxford, 1987) pp. 130–8.

5. N. Rollings, 'The Control of Inflation in the Managed Economy: Britain 1945–1953' (unpublished PhD, Bristol University, 1990).

6. H. Pelling *The Labour Governments, 1945–51* (1984) ch. 12 and K. Morgan *Labour in Power 1945–1951* (Oxford, 1984) ch. 11. See also R. Miliband *Parliamentary Socialism: A Study in the Politics of Labour* (1972) ch. 9; D. Howell, *British Social Democracy: A Study in Development and Decay* (1976) ch. 5 and B. Jones and M. Keating *Labour and the British State* (Oxford, 1985) ch. 3.

7. S. Brittan *Steering the Economy: The Role of the Treasury* (Harmondsworth, 1971) p. 181 and p. 187. Other examples of the first strand are: G. D.N. Worswick, 'Direct Controls', in G. D. N. Worswick and P. H. Ady eds. *The British Economy 1945–1950* (Oxford, 1952) p. 284; and P. D. Henderson, 'Government and Industry', in G. D. N. Worswick and P. H. Ady eds. *The British Economy in the Nineteen-fifties* (Oxford, 1962) pp. 327–9. Examples of the second strand are: G. D. H. Cole *Socialist Economics* (1950) p. 7; Miliband op. cit. p. 305; Howell op. cit. pp. 159–60; Jones and Keating op. cit. p. 83; and J. Eatwell and R. Green 'Economic Theory and Political Power' in B. Pimlott ed. *Fabian Essays in Socialist Thought* (1984) p. 193. Also of relevance here is E. Durbin 'Fabian Socialism and Economic Science' in Pimlott ed. op. cit. pp. 39–53.

8. A. A. Rogow *The Labour Government and British Industry 1945–51* (Oxford, 1955) p. 42.

9. See A. Booth *British Economic Policy 1931–49: Was There A Keynesian Revolution?* (Hemel Hempstead, 1989) pp. 172–3; A. K. Cairncross op. cit. p. 344 and p. 501; A. K. Cairncross and N. Watts *The Economic Section 1939–1961: A Study in Economic Advising* (1989) p. 125; A. Gamble 'Stabilization Policy and Adversary Politics' in A. Gamble and S. Walkland *The British Party System and Economic Policy 1945–1983: Studies in Adversary Politics* (Oxford, 1984) p. 78; P. Hall *Governing the Economy: The Politics of State Intervention in Britain and France* (Oxford, 1986) p. 76 and D. Marquand, *The Unprincipled Society: New Demands and Old Politics* (1988) pp. 42–3.

10. J. Tomlinson *Public Policy and the Economy since 1900* (Oxford, 1990) p. 215.

11. Eatwell and Green op. cit. p. 193. See also J. Eatwell 'Keynes, Keynesians and British Economic Policy' in H. Wattel ed. *The Policy Consequences of John Maynard Keynes* (1985) pp. 61–76; and E. A. G. Robinson *Economic Planning in the United Kingdom: Some Lessons* (Cambridge, 1967).

12. Public Record Office, Kew (hereafter PRO) T229/31 EPB(47)11 'Control of Investment by Trade Associations' by Sir Graham Cunningham 2/9/1947. See also R. S. Edwards and H. Townsend *Business Enterprise: Its Growth and Organisation* (1958) pp. 404–5; and Rogow op. cit. ch. 3.

13. J. Tomlinson, 'A Missed Opportunity? Labour and the Productivity Problem 1945–51', Brunel University Discussion Papers in Economics No. 8904 and S. Blank *Industry and Government in Britain: The F.B.I. in Politics* (Farnborough, 1973).

14. Tomlinson 'A Missed Opportunity?' pp. 22–3.

15. S. Brooke 'Revisionists and Fundamentalists: The Labour Party and Economic Policy during the Second World War' *The Historical Journal* Vol. 32 1989 157–75; E. Durbin *New Jerusalems: The Labour Party and the Economics of Democratic Socialism* (1985). For an example, see G. D. H. Cole *The Machinery of Socialist Planning* (1938).

16. Cairncross op. cit. p. 300.

17. For wartime policy see J. C. R. Dow *The Management of the British Economy 1945–60* (Cambridge, 1964) pp. 162–4; P. J. D. Wiles 'Pre-war and War-time Controls' in Worswick and Ady eds. op. cit. pp. 125–58; W. K. Hancock and M. Gowing *British War Economy* (1949) pp. 156–72 and 335–7; E. L. Hargreaves 'Price Control of (Non-food) Consumer Goods', *Oxford Economic Papers* Vol. 8 1947 1–11 and J. Eaves *Emergency Powers and the Parliamentary Watchdog: Parliament and the Executive in Great Britain, 1939–1951* (1957).

18. The following statistics are all from Dow op. cit. ch. 6.

19. F. W. S. Craig *British General Election Manifestos 1900–1974* (1975) p. 120.

20. Eaves op. cit. p. 132.

21. *Hansard* (Commons) 5th Ser. Vol. 441 Col. 1799.

22. Ibid. Cols. 1805–6 and Col. 1971.

23. PRO BT64/445 various papers July–September 1947 leading to the report by A. Kilroy (Board of Trade) – Sir John Woods (Permanent Secretary to the Board of Trade) 'Prices and the crisis' 12/9/1947. See also PRO BT64/2340 Kilroy 'Price control and the crisis' 2/9/1947.

24. PEP *Government and Industry* (1952) p. 20.

25. PRO T230/323 Robert Hall (Director of the Economic Section) – Edwin Plowden (Chief Planning Officer) 'Have we got a plan?' 21/4/1948 para. 8.

26. For files of the Controls and Efficiency Committee see PRO CAB134/89. For an example of Gilbert's views see PRO T223/89 Gilbert – Edward Bridges (Permanent Secretary to the Treasury) 19/5/1949.

27. A. Chester 'Planning, the Labour Governments and British Economic Policy 1943–51' (unpublished PhD, Bristol University, 1983) pp. 239–46. See also Special correspondent 'What Technique for Price Control?' *The Banker* Vol. XCVII 1951 159.

28. Dow op. cit. p. 166.

29. Ibid. p. 153.

30. Ibid. p. 158 and p. 162.

31. Cairncross op. cit. pp. 343–4.

32. E. Durbin *Problems of Economic Planning: Papers on Planning and Economics* (1949) p. 59.

33. PRO T223/90 Draft memorandum by the chairman of the Wages and Prices Policy Committee leading to WPP(48)7 28/6/1948; and PRO T229/266 Jay – Cripps 17/3/1949.

34. Labour Party Archives, National Museum of Labour History, Manchester (hereafter LPA) Subcommittee on Privately Owned Industry (1948) 2nd meeting 14/10/1948.

35. *Hansard* (Commons) 5th Ser. Vol. 463 Col. 2499 11/4/1949.

36. Ibid. Vol. 468 Col. 182 28/9/1949.

37. PRO CAB134/300 FL(49)1 'Legislative programme: 1950 session' 24/4/1949.

38. Labour Party *Conference Report 1949* 8/6/1949.

39. PRO CAB134/220 EPC(49)51st minute 2 Gaitskell criticising EPC(49)157 13/12/1949.

40. PRO CAB134/225 EPC(50)9 Gaitskell 'Economic planning and liberalisation' 7/1/1950. For draft by Gaitskell and Jay see PRO T230/319. For Dalton's comment see British Library of Political and Economic Science Dalton Papers diary 24/1/1950.

41. PRO T273/311 Alec Johnston – Gilbert 'Economic controls' 20/1/1950. This is a fuller account of the meeting than that provided in the committee minutes, see PRO CAB134/224 EPC(50)5th minute 3 19/1/1950.

42. PRO T273/311 Johnston – Gilbert 'Economic controls' 20/1/1950.

43. Modern Records Centre University of Warwick CBI Predecessor Archive (hereafter CBI) MSS200/F/3/E3/3/9 Final Report by L. P. B. Merriam to the Consultative Committee of the FBI, National Union of Manufacturers and Association of British Chambers of Commerce 22/11/1949.

44. PRO CAB134/640 Production Committee PC(49)14th 31/5/1949. For the papers of the Committee on the Control of Investment see PRO CAB134/63.

45. PRO CAB134/95 CEC(49)1 Paper by Gilbert 'Composition and terms of reference' 9/7/1949.
46. PRO CAB134/95 CEC(49)1st minute 2 20/7/1949 and CEC(50)3 'Report (final version)' 3/3/1950.
47. PRO CAB132/15 Morrison covering the report of the Committee on Economic Controls 'Economic controls – long-term powers' 27/3/1950; and PRO CAB129/38 CP(50)49 Morrison 'Future of emergency powers' 27/3/1950.
48. PRO CAB129/38 CP(50)49.
49. PRO CAB128/17 CM(50)16th minute 3 30/3/1950.
50. PRO CAB132/16 LP(50)65 Morrison covering draft Economic Powers Bill 'Permanent economic powers' 18/7/1950.
51. PRO T229/266 J. G. P. Spicer (CEPS) – D. Pitblado 'Draft Economic Powers Bill' 8/6/1950.
52. PRO CAB132/14 LP(50)13th minute 3 21/7/1950; PRO CAB129/41 CP(50)178 Morrison covering the Bill 'Permanent economic powers' 25/7/1950. This was considered at PRO CAB128/18 CM(50)51st minute 3 27/7/1950.
53. For the papers of the subcommittee see PRO CAB134/635.
54. PRO CAB129/42 CP(50)230 'The Economic Planning and Full Employment Bill' 26/10/1950.
55. PRO CAB21/2145 Gilbert – W. Armstrong (Treasury) 'Economic Planning and Full Employment Bill' 26/10/1950 and PRO T229/323 Gilbert – Bridges and Littlewood 'Economic Planning and Full Employment Bill' 18/10/1950.
56. PRO T228/241 Jay – Gaitskell 27/10/1950 and PRO CAB128/18 CM(50)69th minute 5 30/10/1950.
57. PRO CAB130/60 GEN.324/17 'Report' 6/2/1951 and PRO CAB130/65 GEN.343/4 'Revised draft of the Bill' 6/2/1951.
58. PRO CAB21/2145 Gilbert – Armstrong 'Economic Planning and Full Employment Bill' 26/10/1950.
59. PRO CAB129/42 CP(50)237 Morrison 'The King's Speech on the Opening of Parliament' 20/10/1950. This was discussed at PRO CAB128/18 CM(50)67th minute 4 23/10/1950 and CM(50)69th minute 5 30/10/1950.
60. PRO CAB130/65 GEN.343/2 Gaitskell 'Economic Planning and Full Employment Bill' 9/11/1950 discussed at GEN.343/1st 10/11/1950.
61. PRO CAB128/19 CM(51)15th minute 2 15/2/1951. This had been recommended by the Committee on the Economic Planning and Full Employment Bill at PRO CAB130/65 GEN.343/2nd 9/2/1951.
62. Cairncross op. cit. pp. 352–3.
63. Eaves op. cit. p. 143.
64. PRO T229/456 Vinter (CEPS) – F. F. Turnbull (CEPS) 5/12/1949; PRO CAB128/17 CM(50)16th minute 3 30/3/1950; PRO CAB132/14 LP(50)4th minute 2 21/4/1950 and PRO CAB21/2145 Norman Brook (Secretary of the Cabinet) – Attlee 'Permanent economic powers' 26/7/1950.
65. PRO CAB128/18 CM(50)44th minute 3 10/7/1950.
66. PRO CAB130/65 GEN.343/2 Gaitskell 'Economic Planning and Full Employment Bill' 9/11/1950.
67. PRO T229/323 Douglas Allen (CEPS) and Christopher Dow (Economic Section) – Gilbert 'The Economic Planning and Full Employment Bill. Memorandum by the Minister of Health' 18/10/1950.
68. *Hansard* (Commons) 5th Ser. Vol. 484 Col. 1309 and Col. 1365 21/2/1951.
69. PRO CAB130/65 GEN.343/4 Gaitskell covering the report of the official committee 'Revised draft of the Bill' 6/2/1951 considered at GEN.343/2nd 9/2/1951.
70. Ibid. GEN.343/2nd 9/2/1951.
71. PRO CAB128/19 CM(51)14th minute 8 15/2/1951.
72. PRO PREM8/1395 Brook – Attlee 'Full Employment Bill CP(51)52' 14/2/1951.
73. Craig op. cit. p. 175.

74. *Hansard* (Commons) 5th Ser. Vol. 485 written questions Col. 193 15/3/1951 and Cols. 317–18 22/3/1951 and Vol. 488 written questions Col. 98 5/6/1951.
75. C. A. R. Crosland *The Future of Socialism* (1956) ch. 24; and C. A. R. Crosland, 'The Transition from Capitalism' in R. H. S. Crossman ed. *New Fabian Essays* (1952) pp. 63–4.
76. R. Jenkins *Pursuit of Progress* (1953) p. 139 and J. Strachey 'Foreword' in Rogow op. cit. pp. x–xi. See also LPA Subcommittee on Privately Owned Industry 1952.
77. H. Gaitskell 'The Economic Aims of the Labour Party' *The Political Quarterly* Vol. XXIV 1953 p. 13.
78. Reprinted by the Labour Party as H. Gaitskell *The High Cost of Toryism* (1955) p. 11.
79. Labour Party *Facing the Facts* (1952) and Labour Party *Challenge to Britain* (1953). See also S. Haseler *The Gaitskellites* (1969) pp. 57–8.
80. CBI MSS200/F/3/E3/3/9 FBI Joint Committee on Controls with NUM and ABCC; and CBI MSS200/F/3/D3/5/19 Nuffield College 24th Private Conference on 'The Government's Controls of Industry and Trade' 26–7/6/1948.
81. Ibid. Paper by the Ministry of Supply 'Review of controls', undated; CBI MSS200/F/3/E1/5/4 Note of a meeting with Mr Markwick (Asst. Sec. Central Price Regulation Committee) 'Standstill price control orders' 22/3/1949 and CBI MSS200/F/3/D3/5/6 Summing up report by Norman Kipping of the Ashorne Hill Conference on 'The Next Five Years' 21–3/4/1950 on views of Group V.

Three

Productivity policy

JIM TOMLINSON

The Attlee government was the first in peacetime to put a high and continuing priority on raising the level of productivity in British industry. In doing so it was able to draw on diagnoses, prescriptions and actual institutions from the war period, but otherwise it was entering a policy area previously little explored and one which was both largely unanticipated and foreign to the mainstream of Labour's previous thinking. In pursuing this policy Labour was largely concerned with raising productivity in the private-industrial sector of the economy, so that the focus on productivity necessarily raised a range of issues about how the government was to deal with privately owned firms.

Given this context, this chapter is divided into three parts. The first looks at productivity as a policy *objective* – where it came from and how it was formulated. Second is the issue of policy *instruments* – how did the government think higher productivity was to be attained? The third and largest section looks at the *constraints* on policy, especially those related to the government's attempts to change private-sector firms' behaviour in the name of higher productivity.

I

Prior to and immediately after its election victory in 1945, Labour's central policy concern was with the prevention of unemployment.[2] Whilst this concern never disappeared over the next six years, it quickly became apparent that the most pressing problem in managing the economy was the balance of payments, in turn, at least in the short run, a supply problem.[3] This led to a government 'prosperity' campaign, launched at the beginning of 1946.[4] The initial focus of this was how to 'man-up' certain industries to expand their output, but it quickly became apparent that with a finite supply of labour, most of the expansion of output could only come from increased productivity. By late 1946 it was recognised that the campaign was becoming essentially one concerning the raising of productivity, and Herbert Morrison proclaimed in October that he 'would put this problem of increased productivity first among the current economic problems to which planning must help to find the answer'.[5]

This did not, of course, mean that the concern with full employment disappeared, but now, it was argued, higher productivity was the way to full employment.

> The point to return to is that while the full employment policy is safe from any return of the circumstances that caused it before the war, it is not safe from the consequences of failure in the export drive, and the risks of that failure would be very greatly increased by any failure to improve productivity and to lower costs.[6]

Once established, this concern with productivity never disappeared under Labour. This is apparent in the changing focus of the (published) *Economic Surveys* – that of 1947 reflects the origins of the concern by emphasising the need to finance a full employment level of imports and the consequent need to 'man-up' certain industries. By 1949 and 1950 a direct concern with productivity is absolutely centre stage.[7] But was this emphasis on productivity solely short term, a response to immediate macro-economic concerns? Undoubtedly that is where its origins lay, but there was at least an undercurrent of a long-term aspect. In a brief on 'The Case for Higher Productivity', that case was seen as based on two elements. On the one hand was the immediate need for higher output. On the other was the recognition of a need to produce at lower cost per unit

> we need to hold our export markets securely, and extend them in certain directions, against the rising tide of competition, from European industry as its recovery proceeds, from America as home demand there is overtaken by supply, and possibly also from Japan.[8]

So there was an ambiguity, a possible tension in the productivity campaign, between emphasising immediate output expansion to provide exports and looking at longer-run issues of competitiveness as other producers entered the market. This tension continued to exist throughout the Attlee period.

II

In looking at the instruments brought to bear on the productivity problem it is useful to distinguish between Labour's broad posture on industry and the instruments of industrial policy it was bequeathed by the wartime Coalition.

On the first of these, as every schoolgirl knows, Labour's policy was dominated by nationalisation. Plainly the motives for this were multiple and complex, and only partly aimed at directly economic ends like making possible re-equipment and the realisation of economies of scale. The dominance of nationalisation on Labour's agenda perhaps tended to 'crowd-out' policies on private industry. As of 1945 these consisted of little more than commitments to anti-monopoly policy and to consultative and co-operative relations with the private sector. Anti-monopoly policy was a damp squib under Labour,[9] but the consultative and co-operative emphasis meant that most of the productivity drive (like other policies) was pursued via a range of tripartite bodies like the National Joint Advisory Council, and especially the National Production Advisory Council for Industry. This in turn meant that policy was 'quasi-corporatist' in style, being conducted in the context of intensive consultations with the peak associations of the TUC, FBI and British Employers' Confederation (BEC), but where the government firmly resisted sharing decision-making with these bodies.[10]

Of course Labour's heritage in 1945 was not just a broad ideological position but a complex set of policy instruments built up in wartime. Central to these as regards industry were the control systems for the allocation of raw materials, investment, imports and labour. With the exception of the last, which was largely abandoned in 1945, these controls continued under Labour, their operation still dominated to a large extent by private industry itself, mainly via trade associations. Thus 'quasi-corporatism' was built on a substantial substructure of industrial 'self-government'.[11]

The war also bequeathed a number of other instruments which, whilst designed for a range of purposes, seemed to be usable in the pursuit of higher productivity. Probably best known of these was the idea of industrial boards, advocated by the Board of Trade in 1943, following the example of the Cotton Board and aimed at 'increasing efficiency and interpreting the Government's policy in certain industries'.[12] This proposal drew on the inter-war rationalisation movement and on wartime concentration of production in certain consumer industries. It was mainly aimed at industries which were perceived to have retained a fragmented, small-scale structure and where therefore the state had a role to play in encouraging amalgamation and technical development. This idea was followed through after the war in the setting up of seventeen 'Working Parties', most of which advocated some continuing machinery involving employer, worker and independent membership. This in turn led to proposals for Development Councils, which would fulfil at least some of the purposes of the industrial boards, but without powers of compulsory amalgamation. This proposal was embodied in the Industrial Organisation and Development Act of 1947 which empowered the government to create Development Councils to be established to keep a register of people in the industry, to impose a levy for common services such as research and to collect information.[13]

Development Councils were important as probably Labour's most distinctive policy instrument for industry and clearly originated in a concern for industrial efficiency, though they did not prove to fit easily into the productivity drive. The Cotton Board (later Development

Council) was a channel which the government attempted to use for productivity initiatives, for example investigating the productivity effects of labour redeployment.[14] But by and large the industry retained the initiative. The three other industries where Development Councils were established, jewellery and silverware, lace and furniture were minor industries where the Development Council had little effect beyond a limited provision of common services of research and marketing. In sum, Development Councils cannot be said to have been significant contributors to the productivity drive despite their central role in Labour's approach to the private sector.

Most famous of the bodies associated with this government and the productivity issue was the Anglo–American Council on Productivity. This initiative is discussed elsewhere.[15] But what is clear is that the idea for this body was an *ad hoc* response to US pressure to be seen to be 'doing something' about British industry in the context of Marshall Aid to the UK. From a governmental point of view there were advantages in establishing the AACP as an employer–trade-union body thus 'doing something' whilst passing responsibility elsewhere.[16] Thus the AACP, whilst a government initiative, was not really an instrument of government policy – its activities depended almost entirely on trade-union and, especially, employer policies.

Much more clearly in the hands of government were other, less-publicised initiatives, which also grew very much from wartime experience. Two of these were largely the idea of Stafford Cripps, who had been a wartime Minister of Aircraft Production and became President of the Board of Trade in 1945. First of these is the Production Efficiency Service, which grew out of the wartime Production Efficiency Board of the Ministry of Aircraft Production. In its wartime form the PEB had focused on educating management in the techniques of motion study in firms producing for MAP.[17] Post-war responsibility was transferred to the Board of Trade, the name changed to PES and the function changed to a management consultancy aimed primarily at small firms, headed still by the Director of the PEB, F. E. Chappell.[18] Whilst approached by an average of over 100 firms per annum between 1946 and 1949 the PES had a short and troubled life. Chappell resigned in late 1948 over a 'difference of opinion over its organisation' and it was wound up as an economy measure from January 1950. The archives hint at a considerable degree of opposition to this agency from Board of Trade civil servants.[19]

The PES is interesting as perhaps the government body most explicitly designed to raise productivity. Its stated aims were

> both short-term and long-term. In the short-term it endeavours to
> bring about an increase in the productivity of the individual firm or

group of firms which seek its aid. In the long-term it aims at making industry aware of the possibility of increasing its efficiency by the study and application of up-to-date methods.[20]

In spite of this seeming clarity of purpose, the impact of the PES must appear small partly because of the unwillingness of the Board of Trade to push its activities.[21]

Another body with similarities to the PES was the Board of Trade's Special Research Unit. Like the PES, this was derived from wartime experience, in this case from the application of Operational Research (OR). The brief of the SRU was to apply OR to the problems of industry. Its focus seems to have been on the issue of specialisation and standardisation, conducting some firm-level studies of the relationship between productivity and standardisation.[22]

Standardisation was also pursued by other ministries, perhaps especially the Ministry of Supply, again drawing on experience of the wartime benefits of reduction in the number of parts and products. A Committee on this subject was set up by the ministry, reporting in favour of the potential benefits in 1949.[23] One of the areas of debate under the heading of standardisation was the role of the British Standards Institute in the generation and spreading of standards. In particular the focus was on how large a role government should play in the standard-setting process, and how much should be left to the initiative of the producers.[24]

Alongside OR and standardisation, a popular concern in the productivity campaign was the dissemination of inventions, which led to the establishment of the National Research and Development Council in 1948, with the aim of promoting the *adoption* of inventions.[25] Related to this emphasis on technical change was the expansion of the Department of Scientific and Industrial Research and a partially government-funded increase in the number and size of industrial research associations. However these were certainly not 'instruments' of government policy like the PES, SRU or NRDC but largely controlled by the trade associations in the industries in which they operated.[26]

A further initiative linked to the experience of war was the creation of the British Institute of Management. Such a body had been recommended by wartime committees, and was eventually established in 1946 with a government 'pump-priming' grant.[27] The role of this body was seen as largely educational, and there were other efforts to expand management education in this period, under a scheme drawn up by L. F. Urwick.[28]

Technical education had expanded rapidly during the war, largely at Bevin's, the Minister of Labour's, behest. This priority seems to have been lost after the war when attention and resources were focused on school education as the Ministry of Education reasserted its role in this area.[29] Perception of this neglect is shown by the work of the Percy and Barlow committees on technical education at post-school level, and these did lead to some changes in provision, but leaving a clear excess demand for higher-level technologists into the 1950s.[30]

Central to the productivity drive was the government's belief that if everyone was aware of the nature of Britain's economic problems and desired to co-operate to find solutions, then a large part of the problem would be solved. So in one sense the major 'instrument' of the campaign was exhortation and propaganda.[31] This had two broad characteristics. On the one hand it attempted to link factory-level issues with the fortunes of the national economy, exemplified by the magazine *Target*. On the other hand it focused on what may be called a 'human relations' approach to productivity. In this view productivity was dependent upon a recognition of common interests amongst all those in the enterprise, a recognition which relied on good communications in the enterprise and good leadership. On this basis could be built up a common purpose amongst all the workers and the enterprise, by engaging the workers' concern, could generate higher output. In short 'management had to adopt a participative procedure which on the one hand allowed workers to feel some emotional involvement in the activities of the enterprise, while on the other hand retaining initiative and final authority firmly in managerial hands'.[32]

This approach to productivity suffuses the whole exercise. It is particularly apparent in the discussion of Joint Production Committees. These had been established as factory-level bipartite bodies in many industries, but especially engineering, during the war. As part of its production and productivity campaign, the Attlee government pressed for their expansion, winning employer and union support for this. However, the government made it absolutely clear that these bodies would be voluntary and would not challenge management prerogatives in production.[33] From the government's point of view these bodies were not attempts to extend democracy or citizenship into the enterprise, but rather aimed to engage the co-operative interest of the worker whilst leaving the corporate hierarchy in other respects unchallenged. Hence Joint Production Committees can be seen as perfectly compatible with the 'human relations' approach and its social-psychological foundations, about which Cripps was well-informed and enthusiastic.[34]

From the above list of the 'instruments' of productivity policy a number of conclusions may be drawn. First, much of the productivity drive depended upon pre-existing institutions, largely of wartime origin, which were pressed into service in pursuit of this objective after the war. Second, these instruments did not originate in the Labour Party or Labour government, and some parts of them, for example the emphasis on human relations, fitted poorly with Labour's traditional stance on the economy, in this case because of the anti-union aspect of human relations ideology.[35] Third, the instruments lacked a clear focus, and have the appearance of a range of *ad hoc* measures, often in practice ill co-ordinated and diffuse in impact.[36]

III

This section is concerned with the constraints on Labour's policies on productivity. Constraint is used in a broad sense to embrace not only factors and bodies 'external' to the policy, but also the policy design itself. Plainly a policy can sensibly be described as constrained by bad design as much as by opposition to it from a powerful interest group.

In the context of this paper the concern is with productivity in the private sector. The government *did* concern itself with productivity in the nationalised industries (especially coal) but as in other policy areas found that the Morrisonian corporation provided a powerful inhibition to a direct government role in the industry.[37] Hence, most of what the Attlee government did on productivity *was* concerned with the private sector.

As already noted in passing, the government began in 1945 with few policy ideas for the private sector. This point can be broadened to suggest that Labour as a political party had very little to say about the management of private firms.[38] Labour tended to collapse issues of management into questions of ownership and so policy was dominated by the belief that nationalisation was a necessary, if not sufficient, condition for what Labour wanted to do to change firms. During the debate on post-war policy in the wartime Labour Party there was little specific discussion on post-war industrial policy, the assumption seeming to be that industrial control would operate largely through finance and manpower budgeting – neither in the event proving important.[39]

On parallel lines may be noted the absence of a 'managerialist' ethos or faction in the Labour Party at this time. Whilst individual MPs like Austen Albu or Ian Mikardo took an interest in management, and ministers like Cripps and Dalton were drawn into the issue by the war, industrial management remained largely outside the concerns of Labour *as a party*, even if it could no longer remain so as a government.

This background may help to explain the ease with which, as noted already, 'human relations' approaches to management tended to dominate policy-making in this period. This ideology fitted with Labour's rather herbivore co-operative attitude to the private sector. It could also be fitted in alongside the long-standing commitment of Labour to voluntarism in industrial relations, a theme very strong in the post-war Ministry of Labour. This meant that Labour did strikingly little to reform industrial relations, for example via democratisation of the enterprise. 'Human relations' nicely meshed a non-interventionist stance *vis-à-vis* the governance of the enterprise with an evolutionary view of industrial relations, in which joint consultation, Joint Production Committees and the like could be seen as further additions to 'good industrial relations' rather than a qualitative break with the past.[40]

Of course things never fit so neatly in politics, and there were tensions and strains on such issues as compulsory Joint Production Committees. But the broad point remains that Labour came ill-prepared to the task of reforming the enterprise – this issue was part of the whole government/ private-industry relationship which was, as Harold Wilson was to argue in 1950, 'almost a vacuum in socialist thought'.[41]

Similarly, the 'human relations' approach meshed with the emergent specification of the 'productivity problem'. In principal, productivity can relate to the measurement of output relative to inputs of one or more factors. Modern economics would argue that only total factor productivity measures are appropriate for capturing productive efficiency.[42] But no such measures existed in the 1940s, and when L. Rostas was set to work at the Board of Trade in 1946 to measure productivity the available data made calculations of *labour* productivity the only approach immediately possible.[43] Such a focus also made sense in the immediate conditions of emergence of the productivity issue – the shortage of labour. Higher labour productivity was seen in the short run as the 'logical' alternative to higher labour inputs.

This does not mean that the productivity campaign was based on a belief that labour was the key factor in productivity. Contemporaries were, of course, fully aware that a range of influences determined its level. For example at the beginning of its work the Productivity (Official) Committee produced a list of three main factors in increasing productivity

a) increases in technical efficiency;

b) increase in management efficiency;

c) increases in labour efficiency 'both as a whole through the improvement of relations and increased co-operation between management and workers, and individually through the improvement of technical skill and an increased willingness to apply that skill to the utmost'.[44] And, unsurprisingly, the Labour government was very keen to avoid the implication that its productivity campaign was aimed at getting people to work harder, or that the workers were to blame for any shortfalls in Britain's productivity levels.

> without due exaplanation increased productivity would be connected by many people with longer hours and nigger-driving methods. The campaign is now being attacked overtly by the Communist Party on these lines. It is essential to explain to the public and to all industry the role of the 3 modern factors in productivity – mechanisation, healthy industrial relations, and sound technical management.[45]

Nevertheless, with expansion of the capital stock limited by the diversion of steel and capital goods to export, the focus of the productivity campaign did tend to be on 'labour' in the broad sense – from labour effort through to industrial relations. A discordant note was struck by many of the AACP reports, which tended to emphasise management's responsibility for productivity – but even these were often accompanied by vapid references to the Americans' superior attitude to work.[46] In general the concern with the measurement of labour productivity too easily slipped into the measurement of labour's productivity in a causative sense, a process not inhibited by the emphasis on human relations at the workplace as a key determinant of productivity.

Labour's strategy on productivity was then constrained by its own intellectual and ideological history, which did not predispose it easily to become a party of industrial modernisation in a mixed, predominantly privately-owned economy. No doubt governments to a degree always have to 'make do' with the policy instruments at hand when pursuing their ends, but Labour was particularly constrained by the absence of a clear perception of what could be done about productivity. A unified programme of industrial reform did not emerge, and what little coherence the measures had tended to be centred around human relations ideas, which gave little purchase on many issues, and arguably not a very useful one on the issue – the worker's role in production – on which it focused.

Linked to this lack of a clear view on what was to be done about productivity were divisions within the governmental machine on the issue. For example, the Ministry of Labour was resistant to the idea of seeing Joint Production Committees as largely concerned with short-run productivity issues. It argued for the beneficial effect if the emphasis in the campaign for more Joint Production Committees 'were put on the industrial relations value of joint consultation rather than on its contribution to increased productivity as a direct objective'.[47]

More generally there were clearly divisions in the Board of Trade on the extent to which government should push the productivity drive and enter the traditional domain of responsibility of private-sector owners and management. On the one hand, the Report of the Productivity (Official) Committee declared 'in principle' against a hands-off attitude by government departments to the productivity question in industries under their sponsorship. On the other hand, the Board of Trade argued in its submission to the Committee that departments did not have the technical knowledge to play more than an auxiliary role in such a process. They saw Development Councils as the appropriate body for investigating and disseminating new methods, rather than government departments.[48]

This problem of the capacity of government was reflected in the

SRU's work on the factors affecting productivity. After surveying work on this issue, an SRU report stressed the 'unmistakable impression of the immense detail into which it is necessary to go if the results of productivity research are to be conclusive and useful. It involves the collection of statistics and costings on a scale unattempted hitherto'.[49] So whilst the Productivity Committee's report emphasised a positive role for government, such considerations led it also to stress that 'The decisions which lead to improvement in industrial productivity, whether in the nationalised or private sector, must be taken by managements. Without initiative by, or at least co-operation from, those managements there is little that Government departments can achieve'.[50]

The broad issue of how far government should go in pursuing the productivity issue was not often raised in that explicit form in the debates of those years. But one context in which it did emerge was where there was comparison with the scale of intervention in agriculture. Sometimes this analogy was linked to relatively low-key issues like the mechanisms in agriculture for the dissemination of technical knowledge.[51] Much more fundamentally Harold Wilson raised the issue in his review of the limited effects of Development Councils. He argued that these Councils should be given powers parallel to the County Agricultural Committees (under the 1947 Agriculture Act) to inspect the efficiency of farms and where it was deemed necessary to take possession of the farm in order to run it more efficiently. Not surprisingly, the Board of Trade did not support such a move, and nothing came of Wilson's proposals following the 1950 general election, when Labour's tiny majority seems to have largely put an end to fundamental policy discussion.[52]

The lack of a clear view of the nature of the productivity problem, coupled with its perceived urgency, led on occasion to a search for unlikely panaceas. Most strikingly such a search was involved in the creation of the Committee on Industrial Productivity in 1947. This committee followed from the view of the Advisory Council on Scientific Policy that whilst scientific research would only affect productivity in the long run 'O.R. in the industrial and sociological fields was likely to prove the most valuable type of research for short-term requirements' and that 'collating and publicising of the results of research into the psychological factors affecting productivity should be carried out with the utmost expedition since it appeared to the Committee that these factors were the most important of all'.[53]

Unsurprisingly, such hopes were soon dashed. Whilst the new committee put a lot of effort into investigating the 'Human Factors' in productivity, the chairman of the committee was soon reporting that he was 'very doubtful if the work of this panel can have any early effect on productivity' a view with which it is difficult to disagree.[54]

Whilst the Labour campaign on productivity was constrained by

Labour's own history and the lack of both focus and information in the government on the issue, the biggest constraint was having to work through the private sector. By definition this meant policy had to persuade and/or coerce private economic agents to do things which to a greater or lesser degree they were reluctant to do without government prodding. Not that, of course, productivity-raising measures were obviously against the interests of the private sector. But several factors militated against an enthusiastic embrace for the government's policy. First, and most importantly, this was a Labour government with a programme, above all, of nationalisation, with which few private owners could find much sympathy. Even worse perhaps from the employers' view was the uncertainty attached to Labour's intentions in areas not destined for immediate nationalisation. What scale and character of government intervention did Labour envisage for the unnationalised sector? This was a question to which Labour itself had no clear answer.

In addition to these broad political factors there was the basic economic fact that the Attlee years were a period of a sellers' market for most British producers. However much production may have been disrupted by rationing and shortages, selling was no problem and in consequence profits boomed. In cotton-spinning, for example, profits rose eight times between 1945 and 1951, and the general profits position was extremely healthy, even allowing for the taxation of profits.[55] Such conditions did not provide a 'stick' to drive the inefficient towards productivity-enhancing changes in production methods.

Further, the productivity campaign clearly implied that British industry could do better. This was recognised by the government when, for example, it changed the Committee on Industrial *Efficiency* to *Productivity* to avoid the implication that industry was currently inefficient.[56] This implication was also drawn by economists like Jewkes and Dennison, who argued that the productivity campaign was based on the mistaken premise that British industry was inefficient, and that this was leading to a politically inspired denigration of the private sector.[57] The government in practice was very careful not to let the productivity campaign be used as the basis for an attack on the legitimacy of private-sector management, for example via Joint Production Committees,[58] but clearly such a possibility was inherent in the campaign.

The general political relations between the government and the private sector were subject to significant shifts over the life of the Attlee government. Broadly put, relations between 1945 and the economic crisis of 1947 were relatively amiable, but when that crisis seemed to undermine the government's legitimacy the private sector became more intransigent. This was accentuated by the government's determination to press on with both the nationalisation of iron and steel and legislation to impose Development Councils.[59]

Development Councils were a particular cause of dispute, above all because their imposition was seen as 'backdoor nationalisation' or 'the new despotism' as the President of the FBI proclaimed.[60] Development Councils were important not only because they were Labour's one clear initiative in the private sector, but perhaps even more importantly because they challenged the crucial role of the trade associations in the organisation of the private sector. As Rogow and Shore and, more recently, Mercer have emphasised, trade associations were key actors in this period because of the way they had come to play a central role in running the controls over British industry.[61] Trade associations had grown rapidly during the war, encouraged by this role in the control apparatus, and by a general perception by employers that they were an alternative to an enhanced government role in industry.[62] In the post-war period Development Councils were seen as a threat to this continuing dominance of the trade association in industrial organisation and government–industry relations.[63]

Whilst this crucial role of trade associations is not to be disputed, also important in the government's ability to pursue the productivity drive was the role of the peak associations of labour and capital – the TUC and FBI. The TUC's role is not of great importance in the current context, though certainly at that 'peak' level union support for the government's productivity drive was strikingly enthusiastic.[64] The role of the FBI was much more eqivocal.

Whilst the government was keen to engage all relevant bodies in the campaign for higher productivity, the FBI view, in line with its general policy on industrial organisation, was that trade associations were the proper place for such actions beyond those at individual firm level.[65] The problem with this, of course, was that trade associations (and the associated industrial research associations) were very uneven in their activity on this front. Some no doubt were doing a lot, others less, but the crucial point for the FBI was not their level of activity but that 'proper channels' were being used.[66]

The FBI's role on the AACP has been described elsewhere.[67] The key point in the current context is that the creation of the council was embraced largely in the belief that it would be a useful way to allay 'ill-informed' criticism rather than in a more positive light. Later on the FBI became somewhat disenchanted with the AACP when it focused so much attention on managerial shortcomings as the key problem of British industry.[68]

The FBI also played a rather negative role on the Committee on Industrial Productivity. For example, the suggestion made at the Technical and OR Panel of the committee that government might have an enlarged role to play in spreading knowledge of new production techniques in industry was dismissed. The greater use of management consultants was decried, and the general tone was one of 'industry knows best, and no-one is going to tell us our business'.[69] The FBI also supported resistance to the collection of more data on productivity, despite the almost universal acceptance that existing figures were severely deficient.[70]

Despite this negativism, when in September 1948 Cripps broached the idea of a newly intensified productivity campaign by the government, the FBI argued that they should take responsibility for such a campaign. (The TUC agreed, taking the view that the FBI and TUC together should initiate this intensification of effort.)[71]

The main response to this 'deal' by the FBI was to set up its own Production Committee to look at productivity issues.[72] The first draft report by this committee was received without enthusiasm by the FBI Grand Council, and accused of 'chasing every hare started by the government'.[73] Following further discussion and disagreement amongst the committee, a final report was produced which in many ways neatly summarises the FBI tokenism on productivity. The report, entitled Productive Efficiency, consists of one and a half sides of paper.[74] After running through the FBI's usual liturgy of complaints – high taxation, raw materials shortages, export priority for capital equipment, the report asserted 'Nevertheless, productive efficiency must be a direct responsibility of management'. The two measures which, it was argued, deserved special attention were: productivity measurement, in which they stressed the role of trade associations and individual firms, and mutual aid in industry i.e. interchange of information between firms. This would cover such issues as shop and plant layout, works organisation, management structure, etc. The report urged firms to stocktake on what they had already done and make 'a fresh examination of possibilities'. Finally, it called on trade associations to consider setting up mutual aid schemes.

This rather extraordinary document would seem to be a fairly cynical, lowest-common-denominator production. It was a minimalist, token response to the promise to Cripps that the FBI would intensify the productivity campaign.

In his general account of FBI–government relations in the 1945 to 1951 period Blank disputes the view that the FBI got the better of the relationship, and suggests that in important areas the FBI delivered what the government wanted.[75] He cites as examples the areas of investment controls, dividend controls and export increases. But in each of these cases the FBI had a strong motive for delivering. In the case of investment controls the clear motive was to avoid the government getting directly involved in investment decisions. Thus what may seem the surprisingly warm support by the FBI for cuts in industrial investment in 1947 was motivated in part by a dislike of inflation, but primarily as the lesser of two evils: 'The alternative was increased control, which might slow down the whole of industry'.[76] On dividend controls, as Blank points out,[77] the motive was a bargain to persuade the unions to support wage restraint. The increase in exports was, at least in part, because here government exercised some direct control, via raw material quotas tied to export targets.[78]

By contrast, in the case of productivity, the incentives for the FBI to play a dynamic role were limited. Partly because the government's productivity campaign was so ill-focused it was not tied to any sticks or carrots for the private sector and so often degenerated into repetitive exhortation. The FBI took up the AACP idea, largely for defensive reasons, and similarly set up its Production Committee as a token response to get the government off its back. It offered mild encouragement to the trade associations to do something on the issue, but a central part of its credo was that on such industry-specific issues the trade associations should be the only bodies making the decisions on what was done. In sum, it declined to take the leading role in the productivity drive the government hoped it would take.

IV

Plainly the above account does not provide a full assessment of the productivity drive as it was affected by government–industry relations. Above all, it ignores what was done by individual firms in this period in response to the government's campaign. About this we know very little indeed. No doubt some firms were extremely active in focusing on productivity – for example Courtaulds, Joseph Lucas and the unnamed steel works discussed in the AACP Report on Productivity Measurement.[79] However, this firm-level decision-making was precisely the area in which the government had least formal knowledge and least formal leverage – as Harold Wilson was to stress and to lament in his survey of government–private-industry relations in 1950.[80]

The focus on the representative organs of business – above all the FBI – is not just because its activities are much better documented than the generality of individual firms or even trade associations, but also because the Federation was important in shaping trade associations and firm responses – though certainly not, of course, all powerful. If it had given a powerful lead in the productivity drive then this may have provided one of the necessary, though certainly not sufficient, causes of a rather greater success than that drive actually achieved. The question of how a such a lead from the FBI could have shifted private-sector attitudes was never posed, because the FBI never played such a role.

NOTES

1. I am grateful to participants in the conference on The Labour Government and Private Industry in September 1990 for helpful comments and especially to Neil Rollings, Helen Mercer and Nick Tiratsoo.

2. J. Tomlinson *Employment Policy: The Crucial Years 1939–1955* (Oxford 1987), chs. 5, 6.
3. A. Cairncross *Years of Recovery: British Economic Policy 1945–1951* (1985), esp. ch. 2.
4. PRO PREM8/318 'Prosperity Campaign'.
5. PRO CAB134/189 Steering Committee on Economic Development: H. Morrison address to Institute of Public Administration 17/10/1946; CAB134/188: Steering Committee on Economic Development, Memos. 1946. On the origins of the productivity campaign see also CAB134/509 *Manpower Committee*, Minutes, 2/1/1946.
6. PRO CAB134/591 Productivity (Official) Committee Economic Information Unit, brief on 'The Case for Higher Productivity', 31/8/1948. Wartime discussions on full employment had recognised the link to industrial efficiency, but this point was rather lost in the immediate post-war period.
7. *Economic Surveys* for 1947–50.
8. PRO CAB134/591 Productivity (Official) Committee, EIU brief 'Publicity about Higher Productivity', Annex, 31/9/1948; also PRO CAB132/47 Report from Ec. Planning Board, 31/1/1948.
9. H. Mercer 'Monopoly Policy' in this volume; H. Mercer 'The evolution of British government policy towards competition in private industry, 1940–56' (unpublished PhD, University of London, 1989).
10. This characterisation of policy-making in this period does not imply embracing the overall thrust of K. Middlemas *Power, Competition and the State, Vol. I: Britain in Search of Balance* (1985) on 'corporate bias' in British politics. Indeed, the records of the various tripartite bodies suggest a government eager to consult but firmly attached to the notion of parliamentary sovereignty and hence the government's right finally to make all the decisions.
11. N. Rollings chapter 2 in this volume. A Rogow and P. Shore *The Labour Government and British Industry 1945–1951* (Oxford, 1955).
12. PRO CAB87/63 Committee on Post-War Employment, Board of Trade 'General Support of Trade'.
13. H. Mercer 'The Labour Government and Private Industry' in N. Tiratsoo ed. *The Attlee Government* (1991); PRO CAB134/647 Production Committee Memos, 'Development Councils under the Industrial Organisation and Development Act 1947'.
14. Shirley Institute *Report on Labour Redeployment in the Musgrave Mill Cardroom, Bolton* (Manchester, 1948).
15. J. Tomlinson 'The Failure of the Anglo–American Council on Productivity', *Business History* Vol. 33 No. 1 1991. A. Carew *Labour Under the Marshall Plan* (Manchester, 1987), ch. 9.
16. PRO BT195/19 Committee on Industrial Productivity, Blaker–Lobel 15/6/1949.
17. PRO AVIA15/2525 PEB Motion Study Exhibition, October 1945.
18. Board of Trade *Journal*, 30/3/1946, p. 365; PRO CAB134/642 Production Committee Memos, 1st Report of the Productivity (Official) Committee, 20/9/1949.
19. Board of Trade *Journal*, 2/12/1948, p. 928; ibid., 12/11/1949, p. 883.
20. PRO BT64/2324 The Production Efficiency Service of the Board of Trade.
21. PRO CAB134/642 1st Report of Productivity (Official) Committee, 20/9/1949.
22. PRO BT64/2314–2320 SRU Standardisation and Productivity Research Projects.
23. PRO CAB134/639 Production Committee Memos. Ministry of Supply 'Standardising and Simplifying Engineering Products', 8/9/1948; Lemon Committee Report on *Standardisation in the Engineering Industry* (1949).
24. PRO CAB134/640 Production Committee Minutes, 11/3/1949, 30/9/1949.
25. PRO CAB134/648 Production Committee Memos, '1st Report of N.R.D.C.', 8/11/1950.
26. Much of the work of the Committee on Industrial Productivity was concerned

with operational research and technical efficiency, plus a great deal with 'human factors'. PRO CAB132/28–30 Committee on Industrial Productivity.

27. PRO T228/624–8 'British Institute of Management'.
28. Ministry of Education *Education for Management* (1947). On this see P. Armstrong 'The Abandonment of Productive Intervention in Management Teaching Syllabi: An Historical Analysis', Warwick University Industrial Relations Research Unit (Warwick, 1987).
29. G. A. N. Lowndes *Silent Social Revolution* (1965), chs. 18, 19.
30. Percy *Committee on Higher Technical Education* (1945); Barlow *Committee on Scientific Manpower* (1947); M. Sanderson *The Universities and British Industry* (1972) ch. 7.
31. W. Crofts *Coercion or Persuasion? Propaganda in Britain After 1945* (1989).
32. J. Child *British Management Thought: A Critical Analysis* (1969) p. 116.
33. J. Tomlinson 'Industrial Democracy and the Labour Government 1945–1951', Brunel University Discussion Paper 8702 (Uxbridge, 1987).
34. PRO CAB124/1093 Committee on Industrial Productivity Papers.
35. J. Child *British Management Thought* (1969) pp. 135–6.
36. One reason for the creation of the Productivity (Official) Committee was to try and bring some order to government policy in the productivity area. PRO CAB134/591 Productivity (Official) Committee, 1st Meeting, 2/9/1948. Some of these instruments are discussed in more detail in J. Tomlinson 'A Missed Opportunity? Labour and the Productivity Problem 1945–1951' in G. Jones and M. Kirby eds. *Competitiveness and the State in Twentieth Century Britain* (Manchester, 1991).
37. PRO CAB134/591 Productivity (Official) Committee, 'Organisation of the Committee's Work', 31/8/1948.
38. J. Tomlinson *The Unequal Struggle? British Socialism and the Capitalist Enterprise* (1982); K. Hotten 'Labour and the Enterprise', (unpublished PhD, University of London, 1988).
39. I. Taylor 'War and the Development of Labour's Domestic Programme', (unpublished PhD, University of London, 1977), ch. 4, conclusions.
40. PRO LAB10/722 Ministry of Labour: JPCs Campaign to Develop Joint Consultation Machinery 1948–50.
41. PRO PREM8/1182 'The State and Private Industry', para. 2.
42. R C. O. Matthews, C. H. Feinstein, J. C. Odling-Smee *British Economic Growth 1856–1973* (Stanford, 1982), ch. 7.
43. The first official productivity measures were produced by Rostas at the beginning of 1947. PRO CAB134/190 Steering Committee ED(47)2 'Changes in Productivity in British Industry'. The paper discussed measures of physical output per person, with some industries showing a decline and some an increase since before the war. On the general issue of productivity measurement in this period, see J. Tomlinson 'The Politics of Economic Measurement: The Rise of the Productivity Problem in the 1940s' in A. Hopwood and P. Miller eds. *Accounting in its Social Context* (Cambridge, forthcoming).
44. PRO CAB134/591 Productivity (Official) Committee, 'Organisation of the Committee's Work', 31/8/1948.
45. PRO CAB134/592 Productivity (Official) Committee, OP(49)8 'Publicity About Productivity', 14/3/1949.
46. J. Tomlinson 'The Failure of the A.A.C.P.'; G. Hutton 'British and American Ways of Life – Diverging or Converging?' *Futures* Vol. III No. 6 65–72.
47. PRO LAB10/722 Ministry of Labour, JPCs Campaign to Develop Joint Consultation Machinery, 1948–50.
48. PRO CAB134/592 Productivity (Official) Committee, Draft 1st Report, 10/3/1949; BT64/2982 Board of Trade *Government Organisation for Industrial Productivity*, 1947.
49. PRO BT64/2313 Special Research Unit, 'The Working Party Reports and Productivity' (no date).

50. PRO CAB134/592 Draft 1st Report, para. 142.
51. PRO CAB124/1096 Committee on Industrial Productivity, Nicholson–Tizard, 20/5/1948.
52. PRO BT64/2471 'Amendments to the Industrial Organisation and Development Act', September 1950.
53. PRO CAB132/47 Committee on Industrial Productivity (Technology and Operational Research Panel), '1st Interim Report of the Committee on Research and Productivity', 17/9/1947.
54. PRO CAB124/1096 Committee on Industrial Productivity, Memo by Tizard, September 1948.
55. R. Robson *The Cotton Industry* (1957), Appendix, p. 353; T. Barna 'Those "Frightfully High" Profits' *Oxford University Bulletin of Statistics* Vol. 11 No. 2 July 1949 213–26.
56. PRO CAB124/1094 Committee on Industrial Productivity, Nicholson–Blaker, 15/12/1947.
57. J. Jewkes 'Is British Industry Inefficient?' *Manchester School* Vol. 14 No. 1 1–16; S. R. Dennison 'Industrial Productivity' *Lloyds Bank Review* No. 11 January 1949 37–54.
58. PRO LAB10/721 Ministry of Labour, 'J.P.C.s: Report to the NJAC' 26/1/49.
59. A. Rogow and P. Shore *The Labour Government and British Industry 1945–51* (Oxford, 1955), ch. 3.
60. Modern Records Centre, University of Warwick, CBI Predecessor Archive (hereafter CBI) MSS 200/F/1/1/189, FBI General Council Minutes, 9/6/1948.
61. Rogow and Shore op. cit.; H. Mercer 'The Evolution of British Government Policy Towards Competition in Private Industry, 1940–56' (unpublished PhD, University of London, 1989).
62. J. W. Grove *Government and Industry in Britain* (1962) pp. 58–62; CBI MSS 200/F/1/1/188, FBI Grand Council Minutes, 12/7/1944.
63. CBI MSS 200/F/1/1/188, FBI Grand Council Discussion of Report on 'Trade Organisation', 9/10/1946.
64. J. Tomlinson 'Trade Unions and the Labour Government, 1945–51' in N. Tiratsoo ed. *The Attlee Years* (1991).
65. CBI MSS 200/F/3/TS/27/1, *Committee on Industrial Productivity*, Letter from FBI to Member of Committee, 6/10/1948.
66. On trade association activity in this area, CBI MSS 200/F1/1/190, FBI Grand Council Minutes, 14/9/1949. On 'proper channels' see, for example, the hostile response to productivity research outside the scope of research associations CBI MSS 200/F/3/T3/27/1, Committee on Industrial Productivity Correspondence, October/November 1948.
67. J. Tomlinson 'The Failure of the A.A.C.P.'.
68. Compare this interpretation of the AACP with Carew's argument in *Labour Under the Marshall Plan*, ch. 9 that it focused excessive attention on labour as the basic problem.
69. CBI MSS 200/F/3/T3/27/1, Committee on Industrial Productivity Correspondence, 10/5/1948, 14/6/1948, 12/8/1948. The proposal for an enhanced government role in development is at PRO CAB132/47 Committee on Industrial Productivity, 'Provision for Development', 5/8/1948.
70. CBI MSS 200/F/3/02/1/31, FBI 'Panel on Productivity Statistics', 22/10/1948.
71. PRO CAB134/542 Production Committee, 'Report of Productivity (Official) Committee', Annex IV.
72. CBI MSS 200/F/1/1/189, FBI Grand Council Minutes, 8/9/1948.
73. CBI MSS 200/F/1/1/189, FBI Grand Council Minutes, 13/10/1948, 8/12/1948.
74. CBI MSS 200/F/3/51/14/29, FBI 'Productive Efficiency', 12/1/1949.
75. S. Blank *Government and Industry in Britain: The F.B.I. in Politics 1945–65* (Aldershot 1973), pp. 105–6. In part the criticism is aimed at Rogow and Shore *The Labour Government*.

76. CBI MSS 200/F/1/1/189, FBI Grand Council Minutes, 10/12/1947.
77. Blank op. cit., pp. 94–104.
78. Cairncross op. cit., p. 309.
79. AACP *Productivity Measurement in British Industry* (1950).
80. PRO PREM8/1183 Wilson *The State and Private Industry*, 4/5/1950.

Four

Anti-monopoly policy

HELEN MERCER

INTRODUCTION

'A debate on nationalisation and cartels',[1] so one American observer described the British general election of 1945. The *Financial News* noted, 'All parties in this Election are concerned about Monopolies',[2] and certainly all political parties included policy on monopoly and restrictive practices in their election manifestos.[3] Of these the Labour Party's manifesto was the most hard hitting. It bristled with antipathy to 'the concentration of too much economic power in the hands of too few men . . . bureaucratically-run private monopolies . . . profiteering interests . . .' These were not to be allowed to 'prejudice national interests by restrictive anti-social monopoly or cartel arrangements'.[4] The manifesto's section on industrial policy argued for the nationalisation of coal, railways and iron and steel as the alternative to 'the enthronement of private monopoly'. Immediately after nationalisation proposals came policies for the rest of industry: top of the list was the promise that 'anti-social restrictive practices will be prohibited.'

But the actual policy record was very weak, when compared to the hyperbole of the manifesto. The centre-piece of the government's legislation was the 1948 Monopolies and Restrictive Practices Act. This established an independent tribunal with powers to investigate conditions of 'monopoly', defined as control over production or supply of one-third of the goods in question, either by one firm or by several acting together in such a way as to restrict competition. The Act gave the government power to ban specific practices in a specific industry, found by the Monopolies and Restrictive Practices Commission to be against the 'public interest'. The Commission worked very slowly: by the 1951 election only two reports had been published, on dental goods and cast-iron rainwater goods used in building.

Indeed, Labour's actual policies were no different from the Coalition government's declaration of intent in the White Paper on Employment Policy of 1944.[5] This had promised the investigation of restrictive practices on a case-by-case empirical basis, precisely the outlook of the 1948 Act. The policy was also in line with the Conservative election manifesto, and the Federation of British Industry, the peak business organisation, found the policy 'less objectionable than it might have been'.[6] While Labour's nationalisation programme removed some of the key cartelised industries from the private sphere, the Economic Section of the Cabinet was still appalled in September 1946 when the main outlines of the forthcoming Bill were agreed, describing them as 'less than the minimum urged upon the Coalition'.[7]

Another arm of Labour's anti-trust policy was a series of *ad hoc* investigations: some public, some departmental. The most important of these was an independent committee set up in 1947 to enquire into the practice of resale price maintenance. Its report appeared in 1948 and recommended a blanket ban on collective maintenance of retail prices.[8] The government responded with a White Paper which proposed to ban all resale price maintenance, whether operated collectively, through a trade association or by individual manufacturers acting alone.[9] However business raised so much opposition that implementation was delayed. One of Peter Thorneycroft's first acts on becoming President of the Board of Trade in November 1951 was to shelve the measure.[10]

This chapter looks at what happened to Labour's election pledges. It argues that the Labour movement, broadly defined to include the Labour Party, the TUC and the Co-operative Societies, were divided on the nature of a Labour government's response to oligopolistic structures and practices in British industry. Nevertheless, it is clear that the Labour governments intended to implement strong anti-cartel policies, but legislation was emasculated. The views of their immediate allies were eschewed in favour of a weak policy which, while doing something to carry out election pledges, was geared to appeasing the majority of business opinion. This was generally hostile to any erosion of the right to make restrictive agreements in a post-war world which could witness a repeat of the economic conditions of the inter-war years.

Businessmen were thus a vital constraint on Labour's freedom of action. However, policy was also developed at a time of intense American pressure for removing obstacles to post-war trade, and for international agreements to deal with cartels, as one of these obstacles. Their lobbying was to prove key in both the nature and the timing of the legislation. It will be argued that it was the interaction between these two groups which explains the particular character of Labour policy.

This chapter looks first at the monopoly problem of the 1930s and 1940s. It then looks at Labour's analysis and strategy, the response of businessmen to plans for the 1948 Restrictive Practices legislation and the role of the United States in this. Finally it comments on the story of Labour's failed attempt to outlaw retailing restrictionism.

THE 'MONOPOLY PROBLEM'

There were two aspects to the 'monopoly problem': concentration of ownership in large firms – the trusts; and restrictive agreements between independent enterprises – cartels. For the British economy in the 1930s and 1940s cartels were the most widespread manifestation of the monopoly problem. By 1935 the largest 100 firms accounted for 23 per cent of gross manufacturing output, a level of concentration of ownership on a par with that in the United States. In the 1930s and 1940s the level of concentration stayed fairly constant.[11] However, estimates suggest that between 25 per cent and 30 per cent of gross manufacturing output was affected by trade association cartel agreements in the mid 1930s, and perhaps up to 50 per cent to 60 per cent by 1956.[12] In 1938 about 30 per cent of domestic consumer expenditure was on goods affected by various forms of resale price maintenance and their associated practices.[13]

Government involvement in cartelisation in the 1930s is gaining increasing recognition among economic historians of the inter-war period.[14] Government legislation was responsible for the cartels in coal and cotton, with the Bank of England involved in capacity-restricting agreements in cotton and shipbuilding. The Import Duties Advisory Committee (IDAC) had encouraged domestic cartels elsewhere, like the British Iron and Steel Federation, by suggesting to firms and trade associations that they form international arrangements as alternatives to higher tariffs.[15] Meanwhile a mass of petty restrictions, regarding prices, sales territories and capacity sprang up across a range of industries.[16]

The Second World War, like the First, was a catalyst for the further extension and development of the 'trade association system' or 'movement' as it was called. Their numbers were estimated at about 2,500 in 1944, with 300 export groups additionally established in areas and products previously little organised.[17]

In certain trades, and with direct government cajoling, the war saw a move to vertical integration and rationalisation of the trade association system, with groups representing different stages of manufacture and retailing of related products merging or being brought under 'umbrella' associations. Notable examples were in building materials, radios and parts and tyre manufacture and distribution.[18] The government's purpose was to improve the role of trade associations in the administration of controls and it was with the help of trade associations and export groups that raw materials were allocated, production concentrated, prices fixed and export markets co-ordinated. The controllers were usually businessmen from a major firm or trade association concerned; sometimes their ex-employers paid part or all of their salaries.[19] Restrictionism, in the form, for instance, of price and capacity fixing, could not be carried on independently during the war, but much of a controlling trade association's work, such as allocating materials, had 'many of the vices of the old, pre-war type of cartel'.[20]

On coming to power, Labour did not challenge this system of controls, a point remarked on with surprise by contemporaries, as it had been the focus of much left-wing criticism during the war.[21] The dilemma which the Coalition government had faced, therefore, in developing policy on cartels, was to remain under Labour: how to combat restrictive practices, seen as wholly incompatible with an expansionist post-war economy, without alienating those same trade associations whose co-operation was needed to administer controls and co-ordinate export drives.[22]

An important feature of the pre-war British cartel system was its strong international element. In the 1930s many trade associations came together to provide a national body to negotiate with foreign counterparts, to control prices, sales territories and, sometimes, capacity.[23] In certain industries, notably chemicals, large firms were heavily engaged in international cartels.[24] In 1944 a Board of Trade economist estimated that in the 1930s 16 per cent of British manufacturing output was subject to the control of international cartels.[25] British firms had had a particularly close relationship with German firms, prompting American firms to fear by 1939 that a cartel bloc was being built against them and their exports.[26]

The 'monopoly' problem was not only an economic issue; it had a major political dimension. In the 1930s Britain's involvement in international cartels with Germany became a part of the policy known as 'economic appeasement'.[27] Domestically the growth of cartels was inseparable from the growing political importance of the trade associations. From the end of the nineteenth century, but especially in the 1930s, restrictive practices in Britain had mainly been operated through trade associations. Government estimates of the effectiveness of a restrictive practice were usually based on estimates of the extent to which a trade association was representative of all firms producing or retailing a product.[28] While the effectiveness of these restrictive practices in the 1930s is uncertain, the formation and strengthening of the trade associations was of enduring significance. By the 1940s their role as a part of the wartime state made them powerful economic and political institutions. The machinery, organisation, experience and knowledge of industrial structure were all in place for trade associations to operate effective and wide-ranging restrictions in the post-war world.

The role of Britain's cartels in the 1930s is currently under debate,[29] but in the 1940s this situation was viewed with alarm in many quarters. Economists in the Board of Trade and the Economic Section saw pre-war cartels as a major cause of rigidity in the industrial structure, hindering amalgamation and concentration, hindering the spread of techniques and economies of scale, preferring 'high prices and low turnover' and thus sabotaging efforts to improve efficiency, increase exports and improve the balance-of-payments position.[30] There were also widespread fears of profiteering, through the system of price controls[31] and government contracts: in early 1945 the Ministries of Aircraft Production and of Supply obtained refunds from industries of between £7 million and £10 million, as a result of unduly high profits by contractors.[32] Ernest Bevin made allegations of profiteering by price rings in steel, bricks and cement.[33] Thus large firms, cartels and trade associations had an extensive influence on the British economy by 1945. By then the potential field of monopoly and restrictionism appeared as a major threat to Britain's plans for post-war reconstruction, as the White Paper on Employment Policy of 1944 stated. In addition, the extent of British involvement in international cartels in the 1930s had already aroused American hostility: action to remove obstacles to the expansion of world trade after the war therefore also focused on the problem of cartels.

LABOUR, CARTELS, MONOPOLY AND COMPETITION

A number of different views existed within the Labour movement both in the analysis of the problem and on questions of strategy. However, there was consensus on the immediate measures to be taken by a Labour government against restrictive practices.

Profiteering was an immediate concern in the post-war period. Similar anti-profiteering sentiments during the First World War had prompted an inquiry into the 'trusts' in 1918 and the subsequent Profiteering Acts.[34] After the Second World War, in spite of frequent calls for such an inquiry by the TUC and Labour MPs, no inquiry was initiated partly for fear of business reaction.[35]

However, the second, and more prominent, concern was the effect of monopoly on industrial efficiency, and it was this which focused Labour's attention on cartels. Historically, Labour's attitude towards the 'trusts' had been a combination of strong support for the 'positive' features of large firms – such as economies of scale and the way they prefigured socialist organisation – with warnings about the possible stagnation in economic life, profiteering and the consolidation of vested interests in political life.[36] A Labour Party research paper of 1947 used this approach to single out cartels. Large firms, it argued, covered a relatively small section of the economy, secured certain benefits of large-scale organisation and, being more 'in the public eye' were more sensitive to accusations of monopoly. Cartels, on the other hand, were very widespread, their activities were unpublicised and they were often responsible for retarding efficiency in their industries.[37] Several economists, many of them Labour, had investigated retailing in Britain

and argued that, in the distributive sector restrictive practices were
wasteful of manpower, and so hindered the introduction of self-service,
maintained retail prices and shifted competition into wasteful areas like
advertising.[38]

In developing a policy to deal with cartels and trusts, the Labour Party
displayed a love–hate relationship with the notion of competition.
Historically, Labour was strongly influenced by the work of the early
Fabians, and their rejection of competition as a principle of economic
activity.[39] This tradition was continued into the post-Second World War
period. The TUC saw no future for competition, arguing the move to
concentration meant that control would be either by a public authority
or by 'private groups and individuals'.[40] A paper prepared for a joint
Labour Party–TUC committee on trusts and cartels expressed the long-
held view that free competition produced an unhealthy economy and
inequitable distribution of economic and political power. Any public
supervision of monopoly must therefore be done, not with the aim of
restoring competition, but to ensure that the private sector operated 'in
what may be broadly defined as the public interest'.[41]

However, Labour ministers also indicated that they saw certain
benefits in competition, and indeed in the free-enterprise system itself.
Dalton argued, in a phrase frequently echoed by Labour ministers: 'you
should have either really free, profit-seeking competition, or else a
centrally-planned public enterprise'.[42] In 1948 Wilson argued that
'competition is the public's natural safeguard in any industry which
continues on the basis of private enterprise'.[43] In 1956 the research
department even considered that the Labour Party had the initiative
over the Conservatives in terms of seeking to promote competition.[44]

The Co-operative movement added its voice to this strand of thought.
Co-ops were often 'boycotted' by trade associations and denied the right
to sell certain goods, such as gramophone records, on the basis that the
dividend was a form of price-cutting.[45] The Co-op frequently complained
about the practice of resale price maintenance which encouraged such
boycotts and it was in part their lobbying which prompted the inquiry
into resale price maintenance under Labour. Indeed, its spokesmen
began to look askance at plans for state ownership and state trading,
which were popular in the Labour Party, as a threat to the sphere for
'Co-operation'.[46]

Given these various approaches to the problem within the organisations
making up the 'labour movement' prescriptions for reform also differed.
One strong element argued that it was not monopoly concentration or
even cartels *per se* which were the problem, but who owned them or
operated them: 'If monopoly is the inevitable development in an industry,
it is far preferable that it be public than private.'[47] The Labour Party
research department and the TUC continued to argue that socialisation

was 'ultimately . . . the only satisfactory policy for avoiding those dangers to the life and well-being of the community to which the growth of private monopoly gives rise'.[48] The TUC in its *Interim Report on Post-War Reconstruction* of 1944 had similarly stated that monopoly was inevitable and called for an elaborate system of state ownership and supervision. It proposed corporatist Industrial Boards to supervise industries, which alone should have the power to operate restrictive agreements.[49]

This strand of thought made anti-monopoly policy part of a generally interventionist role for government. The joint Labour Party–TUC committee on trusts and cartels favoured a monopoly tribunal which would be 'an integral part of the Government's economic planning with specialised functions'.[50] In 1950 Wilson was to propose strengthening the Monopolies Act to allow nationalisation of firms criticised by the Commission.[51] In 1951 a draft Labour pamphlet on 'Monopoly' favoured price control to protect the consumer against monopoly exploitation, and nationalisation 'to transform the anti-social character of monopoly power'.[52]

As the Labour leadership imposed limits on further nationalisation, however, the research department was increasingly concerned with making private enterprise enterprising, and hence with a 'competition policy'. The tension between the two elements is evident in a comment by USDAW, the shopworkers' union, in 1950. The Labour government proposed to outlaw resale price maintenance, a move which USDAW feared would lead to pressure on retailers' margins and thus on wages and conditions for their members. The Labour government, they said, had 'rejected the Socialist approach of planning and regulation in favour of private capitalistic unfettered competition'.[53]

Thus, there were divisions: was the answer to cartels *more* public supervision and ownership, or 'freer' enterprise? Nevertheless, it is clear that, in spite of this fundamental divergence, there was broad agreement that private enterprise should not be allowed to operate 'anti-social' restrictive agreements. The phrase in the manifesto 'the prohibition of anti-social restrictive practices' is open to interpretation and may have meant little more than a system of investigation, similar to the 1948 Act, to decide whether a particular practice in a particular industry was against the 'public interest'. However, Labour ministers in the Attlee government wanted something stronger. During reconstruction discussions many of them, including Dalton, Morrison, Cripps, Jay and Gaitskell, had argued for strong legislation against cartels to be introduced as soon as possible.[54] In 1946 Morrison suggested to the Board of Trade civil servants entrusted with drafting legislation that a system of registration of cartels prior to inquiry and prohibition be used, a proposal favoured by the civil servants in the Board of Trade during the war. Again in 1948 Wilson was to propose similar ideas.[55] The TUC in 1944 had called for a very full inquiry into all cartels and monopolies along the lines of the 1918 Committee on Trusts.[56] Ministers in Cabinet and Labour MPs in Parliament expressed regret at the weakness of the Act, especially the powers available if the Commission reported unfavourably.[57] One MP described the Act as a 'puny infant' when he had hoped for 'a lusty and noisy fellow'.[58]

Thus, in spite of divisions, whether public ownership or more enterprising private enterprise was the answer to cartels and monopolies, both analyses tended towards some agreement on a strong line.

It therefore remains to be seen why Labour did not pursue a more active policy on private cartels.

THE PRIVATE SECTOR'S REACTION TO ANTI-CARTEL POLICY

To establish a monopolies tribunal and to investigate cartels and trusts required continuous supervision over the whole of private industry. This businessmen were not prepared to tolerate.

As industrialists turned towards the post-war world, they were agreed on the need to retain the *right* to enter into restrictive agreements. The Principal Assistant Secretary at the Board of Trade during the war, Alix Kilroy, remarked of discussions with businessmen on reconstruction that they 'lead rapidly to questions of Government policy on international cartels and the monopoly of the home market'.[59] During the war ministers, civil servants and temporary economists had been made painfully aware that the overwhelming majority of industrialists would be implacably opposed to any attack on cartels.[60] Civil servants had complained bitterly during the war of the heavily restrictionist outlook of all the major industrial plans for reconstruction, their unwillingness to appreciate the need for a dynamic industry and hence the need for structural change.[61]

There were some divisions among industrialists. A significant grouping was increasingly irritated by restrictions. Large building contractors, for instance, complained at the restrictive practices among their suppliers.[62] In retailing many of the 'multiple' shops, or chain stores were to argue that resale price maintenance could stop larger stores competing through passing on economies of large-scale distribution,[63] and they were supported by the Co-op.[64]

Within the FBI a view was emerging that the industrial consumer needed to be protected from monopoly pricing in components. In 1944 the FBI had conceded that some tribunal for complaint by industrial interests against monopoly practices might be desirable.[65] An FBI paper of 1950 accepted that some monopolistic trade associations, whose prices entered into and significantly affected the 'general cost structure' should be liable to public scrutiny.[66] Thus, on the basis of the need to protect the industrial consumer, the FBI was willing to countenance government power of supervision and investigation. But this was more on the lines of *ad hoc* inquiries, as proposed by the businessman MP, Sir Andrew Duncan, during the war,[67] rather than continuous supervision which the Labour movement generally favoured.

Business hostility to an active and continuous government policy against cartels was rooted in two concerns. The first was fear of a return to inter-war conditions, and therefore the need to have defensive mechanisms to maintain prices and profits and stop 'cut-throat' competition. The rigid clinging to the right to make cartels, was partly inherent in the very *raison d'être* of trade associations, and there was therefore a vested political interest in maintaining the *status quo*.

The second influence on the development of business, and especially of FBI ideas was the American bid to get Britain to agree to a wholesale outlawing of international cartels.

The United States, in line with its general thrust for an 'Open Door' policy in the post-war world, aimed to make Britain a partner in an international 'trust-busting' campaign. Under the terms of the Anglo–American Financial Agreement which accompanied the 1945 loan, Britain had agreed to promote an international conference on trade and employment, at which a code on international cartels would be discussed.[68] A series of conferences resulted in the formulation of the Havana Charter for an International Trade Organisation. The ITO was never ratified, but by 1948 conditions attached to Marshall Aid committed Britain to working actively to limit domestic and international cartels.[69]

This American pressure was crucial to the Act on monopolies coming forward at all under the Labour government. In March 1946 officials explained to the President of the Board of Trade that one reason for resuscitating the whole question of legislation on restrictive practices was because, 'the problem arises in connection with the talks with the Americans'.[70] At that stage it was thought prudent to await the outcome of talks. By 1947–8 American pressure had re-emerged and propelled the Bill along: as Alix Kilroy argued, one reason for ensuring the Bill was discussed that session was 'to make a good impression on the Americans'.[71]

In the years after the Second World War, the FBI was forced to formulate a position on international cartels in response to this American pressure. Ministers and civil servants were particularly responsive to business feelings on international cartels, and took their lead from business reactions to American proposals. Indeed the FBI had a major consultative role throughout the negotiations with the United States, not only on cartels but on tariffs, imperial preference and many other questions.[72]

The FBI set up an Industrial Agreements Committee to consider a submission on the American proposals.[73] Large firms were well represented on this committee. It was chaired by Dr, later Sir, William Coates, then Deputy Chairman of ICI. This committee presented the Board of Trade with a paper arguing that cartels in general were essential to large-scale firms which needed to plan production to secure orderly economic development. Paramount in their defence of international cartels were fears of a post-war recession and foreign competition: 'in the event of failure to avoid a return to inter-war economic conditions, it would be illogical and unjust not to allow producers to take their own private measures where governments have failed'.[74]

Both these arguments were repeated by many other trade associations which submitted replies to the Board of Trade, most of which were, overtly or otherwise, hostile to any international control.[75] A few accepted the need for some national and international supervision of agreements, although they quibbled about the American definition of harmful business practices.[76] British industrialists wished to preserve their right to make international agreements and it was therefore crucial that no outright prohibition of any type of agreement be made, nor that any type of practice be considered a priori against the spirit of the ITO.

This empirical approach had been fought for at the preliminary discussions in London in October and November 1946. The US draft charter presented to this conference suggested that 'Members agree to prevent practices which restrain competition . . . [a list of such practices] and thus have the effect of frustrating the purposes of the I.T.O.' A revision was secured so that the article read, 'Each member shall . . . prevent practices which restrain competition . . . whenever they have harmful effects on the purposes of the I.T.O.'. This revision, 'crucial to the whole chapter', remained and was the wording incorporated in the final Havana Charter.[77]

With the empirical approach secured, negotiations then turned to the question of procedure. It was on this issue that the FBI document submitted to the government, 'Private International Industrial Agreements' was addressed. This insisted that any supervision or investigation of international cartels be vested primarily in the national government. The American draft charter, while committing member governments to take individual action to prevent restrictive practices which limited free trade, made the ITO the body to receive complaints from other members or from commercial enterprises, to require the furnishing of information and to make recommendations to member governments for them to take appropriate action over their nationals.

The FBI was adamantly opposed to this procedure, proposing instead that information on cartels should only be communicated to the contracting parties' respective governments, which should only communicate it to the ITO if there were a complaint.[78]

On this question also the British delegation was quite successful and the final draft of the Havana Charter embodied the thesis that 'Member governments will be allowed a good deal of freedom to deal with problems in their own way', as a Board of Trade memorandum expressed it. The charter obliged member governments to 'take adequate powers within the framework of their legal and economic systems to control any such arrangements'.[79]

This was a very important result. It assured a policy on domestic cartels by obliging the British government, as no other factor in the post-war years did, to establish a national method of supervision and control of restrictive practices. This was a commitment bolstered by the terms of Marshall Aid.

Thus Britain did not 'capitulate'[80] to American pressure but the interaction of American and domestic interests produced ambiguous results. Arguably, British businessmen were more united against limits on international cartels than they were against measures to regulate restrictions in the home market. Thus the coupling of international and domestic aspects of the cartel problem served to harden the industrial response. On the other hand, resistance to international measures prompted the formulation of domestic instruments of regulation.

The point which the FBI would not concede, at either an international or a domestic level was any condemnation of cartels *per se*; the empirical approach was vital, both to resist American pressure, and to allow for certain types of practice to be scrutinised, but not all industrial agreements.

Civil servants had a clear idea of what industry would tolerate, and they played a key role in transmitting industrial feeling and affecting policies. Twice they dissuaded Labour ministers from a *per se* approach. Some civil servants were quite unwilling to accept that pre-war cartelisation was a mistake.[81] But others seemed fairly convinced of the dangers of restrictive practices in an expansionist world. Indeed, during the war the Board of Trade had originally submitted to the Steering Committee on Employment proposals for the registration, investigation and possible banning of practices, foreshadowing the 1956 Restrictive Trade Practices Act. Their paper argued that outright prohibition pointed more definitely at full employment.[82]

Civil servants, however, tended to go for compromise: even G. C. Allen, a leading economist campaigner at the Board of Trade for competition policies recommended a milder policy in the face of business opposition.[83] Just before the Monopolies Bill went before Parliament in

1948 a departmental representative of the Ministry of Supply expressed the view that the Bill should be delayed as the present was no time to 'rock the boat' of government–industry relations.[84]

Civil servants promoted the view, however, that British industrialists had to be persuaded and educated out of their restrictionist habits and into awareness of issues of industrial efficiency and productivity. 'British industry cannot be made competitive by Act of Parliament', Morrison's Principal Assistant Secretary argued.[85] R. C. Bryant, an Assistant Secretary at the Board of Trade, briefing Wilson, argued that 'The conventional view of monopoly in this country is that it is fairly sensitive to public opinion and is unlikely to charge very high prices . . . or to indulge in restrictive practices which are evidently contrary to the public interest.' He hoped that the Monopolies Commission was 'likely to result in recommendations, not for the abandonment of a particular practice but for improved methods of organisation, management, accounting or research.'[86] Interestingly, this approach was almost paraphrased when Wilson introduced the Bill to Parliament. The key sanction in the Act was the use of publicity which would 'cause any of those industrialists who may, without realising it, be acting in an anti-social manner to alter their arrangements'.[87]

Not only did the broad outlines of the Bill therefore conform to industry's empirical approach, but the FBI conducted lobbying around the Bill, both openly through the Conservative Party in Parliament, and through pressure on certain departments. In particular, lobbying concentrated on removing the work of the Commission as far as possible from the public eye. The Conservatives opposed government amendments to introduce a public complaints mechanism, arguing that the mere fact of a complaint would be a slur on an industry.[88] They opposed – unsuccessfully – a government amendment to investigate types of practice, like resale price maintenance, across a range of industries as this would lead the Monopolies Commission into general statements about industry's practices and their relationship to the 'public interest'.[89]

Further constraints on publicity were achieved before the Bill was introduced. Although only reasons of national security should be allowed to prevent the publication of a report, one civil servant noted that 'Industry is, however, likely to press strongly for the withholding of information which might harm "legitimate business interests" . . . and the form of words used is intended to meet this point'.[90] This question of getting hold of necessary information from industrialists was to become a problem in the work of the Commission.[91]

Also of great importance later on was the attitude taken by sponsoring departments outside the Board of Trade. They, both civil servants and ministers, conducted their own lobbying to ensure either that 'their' industries were excluded from the Bill, for instance the Ministry of

28. Office of Fair Trading op. cit.
29. B. Fine 'Economies of scale and a featherbedding cartel?: a reconsideration of the interwar British coal industry' *Economic History Review* Vol. xliii No. 3 1990 438–49; A. Booth 'Britain in the 1930's: a managed economy?' *Economic History Review* Vol. xl No. 4 1987 499–522.
30. PRO BT64/318 Memorandum by G. C. Allen and Hugh Gaitskell 'The Control of Monopoly' 17/7/1943.
31. Rogow op. cit. p. 68; J. Leruez *Economic Planning and Politics in Britain* (1975) p. 64.
32. Morgan op. cit. p. 233.
33. *News Chronicle* 11/7/1945.
34. Cmd. 9236 *Ministry of Reconstruction: Report of the Committee on Trusts* (PP 1918, Vol. xiii).
35. Mercer Thesis pp. 137–8.
36. Labour Party *Trusts and the Public* (1920); H. W. Macrosty *The Trust Movement in British Industry* (1907) pp. 343–5.
37. Labour Party Archives National Museum of Labour History, Manchester (hereafter LPA) R.D.22/April 1946 'Note on the public control of Trade Associations and Combines' for discussion at a meeting of the Joint Labour Party/TUC Sub-committee on Trusts and Cartels 11/4/1946.
38. LPA R.D.89/March 1948 'Should there be a Distribution Policy?'; H. Smith *Retail Distribution* (1937) p. 154; W. Arthur Lewis 'Competition in the Retail Trade' *Economica* Vol. 12 No. 4 Nov. 1945 pp. 230–1; PRO BT64/455 R.P.M.(E)60 Evidence to the Lloyd Jacob Committee on resale price maintenance submitted by R. Cohen, R. F. Khan, W. B. Reddaway and J. Robinson, 1947.
39. N. and J. MacKenzie *The First Fabians* (1977) p. 43.
40. TUC, *Interim Report on Post-War Reconstruction* (1944) p. 8.
41. LPA R.D.44/Feb. 1947 'The Public Control of Monopoly' memorandum for the trusts and cartels committee.
42. Dalton Diaries, LSE I Box 31 4/2/1944; H. Morrison *Herbert Morrison: an Autobiography* (1960) p. 229 for similar views.
43. *Hansard* (Commons) Vol. 449, Col. 2020, 22/4/1948.
44. LPA RE31/Feb. 1956 'Notes on the Restrictive Practices Bill'.
45. PRO BT13/220A MM(46)63 Memorandum by Cripps 'The Effect of Price Maintenance on the Co-operative Societies' 11/7/1946.
46. G. L. Perkins's Presidential address to the Co-operative Congress in 1947, cited in G. D. N. Worswick 'Economic Policy and the Co-operative Movement' in N. Barou ed. *The Co-operative Movement in Labour Britain* (1948) p. 16.
47. E. Davies *National Enterprise* (1946) p. 16.
48. LPA R.D.22/April 1946 'Note on the public control of Trade Associations and Combines' for the Joint Labour Party/TUC Sub-committee on Trusts and Cartels; R.D.33/Nov. 1946 'Criteria for Nationalisation'.
49. TUC op. cit., *passim.*
50. LPA R.D.66/July 1947 'The Public Control of Monopoly'.
51. PRO CAB124/1200 'The State and Private Industry' memorandum by Wilson 4/5/1950.
52. LPA R.53/June 1951 'Monopoly'.
53. LPA R.59/July 1951 'Resale Price Maintenance' paper submitted by USDAW to the NEC.
54. Mercer Thesis p. 116.
55. PRO BT64/251 Note of meeting with the Lord President 26/3/1946; BT64/467 note of President's suggestion for the registration of restrictive agreements 25/2/1948.
56. *Hansard* (Commons) Vol. 408 Col. 954 22/2/1945.
57. PRO CAB128/12 CM(48)21st meeting 11/3/1948 and CM(48)24th meeting 22/3/1948.

58. *Hansard* (Commons) Vol. 449 Col. 2086 22/4/1948.
59. PRO BT64/145 Note Alix Kilroy – G. C. Allen 29/3/1943 and in similar vein, 5/4/1943.
60. PRO BT64/318 Letter Sir Charles Innes – Henry Clay, June 1942.
61. PRO BT64/3497 discussions and comments on 'The Long Term prospects of British industry', May 1944.
62. J. Jewkes, *Ordeal by Planning* (1948) p. 37.
63. There were many divisions in the trade, for a summary of views see, Mercer Thesis pp. 213–14 and 219–20.
64. PRO BT13/220A MM(46)63 'The Effect of Price Maintenance on Co-operative Societies' memorandum by Cripps.
65. FBI *The Organisation of British Industries* (1944) p. 14.
66. CBI, MSS200/S2/14/76, 'Trade Associations: their place in the industrial world', c. 1950.
67. PRO CAB87/10 R(45)8th. meeting 5/2/1945.
68. Cmd. 6708 *Financial Agreement between the United States and the United Kingdom* (PP 1945–6, Vol. xxv); Cmd. 6709 *Proposals for Consideration by an International Conference on Trade and Employment (Dec. 1945)* (PP 1945–6, Vol. xxvi).
69. Cmd. 7469 *Economic Co-operation Agreement between the Governments of the United Kingdom and the U.S.A., 6th. July 1948* (PP 1947–8, Vol. xxxi).
70. PRO BT64/251 note for the President's morning meeting by G. H. Andrew 7/3/1946.
71. PRO BT64/251 letter Alix Kilroy – J. E. Johnson (Private Secretary to Sir John Woods the Permanent Secretary, at the Board of Trade) 28/4/1947.
72. This is according to their own account: CBI MSS200/F/3/S1/13/23, 'Relations between the FBI and British Government' by D. L. Walker 10/7/1947.
73. CBI MSS200/F/3/S1/17/8, Minutes of Committee on Industrial Agreements 1945–48.
74. PRO BT11/3245 FBI memorandum 'Private International Industrial Agreements', February 1947.
75. PRO BT64/307, 'Comments received from firms and associations on Ch. IV of Cmd. 6709, "Restrictive Business Practices"'. Submissions from associations representing tinplate, cement, mechanical cloth, lino, accumulator and electric lamp manufacturers, and one from a firm of accountants claiming to speak for eighteen other trade associations.
76. PRO BT64/307, op. cit. views of tyres, clothing, engineers and steel tube manufacturers.
77. PRO BT64/500, 'Ch. V – Amendments to various articles'. Note for delegate to Havana conference.
78. PRO BT11/3254, FBI memorandum, 'International Agreements'.
79. PRO BT64/484, TN(48)11, 'The Obligations of the I.T.O. Charter and G.A.T.T.', draft memorandum 9/7/1948.
80. P. Burnham *The Political Economy of Post-war Reconstruction* (1990) reviewed by G. C. Peden *Economic History Review* Vol. xliv No. 1 1991 184–5 for a similar view.
81. PRO BT64/145 Kilroy – G. C. Allen 5/4/1943; BT64/318 note by Sir Arnold Overton, Permanent Secretary, Board of Trade, 8/7/1943 and 21/7/1943.
82. PRO CAB87/63 E.C.(43)3 'Restrictive Practices in Industry' memorandum by the Board of Trade 15/10/1943.
83. PRO BT64/394 letter from Allen – G. L. Watkinson 5/3/1945.
84. PRO BT64/467 note by Alix Kilroy of inter-departmental meeting on the Bill, 6/3/1948.
85. PRO CAB124/497 A. Johnstone – James Meade 26/9/1946.
86. PRO BT64/4667 Note by Bryant 10/3/1948.

87. *Hansard* (Commons) Vol. 449 Col. 2027 22/4/1948.
88. *Hansard* (Commons) Vol. 452 Cols. 2054–7 29/6/1948.
89. Ibid.
90. PRO BT64/432 'Notes on the development of restrictive practices policy' by G. C. Andrew 28/1/1948.
91. Mercer 'The Monopolies Commission', p. 83.
92. PRO BT64/466 'Points of principle for decision' 12/2/1948; BT64/467 notes of meeting to discuss second draft of Bill 18/2/1948, and minutes of interdepartmental meeting 6/3/1948.
93. PRO BT64/480 letter Tom Williams, Minister of Agriculture – Harold Wilson 11/3/1948; BT64/467 note of interdepartmental meeting 6/3/1948.
94. Mercer 'The Monopolies Commission', p. 87.
95. PRO BT64/467 minutes of interdepartmental meeting 6/3/1948.
96. PRO BT13/220A MM(46)79 'Distribution Policy' by G. C. Andrew 6/9/1946.
97. Cmd. 7696 *Report of the Committee on Resale Price Maintenance* (PP 1948–9, Vol. xx).
98. PRO BT64/556 letter from Helmore – Sir Norman Kipping 21/6/1949.
99. PRO BT64/556 note by B. Floud (Assistant Secretary, Board of Trade) 26/7/1949, and report of meeting with FBI 28/7/1949.
100. PRO CAB134/133 DM(50)31 'Distribution and Marketing Committee, Resale Price Maintenance' memorandum by President of the Board of Trade. Annex A, 'Official working party on resale price maintenance, Final Report' September 1950.
101. PRO BT64/4665 1st meeting of Policy group 23/3/1951.
102. PRO BT64/4887 paper by Monopolies branch 7/12/1951, and MC/RPM (51)22 8/12/1951.
103. LPA Policy Committee minutes 25/7/1944; R.D.60/July 1947 'The Public Control of Monopoly'.
104. CBI MSS200/F/1/1/188 Grand Council minutes 9/10/1946; FBI/BEC *Trade Organisation* (1946).
105. CBI MSS200/F/1/1/188 Grand Council minutes 10/7/1948.
106. LPA R.D.22/April 1946 'Note on the public control of Trade Associations and Combines'.
107. R. Roberts, 'The Administrative Origins of Industrial Diplomacy', in Turner op. cit. pp. 93–104.

Five

Private industrial investment

MARTIN CHICK

In 1945 the newly elected Labour government possessed a wider range of economic controls than any previous (or subsequent) peacetime British government. Direct controls extended over more than one-quarter of all consumer items. Building licences were required for all but very small building jobs. Licences were also required for the acquisition of most types of plant and machinery.[1] In the financial markets, the Capital Issues Committee continued to vet all requests to make new issues. Ostensibly, it might be thought that an opportunity existed for a Labour government to deploy these controls to initiate substantial restructuring within an economy which had exhibited serious weaknesses both before and during the Second World War.[2] In particular, many of the controls on raw materials, buildings and fund-raising carried particular potential for influencing the level and pattern of fixed capital investment, an area of fundamental importance for the long-term development of the economy. Not only was the increasing capital-intensity of economic production one of the leading character-istics of twentieth-century capitalist development,[3] but also, the management of capital investment had been identified, most famously by Keynes, as one of the principal means of state economic management. Given the extent and apparent potential of the Attlee government's controls, and the subsequent longer-term British economic problems of comparatively low economic growth and productivity, it is possible that later commentators will come to view this early post-war period as a 'missed opportunity'. Such a narrow reading of the use of controls would overlook many of the wider social and economic purposes to which controls were applied. None the less, while examining the nature of the Attlee government's approach to private industrial investment, this chapter will discuss the extent to which such a policy was directed towards effecting a fundamental restructuring of basic sectors of the economy.

One response to perceived structural and operating problems in utility industries was to transfer them to public ownership in the form of nationalised industries. Government policy towards these public corporations, which accounted for just over one-sixth of total investment in this period, has been the subject of considerable study.⁴ In contrast, considerations of government policy towards privately owned industry, which accounted for over half of total investment, have been comparatively uncommon. In part, this may simply be due to the comparative inaccessibility of private industrial archives. Whereas a substantial quantity of records relating to the nationalised industries are centrally collected and classified in the Public Records Office at Kew, those of even large private companies in regular contact with government are scattered and comparatively scarce. Yet, beyond the vagaries of archives, there is a more substantial point affecting the survival of records of relations between government and private industry. Quite simply, contact between government and private industry was often at its most frequent and intense away from the centre of government. Meetings at district or regional level were frequently of more import than any occasional, well-publicised meetings within Whitehall.

In studying the relations between government and private industry, this chapter does not simply concentrate on central-government policy but also attempts to provide some analysis of relations and decisions at a more local and regional level. The first part of this chapter examines central-government policy towards private industrial investment and emphasises the difficulties experienced by government in obtaining information concerning the level and rate of such investment. In addition, it will attempt to identify the main criteria guiding the central decisions on the allocation of resources and the government's general attitude towards private industrial investment. Having noted the pragmatic, frequently short-term and often residual nature of government policy towards private investment, the remainder of the chapter will then concentrate on examining government–private-industry relations at the district and company level. In particular, the chapter will focus on the efforts of the government and the iron and steel industry to plan the rationalisation of that industry.

Although the possibility of nationalising the industry was much discussed during the Attlee government's period in office, it was the 'Plan' for the industry which dominated government–industry attitudes towards investment within the iron and steel industry. This 'planning' option which stopped short of nationalisation, was also attempted to a lesser extent in other industries such as textiles.⁵ In contrast to the pragmatic, often necessitous, short-term approach taken towards aggregate private investment, this 'planning' had the fundamental long-term aim of restructuring and modernising the economy in order to improve its productivity. Although the two Iron and Steel Plans were issued by the Ministry of Supply, the considerations affecting their formulation and implementation were overwhelmingly regional or local. Lacking powers of compulsion, and vacillating over nationalisation, central government, industrial federations and regional organisations struggled to overcome resistance from local firms and companies to their plans for rationalisation. For all the rhetoric of the central planning of investment, planners struggled to influence decision-making at its most local level. Ironically, such wider macro-economic policy concerns as employment policy and the balance of payments allowed local managers to exploit government short-term concern with macro-economic policy, so as to resist the more fundamental, long-term aims of industrial reformers outside Whitehall.

The economic controls deployed by the Attlee government fell, very broadly, into two categories. First, there were those which were simply deemed necessary by the early post-war shortages. Once supply and demand came more into balance, then their *raison d'être* would disappear. Many of these controls were disappearing by 1949. These were short-term controls, primarily concerned to preserve social and economic stability, in part by preventing a repetition of the post-First World War inflationary scramble for decontrolled resources. Second, there were those controls and instruments of economic planning which were intended to have a more long-term life and influence. Many of these longer-term controls and instruments revolved around the factor of investment, both in providing some control over the pattern of investment undertaken by private firms and also in providing some public control over the level of investment and, hence, effective demand within the economy. Planning-minded ministers like Dalton looked to the Capital Issues Committee to provide a long-term means of influencing the pattern of investment, the extension of the life of the Capital Issues Committee into the post-war period being regarded by Dalton as 'part of wider proposals for economic planning' and conferring on the government 'far-reaching powers over investment'.[6] To control the level of demand within the private sector of the economy, some planners looked to such creations as the National Investment Council.[7]

One of the main tasks of the National Investment Council was to organise a 'shelf' of projects during the immediate post-war years, which could then be initiated as information from the planners indicated the approach of a cyclical down-turn. Yet, both the Capital Issues Committee and the National Investment Council were to disappoint the hopes of the early enthusiasts, principally because of the tension which existed between their long-term assumptions and the short-term, immediate problems faced by the Attlee government. The National Investment Council's proposals for collecting shelves of projects rested on the assumption that, as after the First World War, the post-war boom would be short-lived and that a moment would arise for projects to be taken off the 'shelf' and initiated. However, history did not repeat itself and the overwhelming problem faced by the Attlee government was not deficient but excess demand. Few authorities were prepared to devote resources to forming a 'shelf' of projects for future use when current demands were so pressing. In conditions of excess demand, financial controls such as the Capital Issues Committee tended to assume a secondary importance behind the direct controls over such materials as steel. Company investment activity was much more constrained by difficulties in obtaining materials than by problems in obtaining finance.[8] The importance of direct controls was extended by the persistence of excess demand, with the rearmament demands of the Korean War leading to the reintroduction of the recently abandoned steel controls in 1951. The substance of economic planning became predominantly the operation of direct controls, whose primary function was securing short-term economic and social stability, and not in providing the basis for long-term planning. Indeed, one of the key issues affecting such direct controls was how soon they could be confined to the 'bonfire', their life-expectancy being a function of the gap between supply and demand.

In conditions of excess demand, the direct controls, through their influence on the allocation of controlled resources, could be used to influence the pattern of production and investment on the supply side, but their ability to have any impact on the level of demand was much more limited. By 1947, the problem of excess demand and the limited ability of the planning system to cope with the persistent excess demand was becoming clear. Not only was contemporary concern with excess demand finding expression in discussions of 'inflationary gaps', bottlenecks and shortages, but the pattern of shortages and the number of projects in progress were held to be contributions to long construction times. By 1947, the economy was becoming littered with uncompleted investment projects due in part to the large number of projects whose commencement had been authorised in 1945 and 1946. The early failure of planning to check and control demand, indeed the early promotion of demand, resulted in resources being spread too widely across too many projects. In the favoured Development Areas, for example, which accounted for half of all the factory building authorised since 1944, only 40 per cent had been started, a mere 6 per cent completed.

It was in response to the problem of the persistence of excess demand that, in mid-1947, significant changes and additions were made to the structure of central economic planning. As the National Investment Council slipped into irrelevant abeyance, the Central Economic Planning Staff was established to provide some central supervision of departmental expenditure and resource allocation. As a result of a Cabinet decision of 1 August 1947, the Investment Programmes Committee was established under Sir Edwin Plowden to curtail all capital investment projects other than those contributing to the export drive or to import-saving. Largely on the Investment Programmes Committee's recommendations, the

Cabinet approved cuts in the investment programme for the forthcoming year. In 1947, for example, Cabinet sanctioned cuts which were aimed at reducing investment from its previously forecast level of £1,600 million across the whole of 1948, to a new level of £1,420 million.[9] While this represented a cut of some 11.25 per cent in the expected level of total gross investment, the cuts were thought likely to reduce new investment by one-third. Cuts of a similar magnitude were approved in 1949 and, as in 1947, these cuts in investment formed half of the total package of cuts sanctioned by the Cabinet. In 1949, of the £140 million cut in the expected level of investment, £90 million fell on the construction side and £50 million on plant and machinery.[10] The main reductions as allocated between industries were £35 million on new housing, £25 million on fuel and power and £15 million on what was loosely called 'manufacturing industry'.[11]

The government's efforts to establish greater control over the level of gross investment were only partially successful. Efforts to impose greater constraints on the investment programmes of the nationalised industries proved difficult, but more successful than similar efforts directed at limiting private industrial investment. In contrast to the large, heavily concentrated and predominantly monopolistic industries which dominated the publicly owned industries, private industries were much more scattered and heterogeneous. Although chemicals, and to a lesser extent motor vehicles, contained a number of dominant and visible firms among their number, other important sectors such as engineering and construction did not. The government's information about the intended investment plans of much of private industry remained partial. Indeed, as the Investment Programmes Committee acknowledged:

> there are few parts of investment where it is more difficult to get a reasonably sound view of the future, or where it is more important to get it right, than industrial investment. Over a large part of the field it is impossible to speak of programmes in the strict sense.[12]

The problems of obtaining information from private industry on its current and future investment activity were reflected in the composition of the Investment Programmes Committee's reports. While specific details were given about the comparatively small investment plans of the hard coke industry, the chemical, engineering, textile and most other private industries were simply lumped together under the catch-all title of 'manufacturing industry'. Moreover, the government was seeking a type of information which was elusive at the best of times. Although aiming at a target 'level' of investment for the forthcoming year, it was the control of the 'rate' of investment which was fundamental to any approximation to that target being achieved. In addition, before hazarding estimates of any future rate of investment, the current rate of investment had to be established. Estimating the current rate of investment not only involved obtaining information from the scattered, multi-firm engineering and construction industries as well as from their clients (assuming that this was known), but it also required estimates to be made of the rate at which materials currently existing as 'stocks and works in progress' would be converted into completed investment. Completion rates were in turn important, affecting as they did the release of such resources as labour. Completion rates, particularly in the larger, more complex projects, were strongly affected by the availability of resources, something that was in turn affected by the number of competing projects.

The organisational reforms initiated in 1947 marked an intensification of the planners' concern with immediate economic problems and a wider recognition that such fundamental problems as excess demand, inflation and balance-of-payments difficulties were not likely to be eased by a down-turn in the domestic economy. The concern with easing short-term, immediate bottlenecks and increasing the volume of exports was reflected in the broad pattern of steel allocations made in this period. Within industrial investment, the allocation of steel between industrial sponsoring departments remained fairly constant throughout this period, the Board of Trade being allocated 14.2 per cent (home civil and indirect export 3.8 per cent and direct export 10.4 per cent) of total steel allocation between 1946–9, the Ministry of Transport 7.3 per cent, the Ministry of Works 8.5 per cent, the Ministry of Fuel and Power 13.8 per cent (Mines Division 6.1 per cent, Gas Division 1.1 per cent, Petroleum Division 4.8 per cent and Electricity Division 1.8 per cent) and Iron and Steel 1.3 per cent.[13] In allocating resources, priority was given to high and immediate export earners such as motor vehicles, textiles, engineering and chemicals and also to such basic industries as iron and steel, especially those where supply bottlenecks were appearing, an allocation pattern given added emphasis during 1947 by the fuel and balance of payments crises.

Investment resources, as allocated by government, overwhelmingly flowed towards production rather than to infrastructure or long-term reconstruction. One of the few instances in the private sector of resources being allocated to a long-term investment project was the backing given to the expansion of domestic oil-refining capacity. With the United States emerging as a net importer of oil in the post-war period and with Middle East politics becoming increasingly volatile, the allocation of resources to the domestic oil-refining industry received the backing of the Treasury, the Ministry of Fuel and Power and the Defence departments. The programme absorbed considerable resources but was unlikely to produce returns for at least three to four years. When refined oil did begin to flow, its anticipated contribution was not to relieving pressure on fuel resources at home, but, by providing a major export to dollar areas, earning much needed dollars, the dollar shortage, rather than the general trade balance, being the crux of the recurring balance-of-payments problems.

The emphasis on maximising output had its impact, not simply on the allocation of resources between industries but also on resource allocation within industries. Projects which could produce rapid returns in terms of output were favoured, with the result that considerable investment resources were devoted to patching, make-do-and-mend strategies. As the Investment Programmes Committee noted in its report on capital investment in 1949:

> Investment designed to reduce the costs of production will be of increasing importance. In the general circumstances governing investment in 1949, it is unfortunate that such projects will generally have to be deferred unless the prospective economies are unusually large or there are also other grounds for undertaking the schemes . . . A policy of make-do-and-mend, which will be as necessary in 1949 as in 1948, means that extra capital expenditure should be directed to getting more output from existing plant rather than the creation of fresh capacity.[14]

The scope for such a strategy was greatest in those industries which had built up considerable capacity (steel, textiles) and less in the often comparatively newer industries, such as electricity and chemicals, which had faced persistently rising demand. This second group of industries was more likely to be hitting capacity constraints and therefore seeking to build new plant, albeit possibly of technologically sub-optimal size.[15] Elsewhere in industries with traditionally large capacity and with a history of cyclical demand, a patching and incremental investment strategy was most likely. In the cotton and woollen industries, the bulk of the building investment consisted of small extensions and alterations connected with the installation of new, and the respacing of existing, machinery. The largest single scheme was that of J.&P. Coats for complete reorganisation over a ten-year period and involving an ultimate building expenditure of at least £3 million.[16] Even firms in new-product markets within long-established industries were inclined to postpone major investment programmes. Stewarts & Lloyds in the steel-tube market, explicitly opted for immediate profit maximisation in the early post-war sellers' market, with their major new capital investment programme being postponed until demand had subsided.

Such short-term, patching, profit-maximising strategies may have been 'rational' and attractive to ministers and managers alike. There was, however, a tension between such rationality and the government's rhetorical concern with productivity. Much of this concern with productivity centred on the immediate problem of extracting more output from a limited supply of resources. 'Productivity' and 'efficiency' were easily interchanged as objects of improvement. Yet, there were also voices sounding concern at the long-term productivity of leading industries, this concern finding articulation outside, rather than inside, central government with economists, industrial (often American) consultants and a number of reform-minded industrialists being the main advocates of change.[17] This was particularly true of the iron and steel industry which, while always operating under the threat of nationalisation, was of all private industries the one most conspicuously subject to the attentions of government and planners. Although the industry was not nationalised until 1951, before being denationalised in 1953, it was the subject of two Steel Plans, published in 1946 and 1953.[18] The First Steel Plan confronted the issue of the industry's long-term productivity and the perceived associated need for a fundamental restructuring of the industry. While the report bore the imprimatur of government, it was overwhelmingly generated from within the industry itself. The impact of government was to influence the environment in which the plan was prepared and, more importantly, in which its implementation was then attempted. It is here, away from the planning of central government and away from the ambitions of the National Investment Council, that the closest approximation to fundamental long-term industrial planning could be found.

The First Steel Plan emphasised the need for 'rationalisation' and restructuring. Rationalisation on the North East Coast, for example, was intended to replace the existing nine steelworks mostly engaged on a mixed range of production, with five steelworks each specialising in a particular product. Modernisation was to occur at these works, while other less efficient plant was to close. The Skinningrove works, the South Durham plate plant of the South Durham and Cargo Fleet Group and two of Dorman Long's works (Acklam and Britannia) were effectively to disappear. Elsewhere, completely new steelworks were to be built, one in Scotland and the other on the Northamptonshire ore fields in a project to be sponsored by the United Steel Company and Stewarts & Lloyds. Fundamentally, rationalisation would achieve the concentration of demand and thus allow the productivity improvements associated with size to be realised. In addition to building a new beam mill at its Lackenby works, Dorman Long also expected to effect increased concentration of demand from its plants at Cleveland, Lackenby and Redcar. To help meet this combined demand of 22,000 tons per week, three blast furnaces were to be built at the Cleveland works, each capable of making more than 1,000 tons per day. These three blast furnaces were to have hearth diameters of between 25 ft and 27 ft 6 in., comparable in size with the most up-to-date American furnaces. This maximum iron demand of around 22,000 tons per week was a much higher level than was at one time envisaged and much greater than at any other British works.[19]

Such planned rationalisation was not new. Inter-war documents, such as the Brassert memorandum of January 1930 on the regionalisation of the industry and the Bruce Gardner report of the following year, outlined the case for the restructuring of the iron and steel industry, with the small plant operated by small firms being abandoned in favour of a move towards the larger, integrated type of plant then being operated and constructed in Germany and America.[20] The implicit view that the industry's multi-firm, small-plant structure was a major cause of the industry's productivity problems was confirmed and reinforced by the work of Laslo Rostas which began to appear during the Second World War. Using data from the 1930s, Rostas compared the productivity of the iron and steel industries in USA, Germany and Great Britain and ranked their productivity at 168 : 114 : 100 respectively.[21]

Observation of American wartime development simply served to confirm the existing technical opinion that both plant and works were too small.[22] As in the First World War, observers were impressed with the performance of the German iron and steel industry during the Second World War. Individual industrialists like John Craig of Colvilles, who had visited the United States during the Second World War to examine the technical details of the American industry's use of high-pressure furnaces for the increased production of pig-iron and the use of oxygen in steel-making,[23] returned to Britain convinced of the need for the British industry to concentrate production around larger plant. In America, he had found furnaces of 27 ft hearth diameter being operated at pressures of 18/20lbs per sq. in., and producing 1150/1750 tons per day of pig iron in what the Americans, unsurprisingly, referred to as a 1,000 tons-per-day furnace.[24] In contrast, Craig argued that in Britain there were instances of blast furnaces where the capacity per unit needed to be doubled and that, in future, only in exceptional cases should any blast furnace be built with a hearth diameter of less than 25 ft.[25] The recognition of the relationship between size of works, size of plant, capacity throughput and productivity was well recognised by 1945 and formed the fundamental theme of the First Steel Plan of 1946. It was recognised that if all of the existing iron and steelworks were expanded or even retained it would not be possible to reach anything like the minimum efficient scale for efficient operation.

If the need for restructuring was clear in 1945, what was less clear was the ability of government and industry to achieve such restructuring. The experiences of the 1930s were not encouraging. Then, a fundamental restructuring of the industry was supposed to have occurred behind the protective tariff, this tariff being seen as a prerequisite for reorganisation since 'reorganisation required increased loads which could be achieved only from a monopolized home market'.[26] However, the concern that 'protection . . . would . . . actually delay the reforms that are urgently required, as it would lead to the maintenance of a number of plants not designed for efficient production or suitable for amalgamation' proved to be justified.[27] The industry exchanged protection for price stability and compromise, not for rationalisation. It exploited the government's reluctance to intervene in the industry, the Import Duties Advisory Committe's (IDAC) lack of effective powers of sanction, and the IDAC's wish to see the industry organise the necessary rationalisation itself. After all, as the head of the IDAC, Sir George May, told the steelmakers: 'The whole thing rests with you . . . I want you to do it all for your-selves . . . you are all reasonably minded men. If you get together you will surely find a solution'.[28]

Left to themselves, the industry did little other than shore up the industry's structure with price and cost-pooling arrangements, and act so as to deter potential entrants.[29] The ambitions of large and expanding, generally reform-minded firms like United Steel, Richard Thomas and Stewarts & Lloyds were obstructed both by the big, backward heavy steelmakers like Dorman Long, South Durham, Guest Keen Baldwin, and Colvilles and the finishers, smaller firms and re-rollers like Whitehead, Bairds, Skinningrove and the Steel Company of Scotland.

Given that the Steel Plan of 1946 represented the resurrection of government–industry efforts to restructure the iron and steel industry, were there any new reasons for thinking that the restructuring which had proved unattainable before 1939 might be achievable after 1945? There were thought to be some signs of hope. By 1945, the Federation was much stronger than it had been before the war, largely as a result of its involvement in the war-economy. The war had led to the curbing of pre-war critics like Firth (Richard Thomas) and the effective absorption of MacDiarmid (Stewarts & Lloyds) into the Federation, until the latter's death in 1945. By 1945 there remained no significant opposition among the big firms to the British Iron and Steel Federation (BISF). At the same time the industry was viewed as functioning more or less as a semi-autonomous department of government for the duration of the conflict. Andrew Duncan, the post-Second World War President of the Federation, became the first steel controller before becoming President of the Board of Trade in early 1940. All the later controllers were drawn from the steel firms and the administration largely from the BISF. Indeed, as Tolliday notes,

> by the end of the war, the Federation had espoused as its own the role that IDAC would have liked it to play before the war, namely,

one of a strong Federation undertaking more active planning and the elimination of price competition in the context of supervision by an impartial body appointed by the government.[30]

The steady recognition that controls were likely to be a feature of post-war life and the growing concern of steelmen like John Craig at the comparative productivity problem persuaded many steelmen that planning was inevitable and quite possibly necessary, and, that, as such, it was pragmatic to take much of the planning onto the industry's shoulders rather than leave it to government whims and initiatives. Ultimately, it was better to be planning than to be planned against. Such co-operation from the industry might also remove some of the edge from arguments in favour of nationalising the industry.

Whatever optimism attended the First Steel Plan's publication in 1946, it was not clear that the fundamental factors which had obstructed rationalisation in the 1930s had been significantly changed or removed. While the credibility and strength of the Federation may have grown during the war, it still had not acquired the enabling powers which such pre-war critics as Firth and MacDiarmid had regarded as all important. On each occasion that the issue was discussed and questionnaires sent out, the industry stopped short of providing the Federation with such powers. The issue surfaced during the President's Committee meeting of 16 November 1943, when it was concluded that in the matter of the control of capital expenditure and encouragement and regulation of the modernisation of steelworks plant, it was not expedient to seek powers of compulsion for enforcing Federation decisions.[31] The Committee delivered itself of its view of the relationship between the Federation and the industry:

> We agree with the President's Committee decision that there should be no question of compulsion, and that the Federation's functions should be confined to advice and guidance, having no sanction beyond the moral sanction of loyalty to a well-organised and properly equipped body supported by the Trade as a whole, and prepared to give effect to any National Policy which may be laid upon it.[32]

The decision not to provide the Federation with enabling powers, and, in effect, to attempt to secure rationalisation through agreement and consensus within the industry perpetuated one of the fundamental factors underlying the relationship between the Federation and the industry and, as such, ultimately forced the Federation back on persuasion when faced by opposition to its rationalising plans.

The Federation's difficulties in pursuing rationalisation, and in attempting to implement the First Steel Plan, became evident on the North East Coast, particularly in the Federation's dealings with Cargo Fleet and its parent company, South Durham. As part of the process of planning for the post-war industry, the North East Coast producers had met on a number of occasions and by early August 1945 had agreed on a programme for the immediate five years, as well as for a further period of ten years from 1945. Yet, the proposals of the North East Coast producers proved unacceptable to the Federation, which insisted instead that proposals contained in an interim report prepared by the Federation in April 1945 should apply. However, the Federation's proposals were unacceptable to South Durham and Cargo Fleet. Almost from the first, South Durham suspected that the Federation, in a report submitted to the Ministry of Supply but not made available to South Durham, had recommended the ending of the production of pig iron, steel ingots and heavy plates at their West Hartlepool works, the firm only being permitted to operate the four-high light plate mill. Benjamin Talbot (South Durham) made it clear to Andrew Duncan that his firm had not approved such a fate and that they did not voluntarily intend to cease the manufacture of any of their products, particularly plates, at their West Hartlepool works.[33]

Duncan was keen that these disagreements on the North East Coast should be resolved, since the whole question of the site and terms for billet production on the North East Coast was dependent on agreement being reached between Dorman Long, Consett and Cargo Fleet, Cargo Fleet's and South Durham's proposals being in Duncan's words 'bound up together and if one falls down, the other falls'.[34] Yet securing such agreement proved extremely difficult. Discussions, on-site meetings and arguments between the Federation and North East Coast companies were still continuing in 1949, with little sign of agreement. Moreover, the Federation's appeals to the Plan were increasingly regarded as being off-target by many firms, since much of the new investment and development envisaged by the Plan had not emerged and was lagging well behind, while the plant designated for closure had often not only survived but had been improved. As early as July 1947, the Development Committee of the Federation had been forced to reconsider substantial elements of the First Steel Plan, as it was recognised that 'the conditions as they *now* exist were not those at the time the report was drafted'.[35] By 1949, the obvious divergences from the Plan were becoming a standard weapon deployed by firms in battles with the Federation. Consett, in an argument with the Federation over whether Consett should build a plate or billet mill, was arguing by 1949 that all North East Coast makers had departed from the Plan, that for all the talk of Dorman Long's beam mill over the last two years it had not materialised and that South Durham and Skinningrove had become permanencies.

In their opposition to the rationalising ambitions of the Federation, companies like South Durham and Cargo Fleet were also able to exploit the inherent tension between the long-term aim of rationalisation and the immediate political concern with maximising output and minimising unemployment. The virtual contradiction between securing rationalisation and preventing unemployment had influenced inter-war government–industry relations not only in the iron and steel industry, but also in other basic industries such as coal.[36] In their opposition to Federation plans, South Durham and Cargo Fleet were quick to appeal to government concern with the consequences for unemployment. Threatened with closure, South Durham did not hesitate to despatch a letter to Stafford Cripps (President of the Board of Trade) complaining that the firm had not been able to see the early drafts of the Plan and warning him of the problems which the Federation schemes would cause in Hartlepool, an isolated area of 63,000 in which South Durham employed 2,500 and paid wages of £755,000 p.a.[37] The potentially disastrous effects on the rateable value of the town, the reduced spending power of the public and the need to disperse labour in order to allow workers to continue their present specialised occupations with consequent problems for the national housing programme were all emphasised.[38]

South Durham also exploited the government's concern with output.[39] Clearly in the immediate post-war period, the maximisation of output was a leading priority as the First Steel Plan acknowledged. The Plan also acknowledged that while an early increase in the total output of steel was of paramount importance, it was not always possible to reconcile this with the need to attain maximum productivity.[40] While the patching of plant in general was to be avoided, some patching in order to increase output would be necessary in the early years. The duration of such patching was, in part, dependent on the speed with which the modernising and rationalising aims of the Plans were realised and achieved.

The potential for sustained patching to undermine the fundamental rationalising aims of the Steel Plan, was intensified by the scope which existed for firms like South Durham to abuse government controls so as to rebuild plant. In 1946, South Durham was able to rebuild its No. 3 plate mill and extend its output by using the Annual Maintenance Licence for major items of reconstruction.[41] They then intended to construct further blast furnaces (a new store of 150,000 sq. ft to replace two condemned stores each of 63,500 sq. ft) which would allow them to bring their No. 1 blast furnace off for relining and provide a match for its finishing capacity. None of this was provided for in the Plan. Quite apart from this, there was concern that if permission was given for this store to be constructed, South Durham might rebuild their blast furnaces bit by bit. Faced with a *fait accompli*, namely the improvement and extension of a plant due for closure with controlled and allocated steel, the

Ministry of Supply had little option but to issue a licence legalising the work.

The patching and piecemeal modernisation of plant was encouraged by the persistence of the strong post-war demand for iron and steel, and its potential for undermining the main aims of the First Steel Plan was strongly influenced by the length of construction times for the large, new modern plant anticipated in the Plan. The failure of the Federation to secure closures, and the growing awareness that new large-scale investment projects were taking a long time to build, combined to make managers contemplating new projects very uncertain. If closures were not secured, then much of the basis of their original calculations which assumed a greater degree of concentration of demand became highly suspect. Long construction times not only extended the period in which piecemeal improvements were made to the older plant, but it also increased the risks of undertaking such investment, since quite apart from increasing project costs, it also increased managerial uncertainty concerning future demand and market conditions. Not only could they find themselves competing in six years time with plant which, instead of being closed, had been improved, but they could also find that the excess demand of, say, 1947, had given way to excess supply by 1953 when the project was completed. Moreover, although technically more efficient, the new plant would be carrying a high debt gearing, compared with the older smaller plant whose capital costs had been written off some time ago.

That post-war construction times were often twice as long as those in the inter-war period is not surprising, although that they were twice as long as those of their major competitors is notable. Shortages of plant, materials and labour beset most private (and public) capital investment construction projects between 1945 and 1950. In the iron and steel industry, demand for blast furnaces was intense. Whereas planned blast furnace rebuilding was not normally more than 1.5 million tons in a five-year period, in the immediate post-war period rebuilding was running at 4.65 million tons. The severity of plant shortages was reflected in the intensity of the ultimately unsuccessful struggle by firms within the industry to obtain plant from the German Salzgitter works. Plant shortages (both capital and construction plant) affected all private industries. Indeed, there was a general world shortage of capital equipment and prices increased. In part, shortages came from high demand occurring at a time when, as part of the export drive, the engineering industry was exporting one-third of its output. The Korean rearmament effort intensified problems. There were also indications that the British engineering industry was short of capacity and in particular was not geared to high-volume production of standardised capital equipment. However, frequently the modern plant which industries like steel and chemicals required was simply not available in the UK. Applications therefore had to be submitted for dollar import licences which were tightly controlled by the Treasury. The Treasury, for example, was advising ICI in 1947 to provide the Treasury with details of all of the company's capital equipment import requirements up to 1954.

The fierce competition for plant and machinery made the task of co-ordinating demand between and within industries both crucial and problematic. The iron and steel industry and the electricity industry competed for blowers and boiler plant, the principal factors affecting the timing of the blast furnace programme and where delivery times of three years were common. As in the electricity industry, the Ministry of Supply and the steel industry sought to ease this position by matching the demand for boilers and turbo-blowers more closely to the available capacity and by spreading orders away from Parsons, who had 50 per cent of the steelmakers orders, towards other firms such as Richardsons, Westgarth & Co., Fraser & Chalmers and Daniel Adamson.[42] Delays in obtaining plant and machinery also made the managerial task of sequencing and co-ordinating on-site operations difficult, especially on greenfield sites where the retention of labour proved difficult. Before work on the investment project proper could begin housing and a basic infrastructure had to be provided. Building and (more importantly) completed housing in isolated areas proved difficult. Moreover, once built, there was no guarantee that labour would remain on site or on the books during the delays between deliveries of materials. The extreme example from the public sector was that of the Hydro Board but similar difficulties were encountered in private construction projects.[43] The consequences for the implementation of the First Steel Plan was that new plant, such as the beam mill, took longer to build than had been expected, and the knowledge that construction times were long made such companies as Stewarts & Lloyds and Colvilles very reluctant to embark on the building of completely new integrated sites. In the meantime, the patching and incremental improvements to the existing structure of the industry went ahead and the old, small works destined for closure flourished into the 1950s.

The Steel Plan represented one of the few attempts made at securing the long-term industrial restructuring of a private industry during the Attlee government's period in office. While the aims of such long-term planning were never expected to be fully realised during the first six years following the war, the early developments were not encouraging. The planned rationalisation of this basic sector industry had encountered strong local opposition which could not be cajoled into submission. Fundamental gaps were exposed between the ambitions and powers of the Federation and between the general wish of the government to support 'rationalisation' and its unwillingness to tolerate some of the political consequences of such restructuring. As in central policy-making, the government's approach towards private industrial investment became increasingly dominated by its concern to secure maximisation of output, exports and employment, while containing inflationary pressures. In readjusting to the immediate need to secure such goals, much of the early rhetoric and instruments of long-term planning were abandoned.

NOTES

1. J. C. R. Dow *The Management of the British Economy, 1945–60* (Cambridge 1964) p. 149.
2. Correlli Barnett *The Audit of War* (1986); Steven Tolliday *Business, Banking and Politics: The Case of British Steel, 1918–1939* (Harvard, 1987).
3. C. H. Feinstein *Statistical Tables of National Income, Expenditure and Output, 1855–1965* (Cambridge, 1972) Table 2.
4. W. Ashworth *The History of the British Coal Industry* (Oxford, 1986); T. Gourvish *British Railways, a Business History* (Cambridge 1986) and L. Hannah *Engineers, Managers and Politicians: the first fifteen years of nationalised electricity supply in Britain* (1982).
5. M. Dupree see ch. 8, in this volume.
6. A. Cairncross *Years of Recovery: British Economic Policy, 1945–51* (1985); PRO CAB128/2, CM(45)55, 22/11/1945.
7. E. Durbin *New Jerusalems* (1985).
8. B. Tew and R. Henderson *Studies in Company Finance* (Cambridge 1959).
9. Cmd. 7268, *Capital Investment in 1948* (PP 1947) paras. 5 and 9.
10. PRO CAB134/212, Economic Planning Board meeting, minutes, 17/11/1949.
11. PRO CAB134/440, 'Capital Investment in 1950', Report by the Investment Programmes Committee, 10/11/1949, p. 1.
12. PRO CAB134/439 'Report on Capital Investment in 1949', p. 56.
13. PRO CAB134/475–85, Files of Material Allocations Committee, 1946–9.
14. PRO CAB134/439 'Report on Capital Investment in 1949', p. 56.
15. Hannah op. cit. ch. 8.
16. PRO CAB134/440 'Report on Capital Investment in 1950–2', p. 89.
17. C. Miles *Lancashire Textiles: a case study of industrial change* (Cambridge 1968).
18. Cmd. 6811 *Reports by the British Iron and Steel Federation and the Joint Iron Council to the Ministry of Supply* (PP May 1946).
19. Dorman Long 'Blast Furnace Development Policy: New Blast Furnaces at Cleveland Works', 13 May 1947.
20. Tolliday op. cit., p. 204; Bank of England Archive Securities Management Trust, 2/154 H. A. Brassert 'Memorandum on the Regionalisation of the British Iron and Steel Industry' British Steel Archive, 10/1/1930; C. Bruce Gardner 'Confidential Report on the Structure of the Iron and Steel Industry of Great Britain, Incorporating Plans for Rationalisation'.
21. L. Rostas 'Industrial Production, Productivity and Distribution in Great Britain, Germany and the United States' *Economic Journal* Vol. 53 No. 209 April 1943.
22. BISF (1955) *Annual Report*.
23. British Steel Archive, J. Craig 'Notes on a visit to America', 10.11.1947.
24. Ibid.
25. Ibid.
26. Tolliday op. cit. p. 295.
27. Ibid. pp. 295–6.
28. Ibid. p. 301.

29. Ibid. p. 323.
30. Ibid. p. 329.
31. BISF 'Report of the Sub-Committee appointed by the President's Committee to consider control of capital expenditure', 14/2/1944.
32. Ibid.
33. British Steel Archive, Talbot letter to Cripps, 15/2/1946.
34. British Steel Archive, A. N. McQuistan, quoted in a letter to Benjamin Talbot 24/1/1946.
35. BISF Development Committee 21/1/1947.
36. B. Supple 'Ideology or pragmatism? The nationalisation of coal, 1916–46' in N. McKendrick and R. B. Outhwaite eds. *Business Life and Public Policy* (Cambridge, 1986).
37. British Steel Archive, Talbot, letter to Cripps 15/2/1946.
38. Ibid.
39. Ibid.
40. Cmd. 6811 *Reports by the British Iron and Steel Federation and the Joint Iron Council to the Ministry of Supply* (PP May 1946).
41. BISF Development Committee 18/2/1947.
42. BISF Development Committee 18/2/1951.
43. P. L. Payne *The Hydro: A study of the Development of the Major Hydro-Electric Schemes undertaken by the North of Scotland Hydro-Electric Board* (Aberdeen, 1988).

Six

Whatever happened to the British warfare state? The Ministry of Supply, 1945–1951

DAVID EDGERTON

This chapter is concerned with the Ministry of Supply between 1945 and 1951. The Ministry of Supply was perhaps the most important of the many 'production departments' of government: it was the successor to the two most important wartime industrial ministries. And yet, the Ministry of Supply is practically unknown to historians. In the general literature on the Labour governments of 1945 to 1951 there are no more than passing references to the fact that it was responsible for steel nationalisation.[1] In the specialised literature on government–industry relations and economic planning, its role as a 'production' or 'sponsoring' department is merely listed. It is the Board of Trade which was for Rogow and Shore 'the leading production department'[2] and for Leruez 'responsible for most sectors of industry'.[3] For Cairncross, 'the key economic departments were the Treasury and the Board of Trade'.[4] The ministry was neglected by contemporaries as well as historians. Richard Williams-Thompson, the ministry's Public Relations Officer, noted in 1951 that 'I imagine that many people do not know what the Ministry is or does, which is a fine testimonial to my three years' work!'[5] Historians have less excuse especially given that the importance of the ministry in industrial matters was clearly laid out in the major text on the organisation of British central government in the twentieth century.[6]

We may suggest a number of reasons why the ministry has been ignored. First, its name is unfamiliar. Second, it was primarily a defence department which ceased to have civil industrial responsibilities in the mid-1950s, though this does not explain why it was ignored by contemporaries. A more plausible explanation is that the ministry's operations were not reflected in parliamentary politics, as a check through *Hansard* will reveal, and it is thus wrongly assumed to have been economically and industrially irrelevant. It may be that the 'parliamentarism' of contemporary Labour politics and subsequent historiography might well be to blame. The neglect of the post-war Ministry of Supply should be seen as part of a much larger failure. Discussion of the war economy concentrates on the rise of Keynesianism and manpower controls, on the development of the 'welfare state', and very abstract discussions of 'planning' and 'controls'.[7] Even Chester's collection, *Lessons of the War Economy* did not provide an adequate overview.[8] Despite the existence of official histories of wartime arms production, the role of the supply ministries in wartime control of industry is still missing from most commentary on the war economy.[9] It is little wonder, then, that the post-war Ministry of Supply has been ignored by historians.

The Labour government and the Labour Party appear to have failed to understand the significance of wartime supply ministries and of the Labour Cabinet's decision to create a single Ministry of Supply after the war. More surprising still is the fact that the ministry pursued industrial policies which flew in the face of broader Labour thinking. Not only did it not nationalise the arms industry, it 'privatised' huge swathes of state-owned armament capacity. The involvement of trade unions in policy-making was minimal. On the other hand, the ministry did pursue highly interventionist policies, discriminating between sectors and firms, and funded a great deal of civil as well as military research and development. It thus acted as critics said, and say, the Labour government should have but allegedly did not.

THE BRITISH WARFARE STATE

British warfare, contrary to myth, was highly reliant on science, technology and industry, before as well as during the Second World War.[10] Each of the three service ministries, the Air Ministry, Admiralty and War Office, had supply and research branches which maintained very close links with industry and financed a great deal of research and development. In the 1930s, however, it was widely believed that the service ministries were not up to the effort of rearmament and there were thus many calls for the establishment of a civil Ministry of Supply on the lines of the First World War's Ministry of Munitions.[11] As war approached a Ministry of Supply (MoS) was established to supply the army and to undertake raw material control and in May 1940 a Ministry of Aircraft Production (MAP). The Admiralty retained its principal supply roles. Although the creation of the Ministry of Supply and, especially, the Ministry of Aircraft Production, were presented as radical departures from inter-war practice the new ministries were really the expanded and renamed supply organisations of the army and air force. The warfare state had military origins.

MAP and MoS were the two most important wartime industry ministries, responsible for most of what were called the 'munitions industries'. The Board of Trade was marginal: it was responsible for civilian consumption goods like furniture, clothing and so on. Its job, after 1941, was to cut back production. MoS and MAP, by contrast, had to *increase* production. They acted in a thoroughly dirigiste manner making decisions on a product-by-product, firm-by-firm basis, and invested on a massive scale in new industrial capacity. Focusing on these ministries forces us to qualify radically the standard picture of the state of British industry at the end of the war: that British industry was clapped out because investment was deferred.[12] It applies to industries like cotton, which were handled by the Board of Trade and which had often been 'concentrated'. But vast stretches of British manufacturing industry, centred on engineering, but extending to chemicals, were modernised by the war. But because the construction and fitting out of armament plants was classified as part of current defence expenditure the extent of that investment was unknown to most contemporaries and subsequent historians. In 1955 Redfern attempted to allow for some wartime investment[13] but did not capture it all, as Barna pointed out.[14] Indeed it was not until 1964 that some reasonable estimates based upon the official histories of war production were made. Dean estimated that government investment, excluding Royal Dockyards and an estimated £250 million of specialised defence capacity, totalled £680 million in chemicals, engineering, vehicles, shipbuilding and metal goods.[15] Dean provides some other figures which give a good indication of the concentration of wartime investment. He looked at the age distribution of buildings and plant and machinery in 1961. The proportion of plant installed after 1939 was 81 per cent in food, drink and tobacco, 80 per cent in iron and steel, 90 per cent in textiles. But the proportion installed between 1939 and 1947 was only 8 per cent in food, drink and tobacco, 7 per cent in iron and steel, and 8 per cent in textiles. In metal-using and non-ferrous metals industries 40 per cent of plant was installed between 1939 and 1947.[16] That one cannot generalise about the fate of British industry during the war is thus clear.

Neither should we generalise about post-war industrial policy proposals such as the plans drawn up by the Board of Trade under Hugh Dalton (President, 1942–5). These plans envisaged a strengthened Board of Trade, with an Industrial Commission with certain authoritative powers to prohibit inefficient firms from trading. This policy owed a great deal to a critique of pre-war rationalisation schemes and was much more radical than anything the Board of Trade even proposed to do later. The much watered-down proposal found its way into the *Report of the Steering Committee on Post War Employment*,[17] but not into the subsequent White Paper *Employment Policy*, which had no specific industrial policy proposals.[18] The impression has been given that the Board of Trade's were the only ones put forward for consideration,[19] on the assumption, it seems, that the Board of Trade was the obvious candidate for the key industrial ministry. It was not, and Dalton and his young 'post-warriors' deliberately set out to make it the key post-war industry ministry.[20] However, Sir Richard Stafford Cripps (Minister of Aircraft Production, 1942–5) was very hostile indeed to the Steering

Committee Report's central industrial policy recommendations. Cripps, who, we should recall, was not at this time a member of the Labour Party, believed that the Industrial Commission would remove from ministers direct responsibility for industry, which he saw as a return 'to a position in relation to the major industries not differing essentially from the *status quo ante-bellum*':

> Industry is not an undifferentiated whole which can be brought to full employment merely by unselective measures designed to stimulate any and every trade . . . the problems of the major industries are complex, both technically and financially; they involve questions of management and technical organisation; and if the cooperation of industry is to be secured they involve personal contact with the leading men. The Government has acquired through the Departments dealing with these industries the knowledge, the contact and the influence to secure the very varying degrees of assistance, guidance and of reorganisation which the industries if they are severally to contribute their quota to the policy of full employment, will be found to need. I cannot think that we should be wise, whilst committing ourselves to a full employment policy, to jettison the means by which full employment, industry by industry, can be achieved.[21]

Cripps's paper led to a *laissez-faire* response from the Minister of Works, Lord Portal and a further memorandum from Cripps.[22]

Cripps was putting forward an industrial policy which differed radically from that which Conservative ministers would wear, but one that differed from that put forward by Hugh Dalton at the Board of Trade. For Cripps the future lay with the policies and practices of the wartime production departments. Later in 1944 there was discussion about post-war arrangements for defence supply which took place in the context of discussions about future 'machinery of government'.[23] Cripps argued not just for continued existence of separate supply ministries, but for a merger between MAP and MoS. 'The Socialist members led by Sir Stafford Cripps, were eager to preserve the Ministry'[24] recalled Lord Woolton who with Andrew Duncan at Supply, Oliver Lyttelton at Production and the three service ministries rejected the idea. Cripps was against returning to the pre-war practice of leaving supply questions to the relevant service department: as he put it 'The difference between an Industrial Department and a Service Department is a radical one'.[25] Cripps also argued for a peacetime Ministry of Supply with civil industrial responsibilities: Sir Alan Barlow correctly told the chancellor that Cripps wanted the unified supply ministry to be 'the tutelary deity of the engineering industry after the war'.[26] No agreement could be reached and so it was left to the incoming Labour government to decide on the issue.[27] Here, as on general industrial policy, there was no consensus in the Coalition. If it came into office, Labour would have to make up its own mind what to do.

Beyond nationalisation of certain non-manufacturing industries and a continuation of wartime planning and controls, the Labour government had no clear idea as to what to do about industrial policy; that appears to be the consensus in the literature. And yet decisions had to be made about what to do about wartime ministries; should they be kept, and how should their responsibilities be shared out? It is not clear how well Attlee understood the machinery of government in 1945.[28] It appears, however, that he regarded the Board of Trade as the key industrial department in as much as he gave the job to Cripps, who became the only industrial minister in Cabinet other than the Minister of Fuel and Power. John Wilmot was made Minister of both Supply and Aircraft Production outside the Cabinet. Attlee appeared to regard the Ministry of Supply, like the Post Office, as a 'purely administrative' department, which should not be represented in Cabinet.[29]

The Cabinet decided to merge Aircraft Production into the Ministry of Supply.[30] This was to be responsible primarily for the supply to the army and RAF, to have a general responsibility for government purchases and it would also 'carry the primary Government responsibility for the field of engineering', which involved transfer of some responsibilities from the Board of Trade. The combined ministry *lost* some functions: responsibility for the non-engineering munitions industries, notably chemicals, and many raw materials controls, went to the Board of Trade. The Board of Trade also got some of the responsibilities of the disbanded co-ordinating Ministry of Production, whose defence supply responsibilities went to the Ministry of Defence.[31] Attlee's announcement of this policy in October 1945 was 'complicated and not easily understood'; 'the Prime Minister had created, although he probably did not realise it, the most important Ministry in the country.'[32] Neither did *The Economist*. It regretted that the Admiralty was still going its own way and welcomed the peacetime Ministry of Supply in relation to future defence supply. Turning to industrial policy, it said that the Board of Trade was too large and should be split into a Board of Trade, concerned with external trade, and a Ministry of Industry, even though it recognised and welcomed the sponsorship of engineering by the Ministry of Supply, and even noted the wide definition of engineering employed.[33] In 1947 the magazine *Future*, while noting the importance of the Ministry of Supply was equivocal as to why it was created:

> From the political point of view the Ministry was an instrument ready prepared for the shaping of a socialised Britain out of the confusion of the postwar situation, by means of centralised state

planning. Thus the first reason for retaining the Ministry may have been that it would exist to perform certain social and economic duties even if the Services were totally disarmed. Since it would therefore necessarily have great power over the sections of the industry most vital to munition production, it was the best agency to supply the Services. Thus the Ministry that during the war controlled some of the most vital sectors of the national economy in order to supply the Services may in future supply the Services because it controls (for other purposes) these vital sectors.[34]

Interestingly enough, Cripps, in a speech to staff at the Board of Trade in August 1945, declared that 'we shall be a sort of Civilian Supply Department and we must take as close and as intimate an interest in the production methods of industry as have the Supply Departments during the war'. He too seemed to regard the Board of Trade as *the* Ministry for private industry.[35]

But in the period 1945 to 1951 the Board of Trade was just one of the 'production departments': in 1950 the *Board of Trade Journal* listed the Admiralty, Board of Trade and the Ministries of Agriculture and Fisheries, Food, Fuel and Power, Health, Supply, Transport and Works. The Ministry of Supply was easily the most important in terms of the number of sectors covered.[36] It is worth noting that two case studies in this volume (motor vehicles and iron and steel) are about industries which came under the ministry, and a third, shipbuilding, was the responsibility of the other supply department, the Admiralty. We may give another indication of the importance of the Ministry of Supply by noting the number of non-industrial civil servants it had working on non-defence work. While the Ministry of Food had 36,993, the Board of Trade 10,971, the Ministry of Supply had 13,369. The Ministry of Supply had a further 20,053 engaged on defence work.[37] Neither of these indices are particularly good indicators. They do not give an indication of the proportion of industrial output controlled by the ministry – the numbers of staff, for example, is largely an indication of the prevalence and complexity of controls. To measure the 'depth' of intervention is even more difficult, but we can get some indication from figures for industrial subsidies in Table 6.1.

The industrial importance of the Ministry of Supply did not escape the notice of the Board of Trade. There was 'great rivalry' between the two.[38] Furthermore, there appears to have been great hostility in Whitehall which succeeded in keeping the new and potentially very powerful ministry in its place.[39]

The Ministry of Supply was not helped by the fact that neither of the two ministers, John Wilmot and George Strauss, were of a seniority to be Cabinet members.[40] Indeed, 'John Wilmot and George Strauss hardly counted politically – a really strong political minister at Supply would

Table 6.1. Subsidies for trade and raw materials 1946–1951, £m.

	1946	1947	1948	1949	1950	1951
BoT raw materials	11	14	3	—	—	—
MoS raw materials	8	5	15	10	7	6
Assistance to Industry by MoS & BoT	7	8	7	4	4	5
Assistance to Industry by MoS only	7	8	7	4	2	4
Subsidies on Fuel	10	9	5	2	1	—
Utility cloth rebate	8	16	7	—	—	—

Source: CSO *National Income and Expenditure 1946–1953* Aug. 1954 Table 37, except for 'Assistance to Industry by MoS & BoT', which is from CSO *National Income and Expenditure 1946–1951* Aug. 1952 Table 27.

have made it the most powerful Ministry in the country'.[41] Wilmot and Strauss were also dominated by their civil servants. Furthermore, according to Williams-Thompson, when Cripps was at the Treasury, 'Supply had become largely a branch office of Cripps – without decentralised powers'.[42] Wilmot had been sacked in 1947 because he had 'failed to resolve the division of opinion among his civil servants, and to stand up to the steelmasters' over steel nationalisation. Dalton and Cripps, strong supporters of steel nationalisation, wanted Bevan appointed to replace him. Attlee offered Bevan the job, but he refused it.[43] 'What if' questions suggest themselves.

The Tories had been opposed, from wartime, to the idea of a peacetime supply ministry. They particularly objected to the civil functions of the Ministry of Supply and their 1950 manifesto promised to transfer these to the Board of Trade.[44] Within parts of government too there was clearly a desire to separate engineering from the Ministry of Supply.[45] In fact in July 1951 the raw material responsibilities of the Ministry of Supply and the Board of Trade were merged into a new Ministry of Materials. But when Churchill returned to office in October 1951 he kept the Ministry of Supply, then fully engaged in the rearmament effort, and the new Minister of Supply, Duncan Sandys, made it clear that engineering would stay in place.[46] It is significant too that Churchill wanted to appoint Sir John Anderson, as 'Overlord' of the three key economic departments, the Treasury, Board of Trade and Ministry of Supply.[47] However, certain functions of the Ministry of Supply were reduced. Thus, the United Kingdom Atomic Energy Authority (UKAEA) was formed in 1954, and a year later, with rearmament over, the sponsoring function for engineering was put into the Board of Trade. Only then was the Ministry of Supply overwhelmingly a defence department.

THE SCOPE OF THE MINISTRY OF SUPPLY

One of the great difficulties in writing about the Ministry of Supply is that it had a wide range of functions. Thus it was responsible for defence procurement, research and development, much civil supply and was the production authority for the metals and engineering industries. To make things worse these functions overlapped. To take civil aircraft as an example, the ministry was responsible for R&D and buying aircraft for airlines. It saw the support of civil aircraft as a 'war potential' function too, and of course aircraft would make their contribution to exports.

Defence Production

Although the production of armaments was drastically reduced at the end of the war it did not cease. Indeed armaments production was maintained at a high level by previous peacetime standards and was rapidly increased from 1950. Furthermore, the creation of a permanent, peacetime Ministry of Supply was indicative of a commitment to defence production and research. Even though Britain maintained conscript armed services after the war, for the first time in peace, Britain's defence effort was thought to depend on strong defence science, technology and industry.[48] The commitment to new defence production needs stressing because it is sometimes assumed that it was the intention to rely on Second World War stocks until a new generation of advanced equipment was ready for production in the 1950s. One indication of the scale of defence production is the number of workers allocated to it. In early 1946 the Defence Committee of the Cabinet decided on a ceiling of 650,000, a figure Bevin wanted reduced to 500,000.[49] Even in the pre-rearmament plans for defence expenditure for 1950–51, net expenditure was to be £780 million, out of which £250 million was for production and research.[50]

The military aircraft programme provides a good example of the continuation of defence production. Indeed, aircraft and aircraft equipment took 57 per cent of the procurement budget in 1949–50.[51] On the jet fighter side the Meteor, which saw some use in the war, continued in production and new versions were developed right through the 1940s. The de Havilland Vampire, and further developments, were only in service after the war. These are just examples: by 1950 the RAF had been substantially re-equipped with aircraft of post-war manufacture. By the early 1950s it was receiving aircraft of essentially post-war design like the Canberra and the Shackleton. By the mid-1950s it was receiving more advanced aircraft which were the products of late 1940s research and development: the V-bombers, and the Hunter, Swift and Javelin fighters. The aircraft industry of the late 1940s, which produced and

Table 6.2. Some major aircraft in production and development 1945–1951 (single or second date is date of first service or cancellation; first date is beginning of development)

Firm	Military aircraft	Civil	Cancelled
Armstrong-Whitworth			*Apollo (1949)*
Avro	Lincoln (1945) Shackleton (1951) *Vulcan (1947–56)*	York (1943) Lancastrian (1945) Tudor (1947)	
Blackburn	Firebrand (1945)		
Bristol	Brigand (1945)	*Freighter (1951)* *Britannia (1957)*	*Brabazon (1946–52)*
Handley Page	Hastings (1948) *Victor (1947–57)*	Halton Hermes (1950)	
de Havilland	Hornet/Sea Hornet (1946) *Vampire/Sea Vampire (1946)* *Venom/Sea Venom (1952/4)*	Dove (1946) *Comet* (1951)	
English Electric	*Canberra (1951)*		
Gloster	*Meteor (1944)* *Javelin (1948–55)*		
Hawker	Fury/Sea Fury (1947) *Sea Hawk (1953)* *Hunter (1948–54)*		
Saunders Roe			*Princess (1946–52)*
Short	Solent (1948)		*SA4 (1946–50)*
Vickers-Armstrong	*Attacker (1951)* *Swift (1948–54)* *Scimitar (1956)* Valetta (1948) *Valiant (1955)*	Viking (1946) *Viscount (1953)*	

Italics = in development only in period covered   * = jet
Notes: Armstrong, Whitworth, Avro, Gloster and Hawker were owned by Hawker Siddeley. The Hastings and Valetta were military transports.

designed these aircraft was very substantial. In 1948 employment in the manufacture of airframes, engines and parts, as well as guided weapons, but excluding electrical and electronic equipment was 172,000[52] compared to a 1935 figure of 35,000. The aircraft firms themselves were substantial employers. In November 1947 the following firms had more than 5,000 employees: Bristol, de Havilland, English Electric, Fairey,

Avro and Armstrong Siddeley (both part of the Hawker Siddeley Group), Vickers–Armstrong and Rolls–Royce.[53] The industry, and the firms, were about five times as large as in 1935. In 1948 the output of the industry was divided as follows: £21 million government R&D, £75 million government procurement, £8 million home civil and £16 million exports, giving a total output of £120 million,[54] roughly the same as the value of cotton exports and car exports, in that year. As for other industries there were export targets, in this case of £25 million for 1948 and £33 million for 1949, compared with actual exports of £6 million in 1938.[55]

An important feature of defence production in the pre-nuclear age was the maintenance of reserve capacity in case of emergency. This 'war-potential' was to take a number of forms after 1945. The first was the maintenance of surplus specialised production capacity, either by rotating production or mothballing. A good example of the former is the maintenance of massive over-capacity for ammunition filling in some Royal Ordnance Factories. Of around forty-four major wartime ROFs, twenty-one were kept after the war, employing 40,000 workers. There was, on the whole, not enough work for them to do. 'Breakdown' of unused ammunition took up some time, but there was some reluctance within the ministry to use the ROFs for civil work and there were confrontations with the unions on this.[56] But a number of ROFs did civil work in the post-war years – making parts for gas and electric cookers as well as watches.

Another method of maintaining war potential was to find new uses for strategic materials. An excellent, and very important, example of this was the building of a large number of aluminium pre-fabricated houses by the Ministry of Supply. Yet another was to create civil analogues of arms industries. A good example was the creation of a clock and watch industry after the war to preserve fuze-making capacity: before the war the British clock and watch industry barely existed.[57] Another example was the financing of a major civil aircraft programme after the war, one which involved paying for the development of new types and subsidising the operations of the airlines. There was thus an important programme of turning swords into ploughshares, to provide both ploughshares and, in the longer term, swords once more.

The concern with 'war potential' went much further than a concern with particular kinds of industrial capacity and strategic goods. The whole of the engineering industry was seen as a reservoir of capacity and skills for armament production. Furthermore, a ministry paper noted that:

> the Ministry has recognised from the outset that the ultimate determinant of war potential is the economic prosperity of the country, that the engineering industry is of paramount importance

to this and that therefore in the discharge of its responsibilities for the engineering industry it must seek for policies and measures designed to promote a vigorous and efficient structure likely to make an enduring contribution to both full employment and a sound national economy.

It argued further that the ministry differed from the Board of Trade in that it had a great deal of scientific, technical and industrial expertise, as well as close relations with firms.[58]

Civil Supply

The ministry was concerned at being overloaded with responsibilities, in particular about the supply role for other departments.[59] In late 1946, the MoS was responsible for the supply of civil aircraft to the Ministry of Civil Aviation, prefabricated housing and engineering fitments for housing for the Ministry of Works, as well as motor vehicles, hand tools and medical supplies.[60] An official committee under the chairmanship of Sir Alan Barlow, noted that:

> In our view, the primary task of the Ministry in supplying the services and maintaining an adequate war potential in the engineering industry is in itself so great that they should not, in general undertake the supply of any other stores unless it can be shown in each case either that such an arrangement is necessary to discharge their primary responsibility or that there is a substantial balance of advantage from the point of view of the public interest in concentrating supply arrangements, not merely in a single department, but in the Ministry of Supply rather than any other.

Thus it was recommended that future house orders should be handled by the Ministry of Works and medical supplies should be transferred to the Ministry of Health.[61] This indeed happened.

But it is important to note that the ministry fought hard to keep some civil supply responsibilities. The issue of control over the civil aircraft industry illustrates this. This was a subject of argument between MoS, the Ministry of Civil Aviation and the nationalised airlines right through the late 1940s. The MoS was very keen to keep control over both design and production of civil aircraft. They argued, correctly, that as far back as 1938, in response to criticisms of airliner development, the Air Ministry had ordered both prototypes and production of civil airliners.[62] In mid-1947 an interdepartmental committee concluded that the MoS should order prototypes, while the corporations should handle production orders. The MoS, however, wanted control over when a new production aircraft should be ordered.[63] It was clear at a meeting held later in 1947 that there was still no agreement over control of production orders: the corporations still wanted total control over production orders, while the MoS still wanted a say in production.[64] The MoS argued that its technical expertise, its experience of placing contracts and the need to control the aircraft industry meant it should be closely involved in ordering. There was also an important precedent involved: if the ministry lost control of supply to airlines, might it not also lose control of supply to the RAF?[65] The aircraft industry was broadly in favour of a continued MoS role, despite its reservations about the ministry, because it feared that the airlines wanted to buy more American aircraft, rather than support the British industry.[66] However, the MoS was to lose much control over the development of new aircraft. It arose because of great difficulties over the Avro Tudor transatlantic aircraft. A Committee of Inquiry under Air Chief Marshal Sir Christopher Courtney had found a great deal of muddle.[67] A later internal inquiry, chaired by the Chairman of Courtaulds, Sir John Hanbury Williams, recommended that the airlines should take the lead in stating the requirements for civil aircraft, and this recommendation was broadly accepted in the Civil Aviation Acts of 1948 and 1949.[68] But while the intended role of the ministry in procurement for the airlines was reduced in the late 1940s, it did acquire responsibilities for the supply of capital goods to two newly nationalised industries, electricity[69] and coal mining,[70] and tractors for agriculture. Thus the ministry remained a major purchaser, not just of defence goods, but of certain civil goods too.

Research and Development

While there was a radical shift in the output of manufacturing industry from war production to civil production, in the case of research and development there was a much smaller shift. Indeed, the national R&D effort remained overwhelmingly warlike. This has been obscured by the neglect of the Ministry of Supply in discussion of R&D funding. The term 'science policy' has unfortunately been used to describe only 'civil' science policy,[71] and in discussions of this there is a concentration on the small Department of Scientific and Industrial Research (DSIR) from which illegitimate generalisations about the British state's attitude to science and technology are made.[72] Central to any discussion of post-war R&D must be the fact that the Ministry of Supply was overwhelmingly the largest government R&D agency, and spent much more than private industry did on its own R&D, though much of its R&D funds were spent in private industry. The ministry spent some £150 million on current expenditure for R&D in industry between 1945 and 1950.[73] The Ministry of Supply's effort was overwhelmingly defence oriented, but its civil R&D expenditure was much greater than that of any other government department. The civil aircraft programme alone consumed more than the spending of the DSIR. Indeed total expenditure (capital and current) on the nuclear physics establishment at Harwell was greater than the entire budget of DSIR.

Table 6.3. Research and development expenditure 1948–1951, £m

	1945	1948	1949	1950	1951
Ministry of Supply		58	74	89	110
Ministry of Supply in Aircraft Ind.*		21	23	30	35
DSIR		3.2	4.2	5.2	5.3
Harwell**		6.3	5.2	4.7	5.1
Total Government		75	96	115	141
Total Industry-funded	10		24		

Source: *Ministry of Aviation *Report of Committee of Inquiry into the Aircraft Industry* Cmnd. 2853, (PP 1965/6, Vol. iv), p. 119; **M. M. Gowing *Independence and Deferrence* Vol. II (1974) p. 86; other figures from *Civil Estimates* Research and Development Appendix.
Industry-funded research: David Edgerton 'British Industrial R&D, 1900–1970' in P. Mathias and J. A. Davies eds *Science and Industrial Technologies* (Oxford, 1992).

Table 6.4. Estimated Government Expenditure on Civil R&D, £m.

	1945–6	1950–51
Universities and learned societies	1.5	8.3
DSIR	2.3	4.9
MRC	0.3	1.7
ARC	0.3	0.8
Nature Conservancy	—	0.08
Development Fund	0.03	0.3
Ministry of Supply, civil aviation	na	8.0
MAF	0.6	2.0
Other civil departments	0.9	3.0
Navy, civil	0.05	0.2
Air, civil	0.6	0.4
TOTAL	6.58	30.0

Source: Council for Scientific Policy *Report on Science Policy* Cmnd 3007 (PP 1966/67, Vol. 48).

Government R&D expenditure probably did not fall after the war, although no figures are as yet available to compare wartime R&D expenditure with that in the post-war years. In the case of aircraft Winston gives a figure of £19.8 million for 1944–5, a figure which was certainly exceeded in the post-war years.[74] In the mid-1940s aircraft R&D was some twenty times what it had been in the 1930s. If we look at the actual scientific staffs of the Ministry of Supply and its predecessors, even though not all of them were concerned with R&D, it is clear there was a fall in numbers from 7,200 civilians at the wartime peak in both MoS and MAP, to some 4,100 civilians in 1947. The Barlow Committee on Scientific Manpower had put defence R&D as the lowest priority, and had recommended a cut of 50 per cent. The Ministry of Supply fought successfully against it, claiming the need for at least 5,000.[75] It was agreed with the Treasury that the complement of civil service scientists and engineers should be around 5,200.[76] More scientists and engineers were engaged on defence work in industry. In 1947 the distribution of scientists and engineers in R&D was as follows: civil departments, 2,500; research associations, 1,200; defence departments, 5,500; industry 10,000.[77] Perhaps one-third of R&D expenditure in industry was accounted for by defence work in the late 1940s.[78]

Easily the best documented R&D programme is the atomic energy programme, restarted very soon after the war. This project cost £140 million between 1946 and 1953 (it is not clear in what part of the Ministry of Supply estimates this was concealed). In 1953 some 15,000 people were directly employed, with fewer than this employed in private industry.[79] Atomic energy expenditure averaged 11 per cent of total Ministry of Supply expenditure over 1946 to 1953, with a temporary peak of 23 per cent in 1950–51.[80] In real terms this was about half the cost of the equivalent parts of the American wartime Manhattan Engineer District project.[81] But the ministry's R&D programme was very broad indeed. The ministry was responsible for launching the British computer industry.[82] Hendry has noted that

> by 1952 [Ferranti] had reached the stage of being Britian's only commercial computer manufacturer, with six firm orders, without having taken any risks and without having invested any significant resources of its own in the venture. The Ministry of Supply had paid for the bulk of the development work.[83]

One estimate of MoS civil aircraft development spending puts the figure at £78.87 million up to 1955,[84] another at £88.37 million to 1959,[85] the Brabazon alone consuming £13 million.[86] Devons estimated that the Ministry of Supply spent some £30 to £40 million in the immediate post-war years ordering prototype civil airframes, as well as similar amounts for the development of civil engines.[87]

The ministry's R&D programme was the largest the British state had ever funded, even in wartime. It was overwhelmingly a defence programme, even though many defence technologies were expected to have major civil applications, nuclear power being a case in point. It was also a programme of development of useful technologies which would be put into production, but which involved a combination of pure research with engineering and production on a huge scale; the nuclear programme is the best example of this. The research, and especially the development work, was largely carried out in private industry. The research effort, and a smaller proportion of development, was carried out largely within the research establishments of the ministry. There were a great many of these, concentrated in the south of England. Among the most important were the Royal Aircraft Establishment, the National Gas Turbine Establishment, the Telecommunications Research Establishment and Harwell. In sharp contrast to the United States, universities were not entrusted with major defence R&D programmes. This is not to say that British universities were unaffected by the huge defence R&D effort. There was expansion in subjects like nuclear physics and aeronautical engineering, and particular university staff acted as consultants at many levels to the Ministry of Supply.

LABOUR AND THE POLICIES OF THE MINISTRY OF SUPPLY

Was there a distinctively Labour approach to defence supply, R&D and the promotion of civil technologies? At one level the answer must be yes: it was a Labour policy decision to maintain a Ministry of Supply in peacetime and entrust it with major civil industrial responsibilities. But the way in which the ministry exercised its responsibilities does not correspond either to our picture of the policies pursued by the Labour government or to Labour Party thinking on industrial questions. I will explore these issues by considering nationalisation, and the character of relations between the Ministry of Supply and private industry.

Nationalisation

If there is one policy Labour is associated with it is public ownership of industry. But, not only did the Labour government not nationalise the private arms industry, it 'privatised' large numbers of arms plants, sold off machine tools[88] and stopped a nationalised arms firm from competing with the private sector. The nationalised arms industry consisted of plants owned and run by service or supply ministries, known as Royal Ordnance Factories and the Royal Dockyards. The number and scope of the Royal Ordnance Factories had greatly increased since the 1930s as had the quantity of state-owned industrial capacity operated by private firms as 'shadow' or 'agency' factories. In the 1930s the public ownership of armaments production had been a major political issue, to the extent that a Royal Commission was appointed to look into it. The Labour Party in its 1934 programme, *For Socialism and Peace*, called for the abolition of the private manufacture of armaments. The 1935 manifesto was more circumspect:

> Labour will propose to other nations the complete abolition of all national air forces, the effective international control of civil aviation and the creation of an international air police; large reductions by

international agreement in naval and military forces; and the abolition of the private manufacture of, and trade in, arms.[89]

In the late 1930s it merely wanted to see public capacity extended: the 1939 party document, *Labour and the Armed Forces* proposed that:

> The Minister of Supply would be responsible for the existing state armament factories and under a Labour Government he would be under instructions to expand these factories or to set up new factories whenever possible, when an increase in industrial capacity was called for.

The 1945 manifesto contained no reference to the nationalisation of the arms industry, even though wartime Labour ministers had argued that a larger part of the aircraft industry should come under state control.[90] Furthermore, at the Labour Party Conference of 1945 there was a resolution demanding that arms production should become a government monopoly. It drew the following response from Philip Noel Baker for the National Executive: 'Our Party has always stood for the abolition of the private trade and manufacture of arms. We stand for it today. We are pledged to the hilt, and our pledges will be carried through'. The resolution was referred to the National Executive.[91]

In fact, under Labour not only was capacity surplus to defence requirements sold off to private companies, so was much capacity intended for defence production. The proportion of armament production capacity in private ownership was greater under Labour than it had been during the war. This is not just the result of the decreasing importance of Royal Ordnance Factories; this observation applies to the aircraft industry. In that industry in 1944 some £60 million of privately owned capital was used, while the total value of assets used was at least £200 million.[92] These Crown Assets were used freely by the firms during the war, which meant they made high profits in relation to capital employed.[93] From 1946, however, MoS decided to charge a rental on that part of the capacity which firms wanted to keep and from 1947 capacity was sold to the aircraft firms; most appear to have bought some. This policy appears to have been pursued in order to forestall nationalisation of the industry, which was the logical political consequence for an industry in which a very high proportion of capacity was state owned, and the products of which went largely to the government. What price was paid for these assets is not clear, nor whether good prices were achieved. Between 1946–47 and 1949–50 the Ministry of Supply realised £61 million through sales of capital assets.[94]

But more remarkable still was the case of jet-engine design. Frank Whittle's firm Power Jets had been formed in 1936 with private funds, and designed Britain's first jet engines. The production of engines, however, had been turned over to other private firms who also started designing engines of their own. Whittle, then a socialist, urged that the whole jet-engine industry should be nationalised. In a letter to Cripps in April 1943 he noted that:

> The case for nationalisation seems to me to be overwhelmingly strong, so much so that the public would be entitled to raise a vigorous outcry through Parliament if a few private firms were allowed to grasp for the benefit of their shareholders that which should properly be the property of the state.[95]

Cripps, however, nationalised only Whittle's firm, and merged MAP's own gas turbine research establishment into it. Power Jets became a limited company owned by the state which Cripps intended should continue to design jet engines and to manufacture them on a small scale. However, the private firms objected strongly and MAP would not authorise Power Jets to design and manufacture new engines. The election of the Labour government gave hope to Whittle that this decision would be reversed but, in early 1946, the government decided to convert Power Jets into the National Gas Turbine Establishment, a civil service organisation devoted exclusively to research. As Whittle himself put it, it was a 'striking paradox' that a 'Government company was virtually smothered to death while a Labour Government was in office'.[96] Whittle, and his team, resigned, never to design an aero-engine again.

In the Labour Party's review of nationalisation policy in 1948 the aircraft industry was a candidate for nationalisation. The pro-nationalisation argument was that the aircraft industry was an arms industry for which there was a 'moral and political' case for nationalisation; furthermore the state was the principal purchaser of aircraft and did a great deal of research; and, bizarrely, that the aircraft firms could not be considered 'capitalist' in that they were guaranteed against loss by the state. Nationalisation would allow better planning and co-ordination of resources. The case against was that technical progress required a measure of freedom from control; that there was no widespread demand for nationalisation from the trade unions; and that the state as monopoly purchaser had all the powers required to control the industry.[97] John Freeman, the Parliamentary Secretary to the Ministry of Supply, argued that in peacetime waste of resources was unavoidable if 'war potential' was to be maintained, but most importantly of all that 'any undue centralisation on nationalisation would undoubtedly impoverish the main tide of technical thought'; he had little doubt that 'the keen and healthy competition which at present exists between design teams is essential to success'. He concluded that: 'There is no reason arising out of the purely physical difficulties of pursuing research and development, and maintaining or expanding productive potential, which requires the

Government to take any new powers of control over the industry'. Such difficulties that had arisen in the post-war years were 'either inevitable or arise from a weakness in policy or administration on the part of the government and do not arise from an inherent lack of power'.[98] In other words, the whole issue was regarded as an administrative one in which questions of ownership of property were irrelevant. But it is worth noting that the emphasis on competition between design teams was one which would have found no parallel in the nationalised industries. More importantly, the Labour Party's documents show no evidence of awareness of the importance of state-owned capacity during the war or the story of Power Jets.

Tripartism

The Ministry of Supply did not adopt the policy of either establishing Working Parties or Development Councils for the industries under its control. This is not really surprising since the Working Parties were established only for industries the Board of Trade had 'concentrated' during the war and the Development Councils were in most cases an extension of these.[99] There was an attempt to make the Development Councils a general feature of relations with industry, but it did not succeed. The Ministry of Supply dealt with a wide range of bodies in its broad consultations with industry but overwhelmingly with trade associations, and with its own, non-statutory Advisory Councils.[100] Advisory Councils and trade associations were the preferred mode of government–industry relations of the FBI.[101] The Ministry of Supply's Advisory Councils were the Engineering Advisory Council (equal numbers of employees and operatives, and officials from various departments – chaired by the Minister of Supply), the Gauge and Tool Advisory Council, the Machine Tools Advisory Council (which unusually had two independent members), the National Advisory Council for the Motor Manufacturing Industry (one independent member) and the Heavy Electrical Plant Committee. All had different terms of reference.[102] They were significantly different from Development Councils in that they sometimes included government officials, and that independent members, where included, represented a much smaller proportion of membership than in Development Councils. But there were some unique policies and bodies for some sectors, for example the statutory Iron and Steel Board which was established in 1946 as a prelude to nationalisation. It is also worth noting that Political and Economic Planning established an Engineering Group which wrote reports on various parts of the industry, including motors.[103] We are fortunate to have a brief sketch in William Cooper's novel *Sciences from Metropolitan* (1982) of the relations between the ministry and defence contractors.[104] In the novel it is clear that detailed ministry knowledge of capabilities of particular firms, personal contacts between officials and captains of industry loaded down with knighthoods and peerages, and trade associations were all important. There was also a whiff of corruption.

In recent years the view has gained ground that state–trade-association relations were fundamental to government–industry relations in the 1940s.[105] Such a picture certainly does not apply to relations between MAP or MoS and the aircraft industry. The key decisions – on what type of aircraft to produce, where to produce it and so on, were prerogatives of a ministry which made certain that the Society of British Aircraft Constructors (SBAC) did not have a voice in these key decisions.[106] This is, of course, in no way surprising. The state as purchaser had to choose what it wanted to buy – and also had the power to decide who would produce. The key contacts, then, were between individual firms and the ministry. In choosing which firm to place development and production contracts with the ministry took account of many factors – the technical capacity of the firm, its industrial capacity and its current workload. The ministry knew the firms intimately. This is not to say that the SBAC was not important in discussion of general policy, but it is to say that the key relationship was the state–firm relationship. This was one in which the trade association could not interfere because it could not itself afford to discriminate between firms.[107]

The question then arises as to whether this kind of discriminatory approach was used in the case of the engineering industry when supplying the general market, or supplying the MoS with civil goods. As far as the latter is concerned, it was certainly the case with the civil aircraft industry. As far as the supply of engineering goods to the general market is concerned, the ministry could not control through purchasing, but it could control through release of state-owned plant and the allocation of steel supplies. The extent to which these controls were used in a discriminatory way is not clear. But as Tiratsoo shows in this volume (see chapter 9), Standard was the beneficiary of discrimination.

There has been a general presumption that there was no discrimination in the industrial policy pursued between 1945 and 1951. For example, Cairncross has suggested that selection of investment projects was 'largely arbitrary and unrelated to measurable economic criteria such as expected rates of return. There was no question of "picking winners"'.[108] It is generally assumed that industrial policy, at least before the 1960s, was non-discriminatory. Worswick argued in 1952 that discrimination in industrial policy was being abolished:

> During the war it was possible for the Civil Service to discriminate between industries and firms in its treatment of them . . . Since the

war the principle of non-discrimination has been fully restored. Thus policies are scrutinised closely in order to eradicate any trace of favouritism – even in cases where, from the point of view of production, it is known that firms A, B and C are far more efficient, better employers and so on, than firms X, Y and Z. It is not, as some would have us believe, that civil servants are incompetent to judge these things at all. On the contrary, they may sometimes know them only too well; but as things are they are driven to use their considerable intelligence to devise controls which no one can justifiably complain about on grounds of equity. In so doing they often sacrifice efficiency.

This is not to say that the policy has been wrong. But it should be realised that a price had to be paid for ensuring the particular type of equality of opportunity between manufacturers and traders which has been upheld so far. In the light of the overwhelming need for yet higher productivity we may have to reconsider whether the price is not too high.[109]

In the war, of course, there was a major discrimination between industries, between those essential to war production and those which were not, for example between aircraft and cotton textiles. But discrimination between *firms* in wartime was largely confined to the defence industries; it was not a general feature of wartime industrial policy. Thus if we compare like with like we find a continuation of a basic non-discrimination in civil sectors, discrimination in defence sectors and a continuing discrimination between the two. This is a vital distinction, applicable to peace and war, which Worswick, like so many commentators, does not make. To put it another way: the Board of Trade was not a discriminatory ministry, in peace or war, while the Ministry of Supply was. What was new in post-war industrial policy was the allocation of a major portion of civil industry to a discriminatory defence supply ministry. Thus, between 1945 and 1951 state policy did discriminate between sectors, and in some sectors between firms. The state was 'picking winners'. The process may have been largely arbitrary and based on crude criteria, but it was taking place.

CONCLUSION

In this paper I have sought to bring to the fore the role of the unduly neglected Ministry of Supply. In doing so it becomes clear that some commonly held beliefs about state intervention in the 1940s need adjustment. In particular, I suggest that historians have wrongly generalised from the policies and practices of the Board of Trade in their treatment of industrial policy and the study of state–industry relations. During the war it was the supply ministries that played the most active and innovative role and they bequeathed to the post-war years expertise in central direction of industrial resources and a much-modernised industrial base. At the very least then, it is necessary to distinguish between the wartime supply ministries and the munitions industries on the one hand, and the Board of Trade and its consumer-goods industries on the other.

As far as the post-war years are concerned the Labour government pursued a policy unique in British history. It created a unified peacetime supply department, one which was deliberately given very important civil–industrial responsibilities. The history of the ministry highlights the fact that the Labour government decided to maintain a well-developed 'warfare state' and decided also to pursue a policy of exploiting the resources created during the war to build and maintain new civil industries. The Ministry of Supply was at the centre of both the 'warfare state' and the 'developmental state'. It was the scientific, technological and industrial powerhouse of the British state, and pursued the discriminatory, interventionist and technological policies which many critics have said British governments have not, but should have, pursued.

There is another important general issue which arises. How is it that contemporaries and historians have missed such a central element in the history of wartime and post-war economic control? In broad terms, I want to suggest that we should distinguish between British politics and the British state. The industrial policies of the state did not necessarily follow from the industrial thinking of British politics; nor were the actual industrial policies of the state reflected in politics. It is tempting to see this as yet another example of the problems arising from secrecy. There is something in this, but not too much. Availability of information, while a problem was not, and is not, the central issue. Rather the problem was, and is, a failure to come to grips with the fact that in the twentieth century the British state has been a militant, industrial and technological state, just as much as it has been a 'welfare state'. Perhaps the most extraordinary aspect of this is that the Labour Party and Labour ministers on the whole appeared to have missed the significance of Labour's creation of a united Ministry of Supply. To that extent they operated in the realm of politics rather than in that of the state. The appointment of Cripps to the Board of Trade, rather than to the Ministry of Supply, must remain a mystery, at least to me, as are his attitudes to the ministry thereafter. Just as amazing, but no less significant, is the fact that the Ministry of Supply has been ignored in the historiography of govern-ment–industry relations. Government–industry relations were indeed a 'vacuum in socialist thought' but it is significant that many of the positive proposals made by Harold Wilson were descriptions of policies practised by the supply ministries in wartime and the Ministry of Supply after it.[110] It is significant too that Harold Wilson was to recreate the Ministry of Supply in 1967 – in the form of the expanded Ministry of Technology – and that commentators on this ministry have largely failed to note its distinctiveness.[111]

NOTES

1. For example, K. O. Morgan *Labour in Power* (Oxford, 1984).
2. A. A. Rogow with P. Shore *The Labour Government and British Industry, 1945–1951* (Oxford, 1955) p. 55. See also p. 52.
3. J. Leruez *Economic Planning and Politics in Britain* (Oxford, 1977) p. 37.
4. A. Cairncross *Years of Recovery: British Economic Policy, 1945–1951* (1985; 1987) p. 49.
5. Richard Williams-Thompson *Was I Really Necessary?* (1951) p. 3. I am very grateful to Nick Tiratsoo for bringing this book to my attention.
6. F. M. G. Willson *The Organisation of British Central Government, 1914–1964* (2nd edn 1968). The first edition was published in 1957. See also J. M. Lee *Reviewing the Machinery of Government, 1942–1952: A Study of the Anderson Committee and its Successors* (mimeo, 1977).
7. For example, S. Newton and G. Porter *Modernisation Frustrated* (1989).
8. D. N. Chester ed. *Lessons of the British War Economy* (Cambridge, 1951).
9. Exceptions are Alan Milward *War, Economy and Society* (1977) and Cairncross op. cit. pp. 310–14.
10. See David Edgerton 'Liberal Militarism and the British State' *New Left Review* No. 185 January–February 1991; *England and the Aeroplane: An Essay on a Militant and Technological Nation* (1991).
11. D. E. H. Edgerton 'State Intervention in British Manufacturing Industry, 1931–1951: a comparative study of policy for the military aircraft and cotton textile industries' (unpublished PhD, University of London, 1986); G. A. H. Gordon *British Seapower and Procurement between the Wars: A Reappraisal of Rearmament* (1988).
12. For example, Cairncross op. cit. p. 13.
13. Philip Redfern 'Net Investment in Fixed Assets in the United Kingdom, 1938–1953' *Journal of the Royal Statistical Society* Series A Vol. 118 1955 10–182.
14. T. Barna 'The Replacement Cost of Fixed Assets in British Manufacturing Industry in 1955' *Journal of the Royal Statistical Society* Series A Vol. 120 1957 1–36.
15. G. A. Dean 'The Stock of Fixed Capital in the United Kingdom in 1961' *Journal of the Royal Statistical Society* Series A Vol. 127 1964 333–415.
16. Dean op. cit. Table III 348–9.
17. Public Record Office, Kew (hereafter PRO) CAB87/7 R(44)6 'Report of the Steering Committee on Post War Employment Policy' 11/1/1944 paras. 280–9.
18. G. C. Peden 'Sir Richard Hopkins and the "Keynesian Revolution" in Economic Policy' *Economic History Review* Vol. XXXVI 1983 281–96.
19. Keith Middlemas *Power, Competition and the State* Vol. I (1986); J. F. O. MacAllister 'Civil Science Policy in British Industrial Reconstruction, 1942–1951 (unpublished DPhil, University of Oxford, 1986); Correlli Barnett *The Audit of War* (1986) ch. 13, 'Tinkering as Industrial Strategy'. See also Edgerton 'State Intervention'.
20. Lee op. cit. p. 96.
21. PRO CAB87/7 R(44)42 Memorandum by the Minister of Aircraft Production 'Government and the Major Industries' 8/3/1944.
22. Ibid. PRO CAB87/7 R(44)59 Memorandum by the Minister of Works

'Government and the Major Industries', 22/3/1944; PRO CAB87/7 R(44)69 Memorandum by the Minister of Aircraft Production 'Government and the Major Industries' 31/3/1944.

23. Lee op. cit. pp. 11–17.
24. *Memoirs of the Rt. Hon. the Earl of Woolton* (1959) p. 169.
25. PRO ADM1/17794 MG(44)28 Memorandum by the Minister of Aircraft Production 'The Organisation of Supply' 21/11/1944, quoted in P. Winston 'The British Government and Defence Production, 1943–1950' (unpublished PhD, University of Cambridge, 1982) p. 118.
26. Quoted in Lee op. cit. p. 109.
27. PRO CAB66/59 WP(44)713 Memorandum by the Chairman of the Machinery of Government Committee 'Organisation of Supply' 20/12/1944.
28. C. R. Attlee *As It Happened* (1954); Kenneth Harris *Attlee* (1982) p. 402.
29. Attlee op. cit. p. 154.
30. PRO CAB129/2 CP(45)177, 178, 181, 197; PRO CAB128/1 CM(45)37 Conclusions 2/10/1945.
31. *Hansard* (Commons) 5th Series, Vol. 415, Cols. 35–8, 29/10/1945, statement by Prime Minister.
32. Williams-Thompson op. cit. p. 8.
33. *The Economist* 8/11/1945.
34. 'Ministry of Supply' *Future* No. 3 1947 19. This article (pp. 17–25) is by far the most detailed contemporary source on the ministry. I am most grateful to Nick Tiratsoo for bringing it to my attention.
35. Sir Richard Stafford Cripps *Democracy Alive: A Selection of Recent Speeches* (1946) p. 72.
36. *Board of Trade Journal* 26/8/1950, see also 8/9/1951.
37. *Staffs employed in Government Departments* February 1950 Cmd. 7887 (PP 1950 Vol. XVI). The figures are for 1st October 1949. The suggestion made by PEP that for 1949 the number of civil servants doing civil work in Supply was probably half the number in the Board of Trade and Department of Overseas Trade, is thus likely to be an underestimate (PEP *Government–Industry Relations* (1952) p. 98).
38. Williams-Thompson op. cit. p. 8.
39. Ibid. p. 9.
40. Ibid p. 9.
41. Ibid. p. 24.
42. Ibid p. 48. See also p. 166. Of course, many of the other production ministers were under Cripps's thumb: Wilson at Trade, Bevan at Health and Gaitskell at Fuel and Power (Edwin Plowden *An Industrialist in the Treasury* (1986) p. 22).
43. Harris op. cit. pp. 342–4.
44. *British General Election Manifestos 1918–1966*, compiled and edited by F. W. S. Craig (Chichester, 1970). The 1951 Conservative manifesto was silent on the Ministry of Supply.
45. PRO DEFE7/282 *Report by the Committee on the Organisation and Work of the Scientific Branches of the Ministry of Supply and Admiralty* [Chmn. Air Chief Marshal Sir Guy Garrod], 20/4/1951 p. 14.
46. PRO AVIA54/1464 Minister of Supply 'Some Preliminary Reactions to the Garrod Report' 1/2/1952.
47. John W. Wheeler-Bennett *John Anderson, Viscount Waverley* (1962) p. 352.
48. *Statement Relating to Defence* Cmd 6743 (PP 1945–6 Vol. XX). See also Julian Lider *British Military Thought after World War II* (Aldershot, 1985) pp. 509–16.
49. Alan Bullock *Ernest Bevin: Foreign Secretary, 1945–1951* (1985) pp. 128, 240. See also: George Peden 'Economic Aspects of British Perceptions of Power on the Eve of the Cold War' in J. Becker and F. Knipping eds. *Power in Europe? Great Britain, France, Italy and Germany in a Postwar World* (Berlin, 1986) pp. 237–60.
50. *Statement on Defence 1950* Cmd 7895 (PP 1950–1 Vol. XVI Annex II).

51. W. P. Snyder *The Politics of British Defence Policy 1945-1962* (Columbus, Ohio, 1964) p. 89.
52. Ministry of Aviation *Report of Committee of Inquiry into the Aircraft Industry* Cmnd 2853 [Plowden Committee] (PP 1965/6. Vol. iv).
53. PRO AVIA9/138 'Production Information on Certain British Aircraft Firms'.
54. Ministry of Aviation op. cit. p. 119.
55. *British Industries* Vol. 33 No. 10 Oct. 1948 287 and Vol. 34 No. 10 Oct. 1949 274. See also Anthony Sampson *The Arms Bazaar* (1978) pp. 107-8 and Winston op. cit. ch. 5.
56. Williams-Thompson op. cit. pp. 86-95.
57. Winston op. cit. pp. 173-82.
58. PRO AVIA49/75 Memorandum 'Civil Functions of the Ministry of Supply' 20/2/1950.
59. PRO AVIA49/75 Letter A. Rowlands – Bridges, 14/11/1946.
60. PRO AVIA49/75 Memorandum 'Functions and Responsibilities of the Ministry of Supply', November 1946.
61. PRO AVIA49/27. 'Report of the Official Committee on the Civil Supply Functions of the Ministry of Supply', 26/11/1947.
62. PRO AVIA49/1 Supply Council, Note by Permanent Secretary, 'Ordering of Aircraft for the Civil Airline Corporations', 27/11/1947.
63. PRO AVIA55/30, 'Report of the Committee on Ordering Procedure for Civil Aircraft' 13/5/1947; Minutes of Supply Council, SC(47)2nd meeting, 24/6/1947.
64. PRO AVIA55/30, Notes of a meeting held on 10/11/1947.
65. PRO AVIA55/30. Minute from Musgrave US(Air) to Parliamentary Secretary, 12/11/1947.
66. PRO AVIA55/30, Note by SBAC, 'Procurement of Aircraft for the State-Owned Air Transport Corporations'.
67. Peter King *Knights of the Air* (1989) p. 418. *Interim Report* Jan. 1948, Cmd 7307; *Final Report* July 1948 Cmd 7478, both PP 1947-8 Vol. XVII. See also Williams-Thompson op. cit. ch. 8.
68. Keith Hayward *Government and British Civil Aerospace: A Case Study in Post-War Technology Policy* (1983) pp. 18-19.
69. L. Hannah *Electricity before Nationalisation* (1979) p. 322; L. Hannah *Engineers, Managers and Politicians* (1982) pp. 24-5, 27.
70. Winston op. cit. p. 129.
71. For example, N. Vig *Science and Technology in British Politics* (Oxford, 1968).
72. A recent example is an otherwise very useful thesis by MacAllister (op. cit.).
73. Garrod Report, see note 45.
74. Winston op. cit. Table 5.
75. PRO AVIA49/1 Supply Council, Memorandum by Permanent Secretary 'The Staffing of Scientific Services in the Ministry of Supply' 10/1/1947.
76. PRO AVIA49/1 Supply Council Minutes SC(47), 1st Meeting 4/1/1947. The actual staffing in January 1948 was 4,054. Memorandum by Permanent Secretary, 'Staffing of Scientific Services in the Ministry of Supply, 19/2/1948.
77. *First Annual Report of the Advisory Council of Scientific Policy* Cmd 7465 p. 14 (PP 1947-8 Vol. XVI).
78. David Edgerton 'British Industrial Research and Development, 1900-1970' in P. Mathias and J. A. Davies eds. *Science and Industrial Technology* (Oxford, 1992).
79. M. M. Gowing *Independence and Deterrence* Vol. II (1974) p. 37.
80. Ibid. p. 87.
81. Ibid. pp. 56-7.
82. National Archive for the History of Computing, Manchester, FER/B3, Letter B. Lockspeiser – E. Grundy 26/10/1948.

83. J. Hendry *Innovating for Failure* (Cambridge, Mass., 1990) p. 91. On the role of the Ministry of Supply in the development of electronics see: J. Kraus 'The British Electron-Tube and Semiconductor Industry, 1935–62' *Technology and Culture* Vol. 9 1968 544–61.

84. Hayward op. cit. p. 15.

85. Ministry of Aviation op. cit. p. 125.

86. Hayward op. cit. p. 17.

87. E. Devons 'The Aircraft Industry' in Duncan Burn ed. *The Structure of British Industry* Vol. II (Cambridge, 1958) p. 83.

88. *The Economist* 6/10/1946; *British Industries* Vol. 31 No. 9 231.

89. Craig op. cit.

90. PRO CAB87/5, R(43)1st meeting Minutes of War Cabinet Reconstruction Committee, 20/12/1943.

91. Labour Party *Report of the 44th Annual Conference, 1945* (1945) pp. 149–50. See also D. E. H. Edgerton 'Technical Innovation, Industrial Capacity and Efficiency: Public Ownership and the British Military Aircraft Industry, 1935–1948' *Business History* Vol. 26 1984 247–79.

92. PRO AVIA65/1731, Memorandum 'Financial Development of the Main SBAC firms from the beginning of the Rearmament period'.

93. Ibid.

94. *Report to the Comptroller and Auditor General, Civil Appropriations Account (Class IX) 1949/50* p. vii (PP 1950–1 Vol. XXV).

95. Quoted in Sir Frank Whittle *Jet: The Story of a Pioneer* (1953) p. 263.

96. Ibid. p. 302.

97. Labour Party Archive, National Museum of Labour History, Manchester (hereafter LPA) R.D. 182 Memorandum 'The Aircraft Industry 1948'. See also Sub-Committee on Industries for Nationalisation, Minutes, 8/11/1948, 8/12/1948.

98. LPA, R.D. 181, John Freeman MP, 'Memorandum on the Aircraft Industry' 26/10/1948. Quoted in D. E. H. Edgerton 'Technical Innovation', pp. 269–70.

99. David Henderson 'Development Councils: An Industrial Experiment' in G. D. N. Worswick and D. H. Ady eds. *The British Economy, 1945–1951* (Oxford, 1952) pp. 455, 457.

100. A list of bodies the MoS dealt with is given in *List of Committees and Associations which act as a link between the Ministry of Supply and Industry*, Select Committee on Estimates, Tenth Report Session 1950–51, Rearmament, Annex 11 (PP 1950–1, Vol. VI).

101. The definitive statement of the FBI view was 'Trade Organisation – Relationship with Government' printed in *British Industries* Vol. 31 No. 11 Nov. 1946 287–91.

102. Treasury *Government and Industry* (1948).

103. PEP *P.E.P Engineering Reports – II: Motor Vehicles* (1950).

104. Cooper is famous for his pathbreaking *Scenes from Provincial Life* (1950) to which the above is a sequel.

105. F. Longstreth 'State Economic Planning in a Capitalist Society: the political sociology of economic policy in Britain, 1940–1979' (unpublished PhD, University of London, 1983), and some of the chapters in this volume. The great variety of roles of trade associations just in their dealings with industry, the importance of overlapping memberships and the relative unimportance to large firms of trade associations in dealing with government is apparent from PEP *Industrial Trade Associations* (1957).

106. Edgerton 'State Intervention' chs. 3 and 5. See also John Turner 'Servants of Two Masters: British Trade Associations in the First Half of the Twentieth Century' in H. Yamasaki and M. Mijamoto eds. *Trade Associations in Business History* (Tokyo, 1988) pp. 192–3.

107. Snyder op. cit. p. 99.

108. Cairncross op. cit. p. 461.

109. G. D. N. Worswick 'The British Economy, 1945–1950' in Worswick and Ady op. cit. pp. 28–9.
110. The operation of government factories, state purchasing, powers to take over private firms, state information on key firms (PRO PREM8/1183 Memorandum by the President of the Board of Trade 'The State and Private Industry' 4/5/1950).
111. Edgerton 'Liberal Militarism' and *England and the Aeroplane.*

Seven

Taxation policy

RICHARD WHITING

For the Labour governments of 1945 to 1951 taxing business was important both for economic management and political strategy. Britain's post-war position required increases in output for exports along with the restraint of domestic consumption. Businessmen had to be given incentive to produce, but the need for wage restraint also meant that profits could not escape too lightly. Both the actual incidence of business taxation and its political impact, were going to play a part in Labour's tax strategy. The environment for this strategy was shaped by a number of factors. Labour inherited a certain momentum from the war which had seen the raising of large amounts of revenue from companies through Excess Profits Tax (EPT). Assessment of wartime profits continued to bring in revenue well into the post-war years.

The amounts collected under EPT and under the peacetime profits tax are given in Table 7.1. During the war profits taxes (the National Defence Contribution and EPT) contributed roughly 24 per cent to 26 per cent of direct tax revenue. Under the peacetime profits tax which operated strongly from 1948 the contribution was 12 per cent to 13 per cent. None of these figures takes account of the incidence of income tax on company profits, which is dealt with later in this chapter. The NDC was levied at 5 per cent on company profits down to 1947 and was then re-named the profits tax. This was levied at 12.5 per cent on distributed profits and 5 per cent on profits put to reserve. Both rates were doubled in November 1947. While the rate for profits put to reserve stayed at 10 per cent for distributed profits it was increased to 30 per cent from October 1949 and then to 50 per cent from January 1951. EPT figures take account of the 20 per cent post-war refund which was chiefly distributed in 1946–7.

Labour had done little preparation for maintaining this momentum into the post-war period. A memorandum of 1943 from the post-war finance sub-committee of the party assumed that both the National Defence Contribution (NDC) instituted in 1937 and EPT would be repealed and not replaced.[1] Labour's tax thinking prepared it more for dealing with the capital wealth of individuals than with the income of companies.

Table 7.1   Profits taxes, 1945–1951

Tax Year	% of direct revenue	tax receipt	(U. K. £,000)
1945–46	1.7	35,485	Profits tax (N.D.C.)
	21.0	429,345	E.P.T.
1946–47	1.8	32,107	Profits tax
	7.9	141,449	E.P.T.
1947–48	2.0	36,220	P.T.
	7.9	224,234	E.P.T.
1948–49	9.6	199,090	P.T.
	3.4	69,110	E.P.T.
1949–50	12.3	260,760	P.T.
	1.0	21,665	E.P.T.
1950–51	12.6	258,420	P.T.
	−0.04	−852**	E.P.T.

**Refund exceeded receipts in this year.
Source: *Parliamentary Papers 1951–1952 XV Report of the Board of Inland Revenue* Tables 3, 155 and 159.

The other side of the question was how vigorously the business interest was going to respond to taxes levied against it. During the war it had been criticised for being too defensive in its posture: 'the attitude of industry, when E.P.T. was raised to 100%, had been weak. Industrialists appeared to be unwilling on political grounds to fight for what they knew to be right.'[2] But recovery of its position after the war was hampered by internal differences of opinion on key issues. Both the Labour government and private business were to some extent uncertain in their analyses of tax questions, and were to a degree borne along by the war-induced increase in revenue-generating ability at the disposal of the government. It was only near the end of Labour's period in office that some of the problems involved in developing long-term business taxation began to be faced, but these required elaboration after 1951 before they received legislative enactment under Harold Wilson's government.[3] This chapter is going to concentrate in the main upon specific business taxes and will have four areas of interest: the background to Labour's tax thinking, the evolution of the profits tax, the business campaign against taxation and developments in tax strategy at the end of the period.

Labour's tax perspectives in the pre-1939 period reveal a good deal about the attitudes to business wealth of those in the Labour Party regarded as economic or tax experts. Business profits were far from being the prime target; in fact, Labour's aim was to enhance dynamic profit-making at the expense of passive, unearned income, especially inherited wealth. Both Hugh Dalton (Chancellor of the Exchequer 1945–7) and Douglas Jay (Economic Secretary to the Treasury 1947–50) defined their socialism by their predatory attitude towards inherited wealth. Dalton had argued in the 1920s that conventional Marxism ignored a potent source of inequality by giving inadequate attention to capital wealth transmitted across generations. He was particularly interested in Rignano's advocacy of death duties to tax heavily inherited wealth in return for lighter burdens on life-time income creation. Jay's views were similar. In *The Socialist Case* published in 1937 he argued that 'the abolition of unearned incomes and the consequent social ownership of property must be at the centre and heart of socialism', and that 'socialists have been mistaken in making ownership of the means of production instead of ownership of inherited property the test of socialization'.[4]

By attacking inherited wealth or unearned income, Jay and Dalton had to some extent sanitised business profits. As the reward for enterprise and initiative they were far less worrying, or even to be applauded, once their translation into inheritable wealth was blocked. High earnings or profits became a just reward for initiative rather than the subsequent support for an indolent rentier class. The scope for innovation along these lines was limited during the life of the Labour governments but there were signs of these priorities in Labour's tax policies. Dalton was not able to put into practice a scheme for exchanging inherited estates for terminable annuities, but he did make significant increases in death duties in the 1946 budget. Jay was also keen to introduce taxes on wealth, either in the form of a capital levy or as a scheme of death duties along the lines favoured by Dalton.[5] When the Labour Party's finance group contributed its views on budgetary policy the attractions of a capital levy, or death duty taxation on Rignano lines, were spelled out, to which Dalton was sympathetic. It was argued that a levy would be of great 'psychological' value; by this it was meant that workers would feel that the rich were having ill-gotten gains taken away from them, and that a capital tax was an appropriately socialist motif for Labour's budgetary policy.[6]

A capital levy was never implemented by the Labour governments, probably because of the administrative problems of valuation and fears of the intense political opposition it might have raised. However, in 1948 as part of a deflationary budget a Special Contribution was levied, taxing all unearned income above £250 where the total income was over £1,500. Since the effective rate of tax was over 20 shillings in the £ on higher unearned incomes it amounted to a form of capital taxation. In Jay's view, this tax 'followed from the argument of my 1937 *The Socialist case* that large inherited fortunes should be the prime target of direct taxation'.[7] When Labour wanted to use taxation against capitalism in a politically explicit way, it therefore addressed its efforts to capital wealth rather than flows of income.

This segmentation of tax strategy did not mean that the distinction between wealth and income was at all water tight. The Special Contribution and death duties did affect business, the former because it impinged upon private savings, the latter because high duties caused problems for private companies where a partner's liability had to be met by his successors. However, the business interest accepted that, whatever the impact of these taxes upon individuals, they were peripheral to their main political responsibility to represent the campaigns dealing with company taxation. The Federation of British Industries (FBI) lodged its opposition to the Special Contribution as a matter of form, and regarded difficulties caused by death duties as 'not primarily a matter of industrial interest.'[8]

Besides the traditional instincts upon which Labour drew, there were two other factors more to do with the immediate context which bore upon the business interest and which require discussion. In the first place, the Second World War had not been a 'profiteering' war in the same way as the First; the feeling that businessmen had made easy profits and accumulated large reserves was far less prominent, and therefore the virtues of appearing to be punitive had less appeal. Profits of course increased faster than wages overall in the post-1945 period, but references to 'profiteering' are few and far between. A second factor which has to be weighed more carefully is the contemporary awareness of the importance of incentive in the supply of work and enterprise. In the 1920s business had certainly suffered from the view that the weight of taxation did not inhibit risk-taking and enterprise.[9] In the post-1945 period there was greater appreciation of the importance of expectations in the behaviour of businessmen and therefore of the discouraging effects of high taxation. Dalton was anxious at the outset to lighten the burden of direct taxation, claiming that he had no attachment to Philip Snowden's commitment to direct over indirect taxation. These views were shared in the parliamentary party. George Benson, MP for Chesterfield and chairman of the finance group of Labour MPs, expressed them this way in the 1946 budget debates:

> In the next five years it is not the Labour government, it is not socialism that will be on trial. It is private industry that will be on trial, because we should have to demand from it a standard of efficiency, enterprise and initiative which it certainly never showed in the inter-war years. I am not sure we are going to get that with the present colossally high rate of taxation.[10]

Companies were caught up in more general discussions about taxation and incentive which affected the population as a whole because they paid income tax at the standard rate on their profits, once specific profits taxes had been deducted. Even when the 1947 profits tax was in operation income tax payments accounted for 60 per cent of the tax liability of companies.[11] The profits distributed as dividends transferred that part of the tax to the shareholder; the companies deducted the tax at source and retained it. The standard rate fell on the profits put to reserve. Therefore anxieties about the disincentive effects of high taxation in general, or on personal incomes in particular, could in theory have had an effect on company taxation.

Since the main effort in this area was directed to easing tax burdens on working-class incomes, however, the attention was given to reduced rate bands below the standard rate, or to the earned income allowance. The standard rate of tax remained unchanged for the life of the Labour governments at 9 shillings in the pound, although it had been reduced from the wartime level of 10 shillings in the pound. It is true that greater use was made of indirect taxation to ease the burden on direct taxpayers, but again this was a trade-off operating at levels below the standard rate. The most that can be said about the effect on companies of the general concern to protect incentives is that it may have prevented any rise in the standard rate which would, *inter alia*, have fallen on reserves. Despite the pressure to ease direct taxation on grounds of incentive, Labour chancellors never felt it was politically necessary or possible to make the change in the standard rate as opposed to cheaper fine-tuning at the lower levels of tax liability. While the FBI pressed Labour chancellors to put more emphasis upon indirect rather than direct taxation and welcomed the trend when it emerged, it is difficult to detect any beneficial trend for the taxation of company profits. Indeed, businesses felt the impact of working-class resentment about indirect taxation through wage claims. Close watch was kept on the retail price index even by workers whose wages were not formally linked to it, and where indirect taxes contributed to its rise employers felt that they had to resist the pay claims which resulted. The Engineering Employers' Federation argued before a court of inquiry in 1948 that:

> an important factor in the rise of the index of retail prices had been the increased taxation on beer and tobacco, and the purchase tax. It was impossible for the Federation to accept the suggestion that taxation imposed to restrict the consumption of certain commodities was to be recovered by an increase in wages.[12]

Because income tax allowances differentiated workers according to family circumstances, they were far less likely to act collectively over direct taxation.

What sort of business perspective developed within this wider context? Inevitably there were proposals, very often for public consumption, which stressed the national benefits which would follow from the minimal

taxation of industry, and more pragmatic responses which recognised
the necessity of identifying lesser evils rather than ideal solutions. In
1945 the FBI hoped that the transition from war to peace would be rapid
and discontinuous. It did not want the Excess Profits Tax of wartime to
be replaced by a more permanent tax on profits, and it hoped that the
wartime pressure on budgetary policy could be relaxed: 'during the war,
taxation is called upon to perform a service which would be abnormal
and generally unnecessary in time of peace, namely to combat inflation'.[13]
On both counts the FBI was to be disappointed. Fiscal policy under
Labour was concerned with containing inflation; taxes had to be
consistent with the achievement of budget surpluses, and in these
conditions it was highly unlikely that a sector of the economy which had
been successfully taxed in wartime would get off unscathed. The notion
of getting tax relief for business by unbalancing the budget was briefly
essayed but with no success. Provincial business opinion was flatly
against any such move. The Leeds Chamber of Commerce in 1946
deplored 'any suggestion that the Chambers of Commerce should go on
record as advocating any form of deficit budgeting', when an Association
memorandum proposed precisely that.[14] Dalton noted that the FBI's
submission before the 1947 budget was 'irresponsibly inflationist'; it too
had requested reduction in taxation even at the cost of temporarily
unbalancing the budget.[15]

The only alternative to reducing tax burdens was to urge reductions
in government expenditure, a familiar and easy line in business rhetoric
but one which hid divisions of emphasis. While most could agree that
expenditure on social services was too high, provincial opinion harped
on the costs of a swollen bureaucracy and wanted to cut the number of
civil servants by one-third, but those who had more frequent contacts
with government stressed that it was a matter of policies rather than of
the organisation of the administration.[16] Those in the higher levels of the
FBI were also aware that if, say, food subsidies were drastically cut
companies would face increasing wage demands from workers anxious
to maintain their standard of living.[17]

Although the Excess Profits Tax was repealed in 1946, the FBI's wish
to avoid a tax specifically on business profits was not fulfilled. The
Board of Inland Revenue had weighed in on the side of business against
a special profits tax, largely out of a desire to forestall tax innovation
rather than from any special sympathy for business. It argued in
November 1946 that a profits tax would 'have the vicious economic
effect that its incidence would be on the equities, the risk bearers, or
upon the reserves'. Moreover, the Board's feeling was against new taxes:

> it is not the moment to add new taxes of a troublesome and
> contentious kind to the fiscal code. The war should have seen the
> limit of taxation and the taxpayer will resent new taxes and not

approach them with that 'willingness to pay' on which the success of direct taxation in this country so largely depends.[18]

However, the momentum for such a tax was far greater than in the aftermath of the First World War, in that the National Defence Contribution of 1937 continued throughout the war as a flat rate tax and was re-named the profits tax from 1 January 1947. There was no question of instituting a completely new tax, although Dalton did admit that it required modification. What emerged was a tax which introduced the novel principle of differentiation between distributed and non-distributed profits, with a higher rate being levied on the former. The question of differentiating in the profits tax between the amount distributed in dividends and that put to reserve had been introduced by James Meade of the Economic Section. He submitted papers on 'Stabilisation and company profits' and 'The differential taxation of company profits' to the Budget Committee in December 1946.[19] Meade's main argument was that the tax varied according to the broader economic context, a lower rate being levied on undistributed profits in times of inflation and a lower rate on distributed profits in times of deflation. In the context of the post-1945 period, of course, it offered a tax incentive at a time when the general thrust of fiscal policy was restrictive – sums put to reserve seemed to be getting off lightly. The Treasury and the Board had doubts about the sensitivity of a differential tax, but this was the form the profits tax took in 1947, with a rate of 5 per cent on undistributed profits and 12.5 per cent on distributed. The rates both doubled as a result of the supplementary budget in November 1947. The full year's yield of the tax in 1948 was £190 million, of which £120 million was raised from distributed and £70 million from undistributed profits. Income tax at the standard rate on company reserves brought in £280 million.[20] Because profits tax was deducted before income tax was assessed, removal of profits tax would have brought a smaller relief than these figures might suggest, because of the increased liability to income tax.

Meade's view on the differential taxation of profits shows his attachment to fiscal methods of economic management. There were strong political predilections for such a profits tax on the Labour side which gave as much support for it as the more analytical considerations advertised by Meade. On the Labour side there was a good deal of feeling against the distribution of profits as dividends and in favour of them being ploughed back into the enterprise. Meade's preference for a differential in favour of undistributed profits was strictly related to the level of demand in the economy; the Labour preference was more of a political instinct unlikely to shift with any such changes. Had a post-war slump occurred, and the rate on distributed profits been eased, it is fair to suppose that the value of the profits tax for engaging the sympathies of the workers would have been much diminished. The support for the tax from the Labour movement therefore depended on the degree to which economic conditions favoured the restraint of demand, which they did for the life of the Labour governments. In these circumstances the limits on dividends achieved by the tax were seen as valuable for convincing workers that industry – or at least shareholders – were suffering restraints on their incomes comparable to limits on pay. Douglas Jay, in a memorandum presented before the supplementary budget of November 1947, was strongly in favour of a further rise in the profits tax, partly because it was sensible to limit profits in inflationary conditions but also because

> It is the ideal complement, by way of social justice and political practicability, for any sacrifices that must be asked for from the wage earners as a whole. It also partly meets the case for a capital gains tax which in my view is too complex.[21]

Jay was right that profits tax did not substitute completely for a capital gains tax for it was a fiction to suppose that profits put to reserve were nobody's personal income. To the extent that such profits encouraged business performance they led to improved share values which could be realised as non-taxable capital gains. But such a tax which discriminated against the ordinary shareholder had appeal in Labour circles as a second best to the control and limitation of dividends. At the Labour Party Conference in 1950 James Callaghan wanted the tax to go further in the taxation of the ordinary shareholder.[22] Paul Derrick, who at the 1951 Party Conference spoke in favour of permanent dividend limitation, wrote in the Amalgamated Engineering Union's *Monthly Journal* in support of increased taxes on distributed profits and further reductions in the tax on company reserves, to the point where profits put to reserve might suffer no tax at all.[23] These views were pressing a long-established distinction between producers and non-producers, between earned and unearned income. It was the same sort of argument which had been put forward by Dalton and Jay over the taxation of inheritances. It was also the interpretation of the profits tax used by Bevin when the government met the TUC and was anxious to convince the trade unions of the effects of profits taxes to sweeten the pill of wage restraint. Bevin emphasised the virtues of undistributed profits in favour of which the tax operated:

> I want you (i.e. the TUC) to take a sensible view about profits. Some of your best firms are the firms who pay the highest wages and make the biggest profits and they very often adopt the method of putting those profits back into improvements.[24]

In Bevin's mind profits ploughed back were more justifiable, and more likely to come back to the workers in higher wages, than profits distributed as dividends. Another way of convincing the troops that business was being given a rough ride was to stress that over half of company profits went in taxation. Dalton, at the 1948 Party Conference had to

> beg delegates, in quoting statistics, always to distinguish, and to make clear to their audience, the difference between the figures for distribution on the assumption that there are no taxes at all to be paid, and the actual figures for distribution when the taxes imposed by us have been met.[25]

The difficulties of persuading trade unionists and workers that profits taxes were an adequate quid pro quo for wage restraint were twofold: first, there was the view that workers in the main focused on gross profits and earnings, rather than figures net of tax; as one delegate to the 1948 conference rather tartly put it, 'They are not mathematicians, they are not Oxford economists'.[26] The second difficulty was that profits themselves were too high and any limitation of dividends simply deferred rather than removed benefits, whereas trade unionists usually felt that a wage claim deferred was gone for ever. Tibor Barna's article of 1949 told trade union officials that profits were excessive and taxation was merely shutting the stable door after the horse had bolted.[27] But whatever suspicions may have existed within the trade unions about the effects of profits taxes the point remains that the immediate economic and political context required a public display of taxing businesses. How did this affect business? How did it square with the interest in retaining the profit incentive to encourage production?

The FBI and the Chambers of Commerce certainly opposed the profits tax on the grounds that it was unfair to single out business and industry for special taxation in addition to income tax.[28] Fresh criticisms of the tax were pressed at the time of the supplementary budget in November 1947 and in 1951 when the tax was further increased at the time of the Korean War rearmament.[29] However, while the opposition was continuous it does not give the impression of much rigour or coherence. When the differential element in the profits tax was announced in April 1947 it was hardly referred to in subsequent budget debates. Sir John Anderson, leading for the Opposition, regarded the levels as far more moderate than had been expected in some financial quarters, and the wider business reaction was one of relief that the rates had not been higher.[30] While the FBI in particular pressed for the abolition of profits tax this was bound to be weak in the context of suppressed inflation. In the autumn of 1947 the case for a budget surplus was recognised to be overwhelming and 'there was in addition the psychological aspect that if workers were to be asked for longer hours some contribution from employers' profits would be demanded'.[31] It was admitted that companies could not escape taxation in these circumstances. In 1948 the same conditions still obtained. The FBI's taxation committee wanted to press for the abolition of the profits tax and attack the principle of a tax on retained profits but it was agreed that 'at present it was not possible to press for a reduction in overall taxation', and the Federation merely approved the greater emphasis upon indirect as opposed to direct taxation.[32] The FBI, while agreeing that the level of taxation on companies was too high, could not mount a coherent critique nor suggest an alternative to the form which that taxation took.

To attack profits tax constructively required business to decide which category of shareholder it wished to protect. The profits tax fell on the ordinary shareholder, the preference shareholder paying nothing. Profits tax was not directly deducted from dividends, but since it depleted the fund available for their payment it did fall on the equity shareholder. In 1948 the FBI was invited to put its views to the chancellor on profits tax in relation to the financial structure of companies, but it failed to make any headway with the Treasury. And so while the FBI put forward the grievances of the ordinary shareholder it did not positively support them. In fact it was unable to reconcile the grievances of preference and ordinary shareholders and did not want to pursue the step of treating companies as completely separate entities from shareholders for tax purposes.[33] Since the FBI saw dividend limitation as the least objectionable form of company taxation, and since the profits tax discriminated against a class of dividends, it was not the worst form of company taxation as far as business was concerned. Dividend payments certainly lagged behind company profits in the period of the Labour governments, but while the profits tax may account for some of this there is little doubt that many companies were conservative in their distributions.[34] Opposition to the profits tax as a form of company taxation were therefore muted.

Business interests were cramped in their tax resistance by the need to contain inflation, and by the centrality of wage restraint to the strategy of the Labour governments. While provincial business opinion could simply reiterate familiar demands to cut taxes, those at the top of the FBI or the Association of Chambers of Commerce who had a closer view of government knew that they had limited room for manoeuvre. Any concession to business on the tax front would simply elicit demands from the trade unions for tax relief or more likely wage concessions which the government would not have been willing to tolerate. However, business did launch a campaign for tax relief derived from the problems of inflation which is revealing about the political aspects of its tax strategy and also about the particular fears of what taxation might have been like under a Labour government.

The campaign was based upon the argument that profits tax was not falling on real but on money profits. Because of inflation the replacement of assets was costing far more than the original asset on which depreciation allowances were based. Businesses were having to devote increasing proportions of profits to replacement of assets at higher prices. The capital assets of a business had to be maintained before a 'true' profit could be recorded, therefore profits tax was falling on capital rather than on 'real' profits.[35] As the issue emerged in public debate, the proposition was that industry was unable to maintain its capital base. The argument was launched as a major point of principle by some of the leading figures in British industry. Representatives of major companies sitting on the FBI's taxation and home policy committees prepared memoranda and devised appropriate solutions to give adequate recognition to the effect of inflation. Frank Bower of Lever Brothers drew up the most sustained argument in favour of inflation allowances, and he was supported in principle by Paul Chambers who had moved to ICI from the Board of Inland Revenue.[36] Chambers published a paper 'Taxation and the supply of capital for industry' in the *Lloyds Bank Monthly Review* for January 1949. Evidence was placed before the Millard Tucker Committee of Inquiry into Trading Profits (1950) and the Royal Commission on the Taxation of Profits and Income (1951–5). Company meetings were frequently devoted to the inadequacy of depreciation allowances, with the plea that they should be based not on the historic cost of the exhausted asset but on the replacement cost of the new one.[37]

At times it looked like a rather technical debate on accounting principles: should firms treat the extra cost of replacing assets as an appropriation of profits which could not claim tax relief, or as a charge against profits, which could? But this approach served the purpose of taking the campaign from the political to the technical domain of taxation. Bower argued that there had been an irreversible increase in trade union strength which ensured the persistence of inflation: 'the policy of full employment and the political strength of the trade unions were a guarantee that wages would rise more than any real increases in output. A change of government would not alter the situation'.[38] Given that some compensation for inflation was necessary for the foreseeable future, the trick was to locate relief in that part of the tax system which had not been politicised by the policy of wage restraint. As Bower argued:

> Industry's hope of relief of taxation depended not on equity, or on charity or on argument, but on politics. The government proposals for a standstill on wage demands and limitation of incomes was a state of uneasy truce . . . If industry went forward with a plea for the reduction of taxation on the grounds that it could not stand the present level and if the government agreed, the TUC would immediately feel free to advance claims for higher wages. The argument in favour of inflation allowances provided a method of

getting a reduction of taxation which would not start a new wave of wage demands. It was an argument the TUC could accept without appearing to have conceded relief of taxation.[39]

As long as relief was buried in technical questions over re-equipment allowances it would not emerge into the more politically charged arena of incomes and rewards which affected a good deal of taxation at this time.

The experience of initial allowances suggested that this might have been a fruitful approach. In the budgets of 1945 and 1949 the government had tried to give some incentive for re-equipment through the granting of 20 per cent and then 40 per cent initial allowances. These amounted to acceleration of normal depreciation allowances by adding onto the proportion of the cost of an asset allowed against tax a further proportion in the first year of purchase – 20 per cent in 1945, 40 per cent in 1949. This did not increase the amount of depreciation overall, but acted as an interest-free loan to give some incentive to purchase machinery. This was never a feature of political debate in budgets. By focusing on depreciation allowances over the inflation question, business had some expectation of achieving a tax advantage away from the political spotlight.

The FBI's campaign was opposed by Labour and by sympathetic economists. Callaghan argued that the problem of depreciation allowances had been overplayed because of the benefit which industry had derived from excess profits tax refunds and because machinery bought at low prices was now earning a return at higher prices.[40] Barna's article in the Oxford *Bulletin* poured scorn on the claim for higher depreciation allowances, as Kaldor was to do later in his book *An Expenditure Tax* (1954).[41] But business's campaign for inflation allowances stumbled as much from doubts within the business community as from scepticism from outside. These doubts were to do with the technical aspects of the proposed changes, questions of social justice and anxieties about the subsequent vulnerability to capital taxation if the campaign was successful.

There was, in the first place, a very real division within the FBI's taxation committee between those who thought business had every right to claim some preferential treatment and those who did not. According to one member of the committee 'industry had no right to contract out of the effects of a general trend of rising prices'.[42] Even those who felt that industry was in a special position by virtue of its vital role in the economic system saw problems with basing depreciation allowances on replacement and not on historic cost. Replacement cost was essentially a guess about what an item was going to cost at some future date, which was something accountants were unwilling to accept. Replacement, too, rarely involved exchanging like with like. However, it was not merely doubts about departing from conventional accounting procedures which confused the campaign, but also fears that tax relief on changing capital values would open the way for more intrusive taxation of business wealth in the form of a capital gains tax. J. E. Davies of ICI argued that 'the replacement cost solution was unsatisfactory in that it implied additional controls and eventually capital increment taxation', and Bower admitted that if revaluation of assets was accepted 'then there would appear to be no logical reason why capital gains should not be taxed'.[43] By seeking tax relief which required recording the changing value of assets, businesses were providing the very information upon which a new form of capital taxation could be introduced; they would be solving the complicated administrative problems of such a tax in the hope of getting inflation allowances. What might have been gained in one hand would be taken away with the other. Although capital gains tax was usually discussed in the way it trapped personal wealth, the Board of Inland Revenue had little doubt about the likelihood of business opposition to it. In a paper on the tax in 1946 it pointed out that 'the charging of pure capital gains on business assets would weigh very heavily on some industries . . . It would be resented by industry and would certainly not help that re-equipment and modernisation that is so essential for the development of British industry'.[44] When the question was reconsidered for the 1950 budget discussions the Board took the same line: 'It may be taken that the tax would be fought bitterly not only in principle but in every detail. There would certainly be no lack of points of substance around which legitimate dispute could rage'.[45]

The question of taxing capital gains had touched a raw nerve in the First World War and it did so again after 1945. When the Leeds Chamber of Commerce considered the draft submission of the Association of British Chambers of Commerce to the Royal Commission on the Taxation of Profits and Income it 'wanted to avoid the impression that capital profits should be taxed'.[46] When the submission raised the possibility of taxing profits on the sale of assets at a company's liquidation the Leeds Chamber was 'exceedingly strongly of the opinion that the views were most dangerous and should be omitted'.[47] The Chamber did not want what were at that time non-taxable capital gains to be admitted into the ambit of taxable profits.

Within the Labour movement there was some interest in favour of a capital gains tax. Evan Durbin recommended it to Dalton in the budget discussions of 1947 in the light of American experience, as did the TUC in 1951, referring to 'its useful effect on the psychology of working people'.[48] A Labour Party research department draft memorandum of the same year argued that 'there is no doubt that a capital gains tax would greatly increase the measure of justice afforded to workers as against property owners as a whole'.[49] But there was little likelihood of a capital gains tax being introduced in the life of the Labour governments. Dalton was never keen, so the possibility was not given early encouragement; it also looked complicated to administer and it might well have required some lightening of the profits tax as a quid pro quo for ordinary shareholders. In addition, the short-term benefits of the profits tax were not inconsiderable. While a capital gains tax might have allowed a more thorough trawl of business wealth and the capital gains of shareholders, the profits tax achieved a political effect for the spectators (i.e. the workers) without arousing the opposition which the more 'visible' capital gains tax would have done from businessmen and shareholders. The stock exchange reaction to profits tax changes was generally quite muted, *The Economist* noting in 1947 that 'equities found Mr. Dalton's new burdens less arduous than had been expected, and they were quickly counting the blessings of tax increases which Mr. Dalton might have made but did not'.[50] When the tax was further increased in 1949 after the devaluation the real effect was more modest because the tax was allowable against income tax and according to *The Accountant* 'this renewed tinkering with an already highly complicated tax is not for the purpose of raising revenue, it is simply to induce the mass of the workers to refrain from making higher wage claims'.[51]

To some degree then, it might be said that the profits tax met the general political aim of the Labour governments to give a public demonstration that social justice was being done, while not damaging business incentive too heavily. The claims of business that taxes were eating into capital were much exaggerated, and there is not a great deal of evidence that productive investment was being checked.

In the turmoil of post-war adjustment and crisis this represented a considerable achievement, but for the longer term taxation was no different from other aspects of government in suggesting a tension between equity and efficiency. Control over the economy might be accepted as fair by treating even handedly the existing order of things, but in so doing it ran the risk of inhibiting desirable change and initiative. As Nicholas Kaldor put it in a letter to *The Economist* in 1947, 'the egalitarianism of the status quo will ossify the economic structure.'[52] This question was raised very powerfully by taxation. By conventional tax criteria a 'fair' tax was one which treated equally those with similar incomes or forms of income. A tax which fell more heavily on one kind of property rather than another, for example, offended against tax equity. In economic life 'fairness' usually had far less significance; a 'fair' profit was usually what a company could get away with. As taxation became more closely involved with economic management the two interpretations of what was fair were bound to conflict. A clear example arose over working-class taxation. To improve the output of miners and others it seemed a good idea to remove income tax on overtime; but this was criticised for being unfair in a tax sense on those whose jobs did not bring the opportunity for overtime earnings, who would therefore forgo a tax-free segment. The question also arose with business taxation.

The drift of Labour tax strategy to cap the gains of the ordinary shareholder had certain limitations as a long-run policy for achieving fairness in a market economy. In pressing upon the ordinary shareholder it reduced him to the position of the rentier rather than the risk-taker. It encouraged investment by firms with substantial reserves but made the securing of funds from the stock exchange more difficult by diminishing the rewards to risk capital; it hampered the new entrants as against older-established firms. In the view of Kaldor, who by 1950–1 was advising Labour governments, the profits tax and especially rigid dividend limitation approved the *status quo* rather than encouraged dynamic change. This was, as he put it, 'the Socialist version of Baldwinism'.[53] It was Kaldor who came up with the idea of flexible dividend limitation in 1950 as a way of rewarding successful firms but retaining overall control of dividends. As rearmament for the Korean War got under way and dividend distributions increased, the government was under pressure both from the trade unions and from the left to move against dividends by statutory restraint rather than by simply relying on profits tax to have the same effect. When Gaitskell as chancellor met the FBI in July 1951 he told them that

> a new round of wage claims was starting and dividends had increased far beyond what he had wished. The measures taken in the budget (increase in the profits tax to 50% on distributed profits) had not had the intended effect. This had a severe psychological reaction on the unions, particularly when they saw the large profits which were being made.[54]

The purpose of the flexible dividend policy outlined by Kaldor and put before the Budget Committee in 1951 was described critically but accurately by Edward Bridges of the Treasury:

> For political reasons they want a scheme which will enforce something very like a complete dividend limitation but with a certain degree of flexibility to permit a small increase in profits. They want the limitations to satisfy the TUC, and they want the let-out in order to avoid trouble with industry and make it appear that there is still some incentive to companies to make themselves more efficient.[55]

There is some evidence that Kaldor was right in his approach, at least as far as business was concerned. When the FBI's taxation committee considered its preferences as regarded taxation for the Korean War Paul Chambers was strongly in favour of a flexible excess dividends levy as against a more rigid treatment.[56] In the tax treatment of companies Kaldor was trying to achieve the same result which was required in wages policy, namely, how to achieve some flexibility with reward for initiative or contribution while at the same time restraining the overall level of return for wages or profits which full employment required. In wages policy the attempt to get changes for particular occupations within overall restraint came up against the refusal of unions to abandon established relativities.[57] In the taxation of companies the chief difficulty was the customary priority of maintaining equal treatment between similar forms of income, as against rewarding risk through unfair treatment. As Kaldor put it: 'The social justification of dividend payments is as a reward for risk-bearing; it is the essence of this reward that it should be apportioned by the criteria of success, rather than by some criteria of "fairness" or "equity"'.[58] In the end the government made do with uniform dividend limitation, although that was overtaken by election defeat in 1951. The argument that war production was not a suitable environment for flexible dividend limitation won the day.

It is appropriate that this analysis ends with the brutal, less discriminating effect of war conditions on taxation. The tax policy of the Labour governments after 1945 show a combination of political opportunity and analytical uncertainty caused by the Second World War. On the one hand war had drastically extended the limits of taxation. As was remarked in a Labour pamphlet in 1940 'The limit of taxation is what you can get away with – in the atmosphere of war the task is much easier'.[59] But once peace came this new level of taxation had raised questions about its impact, especially on incentives in general but also upon companies in particular. It is not surprising that the Labour governments initiated two inquiries – the Millard Tucker Committee and the Royal Commission – to investigate how the *form* rather than the level of taxation was affecting economic behaviour. *The Economist* noted that the appointment of the Royal Commission 'raises fundamental issues about the incidence of taxation on economic activity and incentive. It is certainly time that these questions should be brought under authoritative examination.'[60] As it turned out the view from the 1950s was that many of these anxieties about the effect of taxation on enterprise and incentive had been exaggerated. None the less, these inquiries point to the uncertainty about the new tax regime, for which Labour's pre-1939 tax thinking had not provided much guidance. The priority from that era – inheritance taxation – was marginal to the questions on incentive and economic management which surrounded fiscal policy after 1945. The proponents of inheritance taxation had not shown much interest in another key question, that of capital gains taxation, which had been raised by the tendency of those suffering high surtax to translate taxable income into non-taxable capital gains. Labour needed a period of catching-up, in order to equate Labour policy with the potentialities of the new tax regime. While there were signs of its beginnings with Kaldor in 1950–1, it was inevitable that the legislative outcome would emerge in a later Labour government, rather than in the 'golden age' of 1945 to 1951.

NOTES

1. Labour Party Archive, National Museum of Labour History, Manchester (hereafter LPA) 'Notes on post-war taxation policy' R.D.R. 222, June 1943.
2. Modern Records Centre, University of Warwick, CBI Predecessor Archive (hereafter CBI) Taxation Committee minutes of Federation of British Industries (FBI) MSS 200/F/1/134 comment by Sir H. H. Williams, MP, 14/8/1940.
3. In particular, the capital gains and corporation taxes introduced in the 1965 budget. See Brian Reddaway 'Tax reform in the United Kingdom' in Tony Lawson, J. Gabriel Palma and John Sender eds. *Kaldor's Political Economy* (1989) pp. 148–9.
4. Dalton's continuing interest in death duties is brought out in B. Pimlott *Hugh Dalton* (1985) pp. 141–4, 625 and D. Jay *The Socialist Case* (1937) pp. 237–8. See also Henry Phelps Brown *Egalitarianism and the Generation of Inequality* (Oxford, 1988) p. 343.
5. Public Records Office, Kew (hereafter PRO) Treasury Papers (T) 171/392 memorandum by Douglas Jay, 10/10/1947.
6. PRO T 171/394, Vol. 1, 'Note of meeting of finance group of Labour Party' 14/2/1948.
7. D. Jay *Change and Fortune* (1980) p. 184.
8. CBI FBI Taxation Committee minutes 27/4/1948 and 5/5/1949.
9. R. C. Whiting 'The Labour Party, Capitalism and the National Debt, 1915–1924' in P. J. Waller ed. *Politics and Social Change in Modern Britain* (Brighton, 1987) pp. 154–5.
10. *Hansard* (Commons) 5th Series, Vol. 421, Col. 1955 9/4/1946.
11. PRO T171/398 Board of Inland Revenue 'Taxation of Corporations' PB 48 (12) 7/10/1948.
12. *Parliamentary Papers* 1947–48 Vol. XII 'Court of Enquiry into Engineers' Dispute', August 1948 p. 12.
13. CBI FBI Taxation Committee minutes 3/4/1945 and 19/9/1945.
14. Brotherton Library, University of Leeds, Leeds Chamber of Commerce minutes 'Memorandum on Finance Bill' 29/10/1946.
15. PRO T171/389 note by Dalton on 'Representation from the F.B.I.' 18/1/1947.
16. For provincial views see Leeds Chamber of Commerce minutes 30/11/1948; for London ones see CBI FBI Taxation Committee minutes 21/12/1950.
17. CBI FBI Taxation Committee minutes 23/9/1947.
18. PRO T171/391 Board of Inland Revenue, 'Notes on Profits Tax and Capital Gains Tax' para. 8 and covering note by C. J. Grigg 1/11/1946.
19. PRO T171/391 B(47)9 and B(47)13.
20. PRO T171/398 Board of Inland Revenue 'Taxing of Corporations' 7/10/1948.
21. PRO T171/392, 'Memorandum by Douglas Jay' 10/10/1947.
22. Labour Party *Conference Report* 1950 p. 106.
23. Labour Party *Conference Report* 1951 p. 125; 'Profits and Progress' and 'Profits and Taxation' in Amalgamated Engineering Union *Monthly Journal* April 1949 and May 1951.
24. PRO T172/2033 'Discussions with the T.U.C.' meeting of 17/11/1947.
25. Labour Party *Conference Report* 1948 p. 150.
26. Padley of the Union of Shop, Distributive and Allied Workers, Labour Party *Conference Report* 1948 p. 146.
27. There was reference to Barna's article by J. Mortimer in *The T.U.C. and Wages Policy* (1950) p. 14. Barna's article was entitled 'Those "Frightfully

High" Profits' and appeared in the *Bulletin of the Oxford University Institute of Statistics* Vol. XI Nos. 7–8 1948 213–28.

28. PRO T171/389 'Budget suggestions by outside bodies' FBI 8/11/1947 p. 2.
29. CBI FBI Taxation Committee minutes 29/11/1947 and 11/4/1951.
30. *Hansard* (Commons) 5th Series, Vol. 436, Cols. 210–11 16/4/1947; *The Economist* 19/4/1947 596.
31. CBI FBI Taxation Committee minutes 23/9/1947.
32. Ibid. 30/12/1947.
33. PRO T171/398 'The Profits Tax' BC 49 (5) 11/1/1949.
34. D. Seers 'National Income, Production and Consumption' in G. D. N. Worswick and P. Ady eds. *The British Economy 1945–1950* (Oxford, 1952) p. 52.
35. CBI FBI Taxation Committee minutes 5/8/1948.
36. Ibid. 24/8/1948.
37. Lever Brothers company meeting, *The Economist* 28/8/1948 356–7.
38. CBI FBI Taxation Committee minutes 8/11/1948.
39. Ibid.
40. PRO T171/397 Vol. 1, letter of 17/12/1948.
41. Barna, op. cit.; N. Kaldor *An Expenditure Tax* (1954) pp. 154, 156.
42. CBI FBI Taxation Committee minutes 24/8/1948.
43. Ibid. 5/8/1948 (Davies); 30/6/1949 (Bower).
44. PRO T171/391 'Capital Gains Tax' 17/11/1946.
45. PRO T171/400 'Taxation of Capital Gains' BC(50)2.
46. Leeds Chamber of Commerce minutes 3/4/1951.
47. Ibid.
48. PRO T171/389 Vol. 1 'Budget suggestions by outside bodies' letter from E. F. M. Durbin 21/2/1947; Modern Records Centre, University of Warwick, TUC archive, Economic Committee minutes 560.1.(7), 14/2/1951.
49. LPA 'Control of Profits' R.32 February 1951.
50. *The Economist* 19/4/1947 596.
51. *The Accountant* leading article, 8/10/1949.
52. *The Economist* 5/4/1947 493. This theme is also discussed in A. Rogow and P. Shore *The Labour Government and British Industry* (Oxford, 1955) pp. 128–9.
53. 'A Positive Policy for Wages and Dividends', 27/7/1951, reprinted in N. Kaldor *Essays in Economic Policy volume 1* (1964) p. 127.
54. CBI FBI Economic Directorate 'Dividend Limitation' E1/5/5, meeting with chancellor of the exchequer 20/7/1951.
55. PRO T171/403 Vol. 1 'Profits Tax and Dividend Limitation' 12/1/1951.
56. CBI FBI Taxation Committee minutes 9/10/1950.
57. Bevin's criticism of the trade unions is in PRO T172/2033 'Discussions with the T.U.C.', meeting of 1/10/1947.
58. 'A Positive Policy for Wages and Dividends' in Kaldor op. cit., p. 120.
59. Labour Party Policy Committee *Prices, Taxation and Saving* April 1940, p. 15.
60. These inquiries published their findings in: *Report of the Committee on the Taxation of Trading Profits* Cmd. 8189, (1951), and *Royal Commission on the Taxation of Profits and Income. Final Report* Cmd. 9474 (1956). *The Economist* 23/12/1950 1154.

I must thank the CBI for permission to draw upon their archive at the Modern Records Centre, University of Warwick, and I gratefully acknowledge financial support from the ESRC (ref. 000 22 11017).

PART TWO

The Sectors

Eight

The cotton industry: a middle way between nationalisation and self-government?

MARGUERITE DUPREE

Let Us Face the Future, the Labour Party's statement for the 1945 election, gave only a general idea of what a Labour government's policy towards private industry would be.[1] Nevertheless, Stafford Cripps brought a distinctive policy to the Board of Trade when he became President in July 1945. He attempted to create a 'partnership' for industrial policy formation among employers, unions and consumers, and an organisational structure embodying that partnership which would promote desired changes in industry and serve as a permanent means of communication between government and industry. He appointed 'tripartite' Working Parties to investigate the major non-nationalised industries, particularly those characterised by small units, producing consumer goods and experiencing concentration during the war. Subsequently Cripps put forward legislation which allowed the establishment of Development Councils, 'Labour's main institutional innovation for dealing with private industry'.[2] Involving neither nationalisation with compulsory public ownership of firms nor reliance on the industrial self-government of trade associations partially representative of employers in an industry, Development Councils offered a type of central statutory organisation covering all firms in an industry financed by a levy on firms and including representatives of employers, employees and independents (representing consumers or the national interest or contributing technical expertise). A Development Council was to have no compulsory powers over prices, nor were wages and conditions of employment part of its functions. Instead, a Development Council was intended as a means for private industries to improve the efficiency of production and distribution, to provide common services such as research, design and statistics and, as Cripps emphasised particularly in introducing the Third Reading of the Bill, to serve as 'that liaison with industry which is now an essential part of any national planning'.[3]

A full account of the Attlee government's policies towards the cotton industry would include the decision not to reopen the Liverpool cotton market and to nationalise the import and sale of raw cotton, creating the Raw Cotton Commission.[4] Although outside the scope of a volume dealing with private industry, this decision which singled out raw cotton from other raw material markets, increased employers' suspicions that the government would nationalise the rest of the industry and influenced their reception of government policy. A full account of government policies would also include the gradual dismantling of wartime controls on exports and prices of cotton yarn and cloth, though in 1951 the much-altered Utility scheme remained in place. The controls together with the government's taxation policies, particularly purchase tax, directly influenced the production decisions of individual firms. The focus of this chapter, however, is on the structure and conduct of relations between the industry as a whole and the Board of Trade, the government department directly responsible for the industry. The nature of this relationship for the cotton industry was central to Cripps's policy towards private industry; it was also fundamental to the detailed formulation and implementation of a range of policies for the industry including those for the industry's long-term reconstruction and exports. Could the Attlee government work with a major private industry?

This chapter will first outline the cotton inheritance Cripps came into on his arrival at the Board of Trade: the position of the industry, the history of its central organisations, and the discussions and decisions regarding post-war policies which had taken place before the Labour government's election. The chapter will next examine: the application to the cotton industry of Cripps's policy for Working Parties, the split in the Working Party, the efforts to keep cotton out of politics, and the Industrial Organisation and Development Act. The third section will argue that, far from being ignored,[5] the Working Party's recommendations served as the agenda for the Board of Trade and the Cotton Board, a rationale for legislation to promote re-equipment and amalgamation in the spinning section, and the basis for a number of more successful but less well-known Cotton Board activities. Contrary to Correlli Barnett's argument that politicians and civil servants shirked the issues of the long-term needs of industry in pursuit of a New Jerusalem,[6] it will be suggested that ministers and officials in the Board of Trade during the first two years of the Attlee government put much effort into searching for and implementing a suitable policy for cotton. After mid-1947 their efforts were superseded by the shift of attention both onto the cotton industry to meet the immediate needs of the export drive and onto longer-term measures to stem Japanese competition.[7] The account will also throw light on the nature of Cripps's leadership and the process of policy-making in the Board of Trade.

I

The Cotton Industry in 1945

During the inter-war years the British cotton industry suffered a disastrous decline in demand. World recession, the falling incomes of primary producers, the development of local industries in former markets, the emergence of Japanese competition aided by depreciated currency in the 1930s and protectionist policies in India, China and Egypt had led by 1938 to a fall in exports of cotton yarn and cloth from the UK to 21 per cent and output and employment to only half their 1913 levels. Thus the industry faced acute problems of surplus labour and surplus capacity on the eve of the Second World War.

During the war shortages of raw cotton and labour resulted in the reduction of the industry's capacity by one-third. Yet care and maintenance schemes, financed out of contributions from running mills to assist the reopening of closed mills at the end of the war, meant that the industry emerged from the war with approximately the same amount of equipment as it had had at the start, albeit increasingly aged. The critical shortage was of labour, which could not easily be filled due to competition for labour from newer industries in Lancashire. Thus, in 1945 Cripps inherited an industry facing the post-war sellers' market with surplus capacity and a shortage of labour.

Central Organisations in 1945 and their Background

On arrival at the Board of Trade Cripps also found two central organisations dealing with the industry: the Cotton Control and the Cotton Board. The Cotton Control, a department in the Ministry of Supply, although much concerned with wartime production and prices, played little role in the post-war organisation of the industry. The Raw Cotton Commission took over its role as monopoly buyer and seller of raw cotton; detailed control over production was ended in December 1945 and government price controls, apart from the Utility scheme, ended in the late 1940s. Afraid of a return to the pre-war buyers' market, the employers in the spinning section of the industry, however, set up a minimum price scheme run by a voluntary trade organisation, the Yarn Spinners' Association, which took the place of statutory controls as soon as they ended.

In contrast to the Cotton Control, the Cotton Board and its history are central to the Attlee government's policy for the industry. In the Cotton Board Cripps inherited an influential body which represented an unusual form of statutory organisation for government–industry relations.

Inspired in part by the First World War's Cotton Control Board,[8] a view emerged in the industry during the inter-war years that the predominantly horizontal organisation both of firms and of the chief associations of employers and trade unions necessitated a central body, representative of all sections of the industry (spinning, weaving, finishing and merchants), to co-ordinate and express the views of the industry as a whole, particularly in negotiations with the government.[9] The effort to create such a body began with the voluntary Joint Committee of Cotton

Trade Organisations (JCCTO) in 1925 and culminated in the proposals embodied in the Cotton Industry (Reorganisation) Act of 1939. Intended as a solution to the problems of surplus capacity and labour during the 1930s, the Act included provision for a statutory Cotton Board to operate an extensive system of minimum price controls, production quotas and scrapping of redundant capacity while providing other services for the industry as a whole.

Thus, the idea and support in the industry for a statutory Cotton Board emerged out of both the disastrous fall in demand during the inter-war years and the horizontal structure of the industry and its trade associations. It was not a creation of government but of the industry.

Considering the industry-inspired Act to be too elaborate and inappropriate for war, the government suspended it in September 1939. Having no pre-war plans for organising the cotton industry in wartime, during the early weeks of the conflict, the Board of Trade assembled representatives of the employers and operatives from the major sections of the industry to advise about wartime arrangements, calling this group the Cotton Board. Using the Manchester premises and experienced staff of the JCCTO and the chairmanship of a civil servant (Sir Percy Ashley), the Board was a consultative body without executive powers. It had no funds of its own; only reluctantly did the Treasury agree to pay for the services of the JCCTO's staff during the early weeks.

Increasing home demand and government orders together with a steep fall in exports soon made it clear that merely advisory powers were inadequate. The Board asked for: (i) control over the allocation of raw material supplies, production price control, statistics of productive capacity, output, stocks, etc and (ii) powers to take measures to promote the export trade. Rather than pass the additional legislation necessary to give these powers to the Cotton Board, the government used existing legislation to create a new organisation, the Cotton Control, endowed with the first set of powers. In November Sir Percy Ashley was appointed Cotton Controller responsible to the Minister of Supply, and the Cotton Control was established as a government department on the same lines as other raw material controls. The Cotton Board continued to act in an advisory capacity under Ashley's chairmanship to promote exports. Yet, as exports of cotton goods fell substantially, in December 1939 the government announced that it would introduce legislation in the next session of Parliament to put the Cotton Board on a statutory basis.

Though encouraged by government rhetoric about maintaining the balance of payments and helping to pay for the war, from the beginning exports generally lost out to military production and home demand for essential raw materials. Alarmed, the Manchester Chamber of Commerce and its Secretary, Raymond Streat, promoted a movement for a Minister of Economic Co-ordination in the War Cabinet responsible for exports.

The government took the view that exports were a function of the Board of Trade. Its new President, Andrew Duncan, early in 1940 established the Export Council, consisting of businessmen and representatives of relevant government departments. Four business members agreed to work full time as an executive committee out of offices in the Board of Trade in London to undertake the detailed organisation of an export drive for all industries. Raymond Streat was asked to be Secretary of the Export Council and the Executive Committee; the Chamber of Commerce agreed to lend him.

Based on support from the industry for a statutory Cotton Board and on his experience as independent chairman of the Iron and Steel Federation, Duncan proposed that the cotton industry should have a similar unifying organisation which would among other things represent it on the Export Council (unlike most other industries which were represented by trade associations). In March Parliament passed a short Act[10] which established a less elaborate wartime Cotton Board than envisaged by the 1939 Act.

Based in Manchester, the Cotton Board consisted of eleven members drawn from employers and operatives in the different sections of the industry and appointed by the President of the Board of Trade. In addition, there was a chairman who had to be an 'independent person' without financial interests in the industry. The purpose of the Cotton Board was to provide services for the benefit of the industry in general, but especially for the maintenance and extension of the export trade. Furthermore, the Cotton Board was to promote research into production and markets, collect and publish statistics and conduct negotiations on any matters affecting the industry, apart from wages and conditions of employment. In addition, the Board was to advise on questions relating to the industry referred to it by any government department. Unlike the Cotton Control in the Ministry of Supply, the Cotton Board was not a government department: its members were not government employees and it was financed by a levy on the industry rather than by the Treasury.

Despite the new statutory status of the Cotton Board, exports of cotton goods continued their precipitous fall. By the middle of June the Board of Trade decided that the lack of effective action by the Cotton Board required the separation of the Cotton Board from the Cotton Control by means of the appointment of a Chairman of the Cotton Board who was not also the Cotton Controller. Raymond Streat's appointment as Chairman of the Cotton Board in June 1940 evolved out of his work at the Export Council, as well as from his broad experience with the problems of the export trade in cotton goods as Secretary of the Manchester Chamber of Commerce for twenty years.[11]

The increasing severity of the war and the advent of Lend–Lease in

April 1941 meant that exports were subordinated to the needs of the war economy and no longer essential to pay for the war. Exports of cotton goods were strictly controlled and limited to what was necessary to meet the needs of the colonies, Dominions and territories dependent on Britain for supplies. Acting as the agent of the Board of Trade, the Cotton Board rationed the small permitted amount of export trade among markets and among the firms of exporters catering for those markets. Thus it kept the complex distribution system in a position to resume the export trade after the war.

While its export role went into a state of suspended animation, the Cotton Board became an integral part of the wartime planning structure, working closely with the Cotton Control. It organised the concentration of the finishing section and it planned and operated the scheme for the care and maintenance of the closed mills. Also in its role as the agent of the Board of Trade, the Cotton Board organised the Utility scheme which supplied standard cotton cloths to meet civilian needs under clothes rationing and price control.

Thus, arising out of the need to increase exports in the early stages of the war and later acting as the agent of the Board of Trade in the concentration and Utility schemes, the Cotton Board emerged from the war with the advantages of an experienced chairman and staff, an established reputation for successful work and the support of the industry for its continuation. The cotton industry was not included in the Labour Party's list of industries to be nationalised. As long as the new government did not change its mind about nationalisation, the industry expected the government to continue the existing Cotton Board and eventually to bring in legislation specific to the cotton industry replacing the 1939 Act. This would retain the Cotton Board, though whether it would have powers of price control and compulsory amalgamation was uncertain.

Wartime Planning for Post-war Policies

In the wartime Cotton Board Cripps also inherited an organisation with three years' experience of discussions with the Board of Trade on post-war plans, some of which were already being implemented. In 1942 Hugh Dalton, President of the Board of Trade, had asked the Cotton Board to put forward proposals for post-war reconstruction of the industry. Dalton made it clear that he did not like the idea of statutory minimum prices but grudgingly he agreed not to rule them out. Beyond that he gave Streat and the Cotton Board's Committee on Post-war Reconstruction little guidance as to possible government policies.

After canvassing a wide range of opinion, at the end of 1943 Streat wrote the report to the Board of Trade of the Cotton Board's committee, including the argument that the necessary reorganisation and re-equipment of the industry would come from minimum prices. This recommendation, like the report as a whole unanimously backed by the operatives and employers on the committee, reflected the industry's perception of its inter-war experience, the existence of similar powers in the untried 1939 Act, and the expectation that the post-war sellers' market would be as short as that after the First World War.

The report received a critical reception from the press and from the Board of Trade, which favoured larger units rather than minimum prices as the key to reorganisation in Lancashire. In September 1944 the Cabinet Reconstruction Committee rejected Dalton's plan for a Spindles Board with powers of compulsory amalgamation for the spinning section, but let Dalton go to Lancashire with a compromise: statutory minimum prices would be possible if the industry started reorganising first. Ultimately Dalton felt frustrated, concluding that 'an All party government, absorbed in the immediate necessities of the war effort, can never give this country a strong policy for Cotton'.[12] Nevertheless, before the war ended the Board of Trade and the Cotton Board had in-depth discussions about the long-term post-war reconstruction of the cotton industry. Also, the chairman of the Cotton Board saw himself and the Board carrying out government policy announced by Dalton in September 1944. For example, alongside the immediate problems of deconcentration and labour shortage during the first half of 1945, Streat talked with Lord Catto about finance for re-equipment of the cotton industry, and the Cotton Board began to set up experimental mills in a search for ways to reorganise production in order to increase productivity.

After the breakup of the Coalition Oliver Lyttelton, the new President of the Board of Trade, saw cotton as one of his 'first priorities'.[13] He had a number of interviews with Streat; they thought they were developing a working relationship that would continue after the general election. Only two days before the announcement of the results Lyttelton travelled to Manchester to discuss with representatives of the employers and operatives possible solutions to the problem of labour shortage in the spinning section. He expected to formulate specific proposals leading to increased wages and improved conditions and to return to Manchester within a fortnight to make them public.

II

Cripps and the Cotton Industry: First Moves

Within one week of taking up his post as President of the Board of Trade in the new Labour government, Stafford Cripps outlined the key elements of his policy for the cotton industry. Displaying his legendary ability to absorb 'intricate cases with miraculous speed and accuracy' and then set out propositions with 'striking lucidity and logic',[14] Cripps revealed to Streat his 'state of mind on the cotton question' by outlining, in order of priority, ten points requiring consideration and action.[15] He took eight of the items from his immediate predecessors at the Board of Trade, including: amalgamations, modernisation of equipment, over-hauling the merchanting system, reform of wage structure, double shifts, employers' statement of good intentions, commission to revise wages, and special freedom for labour experiments.[16] But, he also added two 'fresh points'. One of these, to 'foster confidence by clarity of policy', meant that he would make it clear that the industry would not be nationalised. The second point, 'his pet notion of Joint Industrial Committees' was central to his subsequent policy.[17] The implementation of this policy, important for cotton itself, also illuminates the weaknesses and strengths of Cripps's policy towards private industry.

Two weeks after taking office Cripps was well received by the industry, when he visited Manchester for separate and joint meetings with unions and employers in the spinning section, an address to delegates of all sections and speeches in three cotton towns. With Cabinet consent[18] Cripps made it clear that it was not part of the government's programme to nationalise the cotton industry provided that the industry expeditiously carried through measures necessary for its reorganisation. In addition he assured the industry that in the short term the government would encourage the 'promising experiments which were being tried out at Wye Mill and elsewhere'.[19] Furthermore, with Streat paving the way, Cripps followed up the effort initiated by his predecessors to improve the spinning section in the long term while recruiting labour immediately. He secured the agreement of the Cabinet and of both sides of industry for the Minister of Labour to appoint a joint commission (the Evershed Commission) of representatives of employers and operatives in the spinning section to work out a revised wage structure.

According to Streat, Cripps 'charmed and convinced . . . the very difficult spinners', and he 'expounded government policy most lucidly' at the meeting of delegates which passed 'a unanimous resolution pledging all to work as a team – government and industry, all parties in it, hand in hand'.[20] Cripps made a highly favourable impression on the Chairman of the Cotton Board and 'from all signs on most of my Lancashire friends'. More generally, Streat conceded that

> in many ways, having a Labour Government may prove more bold
> and thorough in certain vital matters than a Tory Government
> would have done. They are not so afraid of justifiable interferences
> with property rights and old established vested interests. And they
> won't be stampeded by the Beaverbrooks and Rothermeres. I feel,
> tonight at any rate, that the Labour majority may prove not a bad
> thing. I have been surprised to find the same feeling in many friends
> in Manchester whose affiliations are mainly Tory.[21]

Within three weeks Cripps shattered this atmosphere with proposals for tripartite commissions or Working Parties whose terms of reference were

> to examine and inquire into the various schemes and suggestions put forward for improvements of organization, production and distribution methods and processes in the industry, and report as to the steps which should be taken in the national interest to strengthen the industry and render it more capable of meeting competition in the home and foreign markets.[22]

The idea for Working Parties was Cripps's; it derived neither from his civil servants nor from the industry, he had not consulted.[23]

Early in September Cripps forewarned Streat that he would disclose his plans for the cotton industry at meetings in Manchester before he announced government policy on industry generally in a speech at Blackpool. Cripps told Streat that

> there were several industries which, though they were not to be nationalised, were in need of positive action either to remedy conditions or to make them fully efficient. The idea was to set up for each such industry a tripartite commission, one-third owners, one-third workpeople, one-third government, to decide what should be done. Probably a tripartite body would continue afterwards to concern itself with the carrying out of the chosen policy. But it would not have 'powers'. All 'powers' must be vested in the Board of Trade. The Labour government were against so-called 'self-government' for industry – that would only lead to a corporative state. The new bodies would be advisory though they might have executive responsibilities for such things as the Colour, Design and Style Centre and the Recruitment and Training Department. The Labour government therefore aimed neither at the present Cotton Board, where the representation was not equal nor at the 1939 formula, which conferred powers which ought to reside only in the government.[24]

Cripps believed that it was important to move ahead now rather than wait while the industry met its most urgent needs by building up its labour force and exports, because '12 million voters had put them in power to do positive things, not wait and see'.[25]

Streat told Cripps that the 'announcement of such a policy in such words would plunge all concerned into a state of uncertainty in which nothing would be done in the vital weeks and months immediately ahead of us to re-employ the people and to get exports moving.' He went on to point out that 'as to cotton, we had had committees ad nauseam and all that could be said had been said.' Streat argued that 'a new "Commission" would appal the Cotton folk. They wanted decisions, not new machinery for reaching decisions'. He told Cripps that he feared the good impression he made on his previous visit to Manchester 'would be dissipated by this new move'. It seemed to Streat that 'the Post-War Committee was already on the field and the obvious body to agree with the government on a programme of next steps.' According to Streat, Cripps's objection to this was that the Cotton Board was not equally divided, owners and workers. 'He seemed to be quite set on his "tripartite" conception', though he admitted that many of the Cotton Board's present activities 'were quite excellent and an example to other industries'.[26]

Cripps's announcement of government policy towards the cotton industry[27] was met with the dismay, criticism and hostility which Streat predicted. At his meeting with the executives of the trade associations Cripps was asked 'why the new body and why override the Cotton Board . . .   they had a Chairman who had gained their confidence and obtained unity and asked why the existing man and existing organisation was [sic] not good enough'. The meeting refused to vote on a resolution agreeing to Cripps's plan even in broad terms and signs of division between trade-union representatives and employers appeared. In the afternoon Cripps faced hostility from the members of the Cotton Board's Post-war Committee. He was told that 'Sir Raymond Streat as a man and the Cotton Board as an organisation had united the industry as never before and done work which could not be replaced . . .   If he dislodged Raymond Streat he would put the cotton industry back five years.' Furthermore, Cripps was asked if he 'intended to coerce them whatever their views or if their advice mattered to him'.[28]

Their advice, probably reinforced by pressure from his civil servants,[29] did matter. Altering his schedule, Cripps discussed the situation with his officials immediately after the meeting of the Post-war Committee and soon after with Streat. Cripps refused 'to depart from his plan. He had got it through the Cabinet with some difficulty and he was not going back with variations'.[30] The Cabinet insisted on an impartial independent chairman, and for Cripps this had eliminated Streat. Moreover, he thought Streat

> believed in persuasion, education, progress by consent and compromise. The condition of England required drastic measures. His party had been elected to do things and do them quickly. He somewhat feared [Streat] . . . might be neither willing nor temperamentally suited to operate a policy of strong compulsion.

But after the hostile reception and after Streat pointed out that he was independent and that a trade unionist as chairman would not be as impartial as himself since the TUC had a declared policy, Cripps suggested a compromise. He realised that if he could persuade Streat to support the plan and recommend it to his supporters it would attract a sufficient majority. The compromise was to offer to nominate Streat as one of the four government members of the Working Party under a chairman without previous connections with the industry. Cripps would say openly that the Working Party would be 'entirely a temporary affair'; and, although there is evidence that Cripps was disingenuous,[31] Cripps told Streat that if at the end a policy emerged which Streat felt willing to operate, he would be glad to see him at the head of the permanent organisation in whatever form it took upon the Working Party's recommendation. Moreover, Cripps

> intended that the permanent organisation should be most powerfully supported. It might have less legal powers than the 1939 Act proposed but he would make it the only channel upwards and downwards. The Board of Trade would not hear or receive through any other channel.[32]

After their discussion Cripps put his compromise proposal on paper in a handwritten letter to Streat.[33] Consulting the Cotton Board's Post-war Committee before replying, Streat told them that he had decided not to accept the place on the Working Party. He still thought Cripps should use the Post-war Committee as the Working Party, adding some independent members to represent the government and the consumer's points of view, renewing the mandate given the committee by Dalton and providing the committee with some main lines of government policy for guidance. Also, he believed that his presence would be awkward for the chairman. He said that he would continue to run the Cotton Board organisation until a new body was in place and he would be a witness for the Working Party. But, he felt that for any evidence he gave the Working Party to be untainted by any suspicion of self-interest, he had to say that he would not be part of any future permanent organisation. Yet, he did not feel that the industry should oppose Cripps, and he promised that the Cotton Board would provide any assistance it could to the Working Party. Various opinions were expressed at the Post-war Committee meeting: unions were in favour of the Working Party; spinners and manufacturers were against; finishers and merchants were not keen but willing to nominate members.

At the end of September Cripps returned to Manchester, and secured the Post-war Committee's agreement after announcing that Sir George Schuster, an independent, would be chairman of the Working Party. Schuster, a barrister and company director who had been a Liberal National MP before losing his seat in the 1945 election, was not completely new to cotton as he had been Finance Member of the Viceroy's Executive Council in India 1928–34 and thereby knew of Lancashire's problems in the Indian market. Nevertheless, by insisting on including the cotton industry in his general proposal for industries which were not to be nationalised, Cripps seriously weakened the unity of the industry, opening up old divisions between producers and

merchants, employers and unions. When he bypassed the Cotton Board
he left impotent the organisation and its chairman whose function it was
to promote co-operation among sections and to provide the Board of
Trade with a link to the industry.

The Working Party

The Working Party report was due by Christmas 1945, but did not
appear until the end of May, long after Cripps had left for India as head
of a Cabinet mission. Some delay in the report was inevitable, owing to
the way in which Schuster chose to approach the task. Cripps envisaged
that the Working Party would go through already published proposals
regarding the industry and produce recommendations, but Schuster
undertook a more extensive investigation. The Working Party not only
went over previous reports, but also took evidence from most of the
organisations associated with the industry; four sub-committees
investigated costs and costing methods, machinery, scientific research
and distribution.

The delay, however, was due primarily to Schuster's inability to
reconcile disagreements among the members of the Working Party. At
one stage there was a rumour that Schuster 'might not get any signatures
except his own'.[34] In mid-December Schuster presented a draft report to
the Working Party for discussion. A month and a half later he conceded
that the members would not accept his proposal for a single statutory
corporation to replace the Cotton Board and undertake additional
functions including compulsory amalgamations. Nevertheless, despite
the continuous principled opposition from Professor Jewkes, Schuster
persisted with proposals for amalgamations, a scheme to eliminate
'redundant' capacity, and a re-equipment levy. Eventually all active
members signed the report, but it contained a 'dissenting memorandum'
in which six members (three employers and three independents including
Jewkes) dissented from six of the thirty-four recommendations. This
dissent provoked a critical retort from the operatives and a reply from
the remaining employer. Board of Trade officials referred to it as 'very
much an affair of "six of one and half-a-dozen of the other"'.[35]

Conflict within the Working Party focused on three major and three
associated recommendations, known as the three 'Rs': re-equipment,
reorganisation and redundancy.[36] First, re-equipment should be assisted
by contributions from a fund built up by a compulsory levy on the
industry, counterbalanced by an increase in controlled yarn and cloth
prices. Cheap money should also be made available to finance approved
schemes of re-equipment and consolidation. Second, the industry should
aim at consolidation by grouping or amalgamating separate units into
units (not necessarily complete financial amalgamations) large enough

to handle their own problems and to co-operate effectively in a concerted policy for the industry. Finally, provision should be made for immobilising a moderate proportion of existing plant in order to restore the balance of the industry in view of the labour shortage. The industry should be given three months to work out its proposals for giving effect to these three recommendations or to submit alternative measures to achieve the same results. What would happen at the end of the three months if the industry's proposals were not satisfactory was unclear, but it was interpreted in the industry as a threat that there would be government compulsion.

The six members who signed the 'dissenting memorandum' accepted the need for re-equipment. However, they stressed that this was a matter for each firm to decide for itself without external pressure. They recommended that, rather than a compulsory re-equipment levy, the price control on cotton goods should be relaxed so that firms engaged in exports should receive a larger share of the current high export prices and firms could finance re-equipment from profits. To the dismay of the trade-union members, the dissidents also recommended that special attention be given to the possibility of increasing mechanisation without re-equipment. In addition, they argued that it was unlikely that a widespread process of amalgamation would bring any gains; compulsory amalgamation in particular would defeat its own objects. Finally, they directed some general criticisms against schemes for the immobilisation of plant and argued that the present time would be highly inappropriate for carrying out such plans. The underlying attitude was that management decisions were best left to individual businessmen.

In the end, therefore, despite much painstaking work and agreement on twenty-eight of the thirty-four recommendations,[37] Schuster failed to get members with conflicting interests to work together. The dissension in the Working Party left the Board of Trade with 'an exceedingly awkward situation in Lancashire'. Officials feared that 'unless matters are carefully handled suspicion and mistrust between the employers and operatives will spread over all sections of the industry to hamper progress in the next two or three years.'[38]

Picking Up the Pieces After the Working Party

Because Cripps was in India when the Working Party report was signed, officials at the Board of Trade had to communicate with him by telegram, complaining that 'it was terrible . . . to have to put everything in writing and never to be able to talk things over. Cripps replied and that was that – no room for adjustment to circumstances.'[39] But as a result, a particularly detailed record of the formation of the Board of Trade's response to the report survives in the 'Woods' and 'Trees' telegrams between respectively 'John Henry' Woods, the Board of Trade's Permanent Secretary and Cripps in India – and from a different perspective in the diary of the Chairman of the Cotton Board.

Board of Trade officials at the end of April were worried that the report 'was obviously going to leave a terribly messy and dangerous position'. In addition to their own assessment, officials were subject to pressure from outside the Board of Trade. Disgusted with the Working Party's chairman, one of the independent members went to Cripps's wife (who had not accompanied him to India), who in turn approached G. L. Watkinson, Under-Secretary at the Board of Trade and the key figure in cotton policy. Watkinson urged Woods to recommend to Cripps that everything possible should be done to secure Streat's services 'to keep Parliament at rest', secure greater support from the industry and generally to clear up the mess. Watkinson, who believed that the Working Party report's recommendations failed to acknowledge clearly the steps which the Cotton Board had already taken in many areas, was particularly aghast at the proposal to change the name and personnel of the Cotton Board, because 'there was no chance of legislation until next Spring and the Board of Trade must rely on somebody in the interval'. The term of office of the members and chairman of the wartime Cotton Board would expire on June 22nd unless renewed.[40]

Watkinson convinced Streat to agree to head whatever organisation was at the head of the cotton industry on a five-year contract on condition that there should be no compulsory amalgamations. Streat felt released from his decision in September 1945 not to be part of the permanent organisation, because Schuster had ignored him for six months apart from an initial statement in October, asked for his support after completion of the report, and then accused him of encouraging the dissenters.[41] Watkinson had Woods telegraph to Cripps saying

> the extent to which the Cotton Board will fill the gap depends largely on Raymond Streat. Without him the Cotton Board would be ineffective; if he stays on, however, something useful might be done . . . I am bound to say that we shall not find anyone who has anything like Streat's following in Lancashire and capacity to get conflicting interests to work together. That, of course, is where Schuster, notwithstanding a vast amount of painstaking work and great ability, has failed. We are very much afraid that the field is so limited that we may make matters worse in Lancashire by choosing the wrong man.[42]

From India Cripps's initial reaction was to question whether Streat would follow government policy which might require faster methods. However, Watkinson and Woods persevered, getting Streat to state that he could not tell what government policy was. He would not agree to take the post if the government wanted to refer the report to him with its backing on every point from the start. But, 'if everything is open for further consideration and discussion and if I am free to state my own views, both to the industry and the government, then I might conceivably do some good for both.'[43]

One of the faults of the Working Party report was that it left the issue of compulsory amalgamations ambiguous. Streat argued that, although the report carefully avoided saying so, the three-month limit implied a threat of compulsion; moreover the Working Party had taken six months to produce its report.[44] Streat told Woods and Watkinson that he would not have the three-months threat under any circumstances. Nor would he have the threat of compulsory amalgamations, though

> I believe in more and better groupings and will join in the firmest persuasion in that direction. As a matter of principle I have no conscientious objection to government influencing industry in directions required by national policy, and in suitable cases I would face up to compulsion. But only when you know what you want to compel and how you can work compulsion neither of which you know in the slightest today as regards cotton.[45]

This satisfied Woods and Watkinson. Cripps took their advice and agreed 'to take on Streat and use the Cotton Board'.[46]

Preceded by the government's decision not to reopen the Liverpool cotton market and to nationalise the buying and selling of raw cotton, as well as press reports of 'heated exchanges' at the final sitting of the Working Party, publication of the Working Party report still threatened 'a period of clash and antagonism, employers saying, "Hands off the industry", operatives saying, "Nationalise", moderate elements on both sides being submerged'. Streat urged the Board of Trade officials to take steps 'to prevent the opposition making the cotton Report a Party issue ... [and] smother the danger of poor Lancashire being made a political football'.[47] In Lancashire with some help from the Board of Trade he obtained the full support of both union and employer members of the Cotton Board. As a result when the report was published attention focused on Streat, and he was able to defuse the threat of direct confrontation and turn attention to future policy such as 'the need for serious study of efficient labour utilisation'.[48] After a government statement in Parliament on the report and the approval of a meeting of 200 leaders of all sections of the industry and operatives, the Cotton Board and the Board of Trade set to work implementing the recommendations in the Working Party report that were generally agreed. Meanwhile, discussions of the controversial recommendations began both in the Board of Trade and in the industry's organisations.

Industrial Organisation and Development Act
Among the Working Party recommendations was one for a permanent

central organisation for the industry. The details of the Working Party recommendation (for a part-time chairman with a full-time director-general under him) were already superseded by Streat's appointment, though the central organisation's composition and powers remained to be settled. Moreover, rather than follow the precedents of the legislation in 1939 and 1940 with a separate Act for the industry, the government decided to make the industry the subject of the first Order under its more general Industrial Organisation and Development Act.

Passed in mid-1947, the Act provided enabling legislation which empowered any one of eight ministers, if satisfied that a particular industry or group of industries wanted one, to establish a Development Council by an Order subject to approval by a resolution in both Houses of Parliament. Intending not to supersede existing trade associations and unions, the minister appointed members of a Development Council only after consultation with representative trade organisations; members included representatives of employers and workers (who together had to form a majority of the council) and independents.

The Cotton Board established in 1948 under the Act differed little from its predecessor. A statutory organisation which in contrast to trade associations represented 100 per cent of the firms in the industry, the Board now had equal numbers of employer and trade-union representatives and two independent members in addition to an independent chairman; also it had no representatives of raw cotton or of rayon. Otherwise its functions were the same, providing common services (for example, scientific and technical research, design, home and export trade promotion, improvements in marketing and distribution arrangements, recruitment and training, the improvement of working conditions, and the collection of statistics) and serving as a single channel for representation of the industry's view to government and the government to industry. The Act excluded questions of wages and terms of employment. In the case of the Cotton Board the Board of Trade was careful to keep it out of any role in price controls, even though the Board of Trade's view of the minimum price scheme of the new Yarn Spinners' Association was ambiguous, refusing to make a public statement in support of the new association but at the same time wanting to agree and supervise its prices and being ready to co-operate generally with it.[49] Finally, the Act gave the Cotton Board only three compulsory powers: registration of firms, collection of statistics and the imposition of a levy on the industry in order to cover expenses.

Implications

Thus, contrary to Barnett's criticism that politicians and ministers lacked the will to design an industrial strategy, Cripps's policy of tripartite Working Parties was an explicit attempt to do just that. Also, it was successful in the cotton industry, though less so elsewhere, in so far as it produced a comprehensive report and recommendations that the Board of Trade used, albeit after significant modifications, as rationales for action.

In the case of cotton, however, Cripps failed to recognise the particular circumstances of the industry. It already had a statutory organisation representative of all sections and both sides of industry which had an experienced staff and most important a consensus within the industry in support of its continuation. The industry had long recognised that its sectional structure required a statutory central organisation like the Cotton Board. Already in 1945 the Cotton Board had discussed long-term post-war plans and was implementing them as far as it could. The evidence suggests that Cripps initially thought it likely that government policy would include compulsory amalgamations and that the Cotton Board and its chairman would be insuperable obstacles. But, because Cripps eventually had to turn back to the existing Cotton Board and its chairman, it is hard to avoid the conclusion that the Working Party in the cotton industry was a mistake. It unnecessarily delayed the detailed formulation and implementation of policies, came close to creating a disaster for industry–government relations in the industry and made the subsequent job of the Cotton Board more difficult.

Again in the Industrial Organisation and Development Act which allowed for the creation of Development Councils in private industry, Cripps failed to appreciate the particular circumstances of cotton, despite his intention that the Act be flexible enough to take account of differences among industries.[50] However, if the Cotton Board was the model for the post-war organisation of government relations with private industry, the cotton industry, with its sectional divisions, corresponding sectionally divided trade organisations and long experience with a statutory central organisation, was atypical of other private industries. With the sellers' market continuing longer than expected, the advantages of a central statutory organisation disappeared in industries lacking either an urgent structural need for such a body or an organisation of this kind already successfully in existence.[51]

Even for the cotton industry the Development Council idea had two major weaknesses. First, because it had no executive powers, the Cotton Board was vulnerable, on the one hand, to conflicts between sections within the industry, and on the other hand, to disagreements within the Board of Trade and between the Board of Trade and other government departments. Streat was particularly aware of the latter in September 1946, commenting that

> we shall get ourselves set up as a permanent body; . . . Stafford will argue that all the varied problems should, and must be, dealt with by the new body. This will excuse him from the immediate necessity

of doing things he knows he can't do, either because of his ministerial colleagues, or trade union stops, or just unalterable circumstances. After that, failure will lie at the door of the new body, not at his. He doesn't say this: give him his due, I doubt if he even thinks it today: but it is what it amounts to . . . only Lancashire can save Lancashire . . . I obviously will never fulfill all Schuster's elaborate dreams, but we can do a lot and, item by item, get a lot of help from Stafford. So let it go like that – especially as I know of no way of changing the prospect.[52]

Sectional divisions within the industry only became a problem for the Cotton Board in 1952, after the Labour governments and the sellers' market had ended. However, Streat believed that they were exacerbated by the provision in the Act requiring renewal of the organisation every five years after consultation between the industry and government, as it encouraged the raising of difficulties when often there were none.[53]

Second, where the industry's support for the Cotton Board was based on recognition of the weakness of sectionally divided trade organisations for representation of the industry and provision of common services and facilities, it could be argued that the success of the Cotton Board contributed to the problems of the industry by perpetuating its horizontal structure. However, the horizontal structure did not stop some, such as the flamboyant Cyril Lord, from building a large textile empire after the war. Furthermore, alternative proposals involving compulsory amalgamations put forward during the 1940s, such as Dalton's 1944 proposal for a statutory Spinning Board, were for horizontal amalgamations.

III

Out of the discussions of the Working Party recommendations between the Cotton Board and the Board of Trade came, during the last half of 1946, proposals for legislation relating solely to the spinning section of the cotton industry. The Cotton Spinning (Re-equipment Subsidy) Act 1948 substituted a Treasury grant of 25 per cent of the cost of re-equipment for the Working Party's recommendation of a levy, and it used the carrot of the grant administered by the Cotton Board rather than the stick of compulsion to encourage amalgamation into units of approximately 500,000 spindles. The way in which this legislation developed provides an example of the methods and style of Cripps's policy-making for private industry and more generally for policies not derived directly from party programmes.

While civil servants in the Board of Trade sometimes took the initiative in recommending policy, major decisions rested with Cripps. For a meeting between Streat and Cripps in September 1946 the Board of Trade officials prepared documentation for the minister consisting of the headings of the Working Party report's recommendations and concise

notes under each describing the present state of that particular matter.
Streat observed that

> they were all much concerned and interested to discover by
> attendance at my interview, what their own marching orders were
> to be . . . I was impressed by the way high officials wait with
> disciplined loyalty for the Minister to determine his line and regard
> their responsibility as limited to comment on the general feasibility
> thereof.[54]

In a similar vein Streat commented

> how strange are the workings of our system of government – one
> man sits at a desk, four others sit round, convention restrains the
> four men largely to comment and such modifications as comment
> can evoke; the single man knows less than any of them and has
> spent least time on it. When decisions emerge, the entire resources
> of the official machine and the party majority will be deployed to
> carry them into effect . . . I must add, of course, that my analysis
> omits to cover the factor of great general reforms like health,
> education or coal nationalisation, which are evoked out of party
> political programmes. Board of Trade work does not seem to be
> affected by issues of this magnitude – hence the peculiar power of
> the Minister and the peculiar significance of these odd hours in his
> room.[55]

Streat also observed that the stimulus to policy decisions was often a
visit or speech.

> Much time is spent on discussing the date of, and programme for, a
> visit. This may seem quite absurd, but in practice, a commitment to
> make a visit or a speech is often the way in which the machine of
> state is geared up to produce policy decisions.[56]

Streat later remarked further on the importance of the speech in policy-
making and Cripps's use of it saying that

> Cripps is a curious man . . . so satisfied that a lucid speech is
> equivalent to achievement of real purposes: so content with planning
> in general and his planning in particular; so content with an
> argument that is sound regardless of whether sound action will
> really ensue. Hence it leaves me troubled with a vague sense of
> unreality.[57]

The problem was whether effective action would result after the speech.
Ironically given Cripps's sense of urgency in 1945 and concern that
Streat was too prone to rely on persuasion, by late 1946 Streat was
critical of Cripps's advocacy of joint consultation.

> He thinks everything should be done by joint consultation. This
> frightens me. I know that joint consultation in our world today
> means endless meetings delays, and ultimately compromises. One
> longs for men of action to do real things within their own field of

power and responsibility and this is not a picture which is conjured up by the spectacle of joint consultation.[58]

To a meeting of 200 representatives of the main organisations of the cotton industry in Manchester on 3 December 1946 Cripps set out the government's attitude towards the Working Party's proposals, and he announced an offer of financial assistance for the spinning section of the industry. He asked both sides and all sections of the industry 'for a yes or no as regards the whole broad scheme' stressing the need for a quick decision and asking to have the replies of employers' and operatives' organisations before the end of the year.[59] To the industry Cripps's new policy for the cotton industry came 'as something unexpected and portentous. They all recognised that it might have been worse. There was no nationalisation: no absolute compulsion: there was a subsidy for re-equipment of spinning mills: but with conditions which gave people furiously to think'.[60] Later in December Streat met a large meeting of spinners to explain the policy further, and in January he met the unions. Reaction from the industry was not all favourable, but the government decided to go ahead with the legislation.

Much to the disappointment of Cripps and the Cotton Board, and contrary to the example of the Lancashire Cotton Corporation whose Chairman Frank Platt supported the scheme,[61] spinners in general opposed the clause requiring firms to amalgamate or form close groupings in order to be considered for a grant. Also, some sections of the unions, particularly the cardroom workers were reluctant to accept shift working. Although twenty-nine groups were registered covering over half the spindles in the industry, spinners were reluctant to take up the re-equipment grant; only £2.6 million in subsidy was paid out on an expected expenditure of £15–16 million.[62]

Even Cripps tired of joint consultation. Frustrated with the 'ridiculous fools' among both unions and employers, he rejected the idea of a 'tripartite partnership meeting', saying 'if they wouldn't have what he had offered . . . Lancashire must take the consequences of putting such men in office'.[63]

Nevertheless, it is possible that cotton spinners acted rationally. Singleton, for example, argues that they lacked confidence in Lancashire's future in the face of competition from low-wage producers.[64] Alternatively, it can be argued that in the face of the persistence of high demand in a resource-constrained economy employers were rational to follow short-term, output-maximising investment strategies.[65] Also, in the cotton industry a survey of machinery in mid-1947 suggested that output could be increased without new equipment by improving or 'converting' existing machinery. In light of the national financial crisis in mid-1947 which was seen to offer a choice between 'flagrant inflation and cutting down capital expenditure', the argument for re-equipment, two-shift working and grouping disappeared.[66] In any case, what is not recognised is that the legislation offering financial assistance for re-equipment in the spinning section, although a significant part, was still only part of the Board of Trade's response to the Working Party recommendations[67] and only part of the continuing useful work of the Cotton Board.

The Cotton Board was a channel which the government attempted to use for productivity initiatives. Not only did the Cotton Board commission mill experiments in methods of reorganising production to increase productivity between 1944 and 1948, but it also took the initiative in organising a series of conferences, attended by directors, mill managers and trade-union officials, for the discussion of current issues. Among the first of these conferences was one in 1947 devoted to the question of increasing productivity by means of the redeployment of labour. From this sprang a succession of further conferences and instructional courses set up by the Cotton Board for the training of managers and foremen.

In 1940 the Board had set up a Colour Design and Style Centre in Manchester in order to raise the standard of design in the industry and to promote the use of cotton fabrics among fashion and interior designers. It was a well-established and highly successful feature of the industry, holding numerous exhibitions.

The Cotton Board established during the war a Recruitment and Training Department which encouraged owners to improve amenities in mills, notably instituting advisory services to help in the equipment of canteens, rest rooms, mill nurseries and first-aid rooms. Recruitment campaigns stressed the attractions of the industry as a career for school leavers, including mill visits, film shows, exhibitions of products and demonstrations of the machinery and processes. The proportion of school leavers entering the industry was increased. In addition, the Board assisted firms in employing 15,000 volunteer workers from European countries under Ministry of Labour schemes by selecting workers in Europe, receiving them on arrival, and providing interpreters and subsequent guidance to the community. In no small measure due to these efforts of the Board, the labour force in spinning and weaving rose from 189,000 in 1945 to 296,000 in 1952 when checked by the recession, nearly 50,000 more than the Working Party report's most optimistic forecast.[68]

The Board also promoted relevant scientific research. It supported the British Cotton Industry Research Association which ran the Shirley Institute, one of the foremost industrial research establishments. Approximately half the Board's income from the levy went in support of the Shirley Institute.[69]

Finally, the Cotton Board was still important after mid-1947 as short-term problems swamped the government's efforts to encourage long-term changes in the organisation of production. If less was done regarding re-equipment, this was due to government policy more than lack of drive on the part of the Cotton Board. In September 1947 the government made the cotton industry the 'spearhead of the export drive', encouraging increased output whatever the methods even if they did not increase productivity. The Cotton Board helped the industry reach its targets by propaganda, by recruitment campaigns and by encouraging increased exports to dollar countries. Also, in October 1947 the new President of the Board of Trade, Harold Wilson, was able to turn to the Cotton Board to pursue attempts to preserve export markets from Japanese competition by seeking to limit Japanese production.[70]

CONCLUSION

The experience of the cotton industry demonstrates that the Labour governments were able to work with a major, long-established private industry once they gave up hopes of coercing it. The cotton industry was the subject of the first Working Party appointed by Cripps. Once its structure and recommendations were modified, the Cotton Working Party provided a rationale for subsequent government policy towards the industry; and Cripps hailed the Cotton Board, a statutory body established during the war including representatives of the employers and unions, as the model for Development Councils.

The experience of the cotton industry does not reveal a powerful government controlling and regulating a subordinate private sector, nor even a government promoting a policy of tripartite partnership with much success. Instead, the Working Party left bitterness and division in relations between employers and unions, and it left government–industry relations near chaos. The Working Party offered nothing new in the way of feasible policy recommendations and undermined the sense of co-operation that had been built up during the war through the structure and activities of the wartime Cotton Board. Civil servants rescued the situation by persuading Streat, the chairman of the wartime Cotton Board, to agree to head the post-war organisation, and by persuading Cripps to appoint him. It was by no means inevitable that Cripps would introduce the second reading of the Industrial Organisation and Development Bill in February 1947 with praise for the Cotton Board, saying

> [the provisions] are not novel in their conception: they have been anticipated by the structure of the Cotton Board which is undoubtedly proving of great value. What we are seeking to do by this Bill is to make similar conveniences and advantages available for other industries.[71]

Although this legislation led to slight changes in the Cotton Board's composition[72] and the Working Party recommendations initially dominated its agenda, Cripps in effect continued the wartime Cotton Board and its activities, already supported by the industry. This accounts in large part for its subsequent survival; by the mid-1950s it was one of only two Development Councils left.[73] Contrary to Andrew Duncan's prediction in 1942 that the Cotton Board would prove generally to be a 'model for the post-war form of relationship between industry and the State',[74] a middle way between nationalisation and voluntary trade associations, it was the product of the circumstances of a particular industry with a sectionally divided structure and trade organisations, a disastrous fall in demand during the inter-war years and a successful wartime Board and chairman supported by employers and unions. When the post-war sellers' market continued employers in other industries, lacking these circumstances and afraid of a thin end of the wedge for nationalisation, saw no need for such central organisations despite the recommendations of most of the seventeen Working Parties.

The experience of the cotton industry with the Working Party and with subsequent legislation to promote re-equipment and amalgamation reveals much about the difficulties of effective articulation between government and industry. Nevertheless, once re-established with the backing of the government and both sides of the industry, the Cotton Board proved a successful mediator between the Labour government and the industry. In contrast to some industries,[75] relations between the cotton industry and the Labour government were more harmonious in the later years than in the first two years of the government. Moreover, looking back the chairman of the Cotton Board was able to contrast the sympathetic attitude of ministers and friendliness of the officials at the Board of Trade during the Attlee governments with their successors after 1951.[76]

The Attlee governments' policy towards cotton was a partly failed attempt at a middle way in Labour's terms between nationalisation and *laissez-faire*. Its experience suggests that continued private ownership in effect meant both that an industry needed to have its own influential organisations, whether facilitated by government as in the case of cotton or in the form of a trade association as in most industries, and that as a result the industry must largely have its way. Lancashire was not just 'conservative' but also consensual. A consensus within the industry regarding the usefulness of the Cotton Board led to real achievements for a middle way, but on Lancashire's terms.

NOTES

1. A. A. Rogow and P. Shore *The Labour Government and British Industry 1945–1951* (Oxford, 1955) pp. 3–5.

2. K. O. Morgan *Labour in Power 1945–51* (Oxford, 1984) p. 129.
3. *Hansard* (Commons) 5th Series, Vol. 438, Col. 91, 3/6/1947; *Hansard* (Commons) 5th Series, Vol. 433, Cols. 547–55, 13/2/1947; *Hansard* (Commons) 5th Series, Vol. 438, Cols. 90–9, 3/6/1947. For an assessment of Development Councils see P. D. Henderson 'Development Councils: An Industrial Experiment' in G. D. N. Worswick and P. H. Ady eds. *The British Economy 1945–50* (Oxford, 1952) pp. 459–60.
4. J. Wiseman and B. S. Yamey 'The Raw Cotton Commission, 1948–1952' *Oxford Economic Papers* Vol. VIII 1956 1–34; R. Robson *The Cotton Industry* (Oxford, 1956) pp. 259–60; J. Singleton 'Planning for Cotton, 1945–51' *Economic History Review*, 2nd Ser. Vol. XLIII 1990 73–4.
5. C. Miles *Lancashire Textiles: A Case Study of Industrial Change* (Cambridge, 1968) p. 30.
6. C. Barnett *The Audit of War: the Illusion and Reality of Britain as a Great Nation* (pbk edn 1987) p. 275.
7. M. Dupree 'Struggling With Destiny: The Cotton Industry, Overseas Trade Policy and the Cotton Board 1940–1959' *Business History* Vol. XXXII 1990 106–28.
8. H. D. Henderson *The Cotton Control Board* (Oxford, 1922).
9. G. W. Killick 'The History and Work of the Cotton Board' *Empire Cotton Growing Review* Vol. XXXI 1954 1.
10. Cotton Industry Act, 1940.
11. For Raymond Streat's role as Secretary of the Manchester Chamber of Commerce and in the industry more widely before the Second World War, see M. Dupree, 'Fighting against Fate: the Cotton Industry and the Government During the 1930s' *Textile History* Vol. XXI 1990 101–17 and M. Dupree ed. *Lancashire and Whitehall: the Diary of Sir Raymond Streat 1931–1957* Vol. I (Manchester, 1987).
12. Dupree ed. *Lancashire and Whitehall* Vol. II pp. 261–2; Singleton op. cit. 64–5.
13. Dupree ed. *Lancashire and Whitehall* Vol. II p. 263.
14. Streat was well aware of Cripps's reputation when they first met. See, Dupree ed. *Lancashire and Whitehall* Vol. II p. 268; Woodrow Wyatt 'Richard Stafford Cripps' *The Compact Edition of the Dictionary of National Biography* (Oxford, 1975) p. 2586.
15. Dupree ed. *Lancashire and Whitehall* Vol. II p. 269.
16. Ibid.
17. Ibid.
18. Public Record Office, Kew (hereafter PRO) CAB128/I, Cabinet Minutes, 7/8/1945 pp. 9–10.
19. Ibid., p. 10.
20. Dupree ed. *Lancashire and Whitehall* Vol. II p. 274.
21. Ibid.
22. Board of Trade *Working Party Report – Cotton* (1946) p. v.
23. Dupree ed. *Lancashire and Whitehall* Vol. II p. 281.
24. Ibid., p. 279.
25. Ibid., p. 280.
26. Ibid.
27. PRO CAB128/I, CM(45)28, Cabinet Conclusion, 4/9/1945.
28. Dupree ed. *Lancashire and Whitehall* Vol. II pp. 282–3.
29. Ibid., pp. 283, 285. [Bruce-Gardner and Watkinson].
30. Ibid., p. 283.
31. G. Schuster *Private Work and Public Causes: A Personal Record, 1881–1978* (Cowbridge, Glamorgan, 1979) p. 141.
32. Dupree ed. *Lancashire and Whitehall* Vol. II pp. 283–5.
33. Ibid., pp. 285–6.
34. Ibid., p. 341.

35. PRO CAB127/103 Trees 53 2/5/1946. For a contemporary assessment of the report see G. C. Allen 'The Cotton Industry Working Party' *The Manchester School* Vol. XIV 1946 60–73.
36. Board of Trade *Working Party Report – Cotton* pp. 214–49.
37. See Ibid., pp. 169–213.
38. PRO CAB127/103 Trees 55 2/5/1946.
39. Dupree ed. *Lancashire and Whitehall* Vol. II p. 343.
40. Ibid., 341–2.
41. Ibid., pp. 344–8, and see above p. 147.
42. PRO CAB127/103 Trees 55 2/5/1946.
43. Dupree ed. *Lancashire and Whitehall* Vol. II p. 348.
44. *Manchester Guardian* 29/5/1946 p. 6.
45. Dupree ed. *Lancashire and Whitehall* Vol. II pp. 348–9.
46. PRO CAB127/103 Trees 76 17/5/1946.
47. Dupree ed. *Lancashire and Whitehall* Vol. II p. 350.
48. PRO CAB127/103 Trees 84 29/5/1946.
49. PRO BT64/420 Letter Streat – Watkinson, 25/10/1946; Minute [by Andrew ?] [n.d.]/11/1946; Minute [Hughes?] – Andrew 5/11/1946; Letter Streat – Watkinson 5/11/1946; Minute Kilroy – Watkinson, 8/11/1946; Letter Watkinson – Streat, 9/11/1946; Letter Woods – Platt, 1/1/1947.
50. *Hansard* (Commons) 1946–7 5th Series Vol. 433, Cols. 552–3, 13/2/1947; Vol. 438, Col. 91, 3/6/1947.
51. Rogow and Shore, op. cit. pp. 82–96; P. D. Henderson, op. cit. pp. 459–60.
52. Dupree ed. *Lancashire and Whitehall* Vol. II p. 370.
53. Ibid., p. 794.
54. Ibid., p. 367.
55. Ibid., p. 370.
56. Ibid., p. 367.
57. Ibid., p. 411.
58. Ibid.
59. Ibid., p. 376.
60. Ibid., p. 380.
61. PRO BT64/420/19 Letter Platt – Woods, 20/12/1946.
62. Robson op. cit. p. 219; P. D. Henderson op. cit. p. 436.
63. Dupree ed. *Lancashire and Whitehall* Vol. II p. 398.
64. Singleton op. cit. pp. 69–71.
65. For this argument applied to the iron and steel industry see M. Chick 'Private Industrial Investment' in this volume.
66. PRO BT175/4 Letter Lacey – Streat, 28/8/1947.
67. PRO BT64/2714 Cotton Industry Policy, 13/8/1946 p. 5.
68. *Working Party Report – Cotton* p. 61; Robson op. cit. p. 247.
69. PRO BT175/3 Cotton Board Minutes 5/6/1945 pp. 4–5; Killick, op. cit. p. 11.
70. See Dupree, 'The Cotton Industry, Overseas Trade Policy and the Cotton Board 1940–1959', esp. pp. 113–17.
71. *Hansard* (Commons) 1946–7 5th Series Vol. 322, Col. 560, 13/2/1947.
72. P. D. Henderson, op. cit. p. 459.
73. P. D. Henderson op. cit. pp. 459–60; 'Government and Industry' in G. D. N. Worswick and P. H. Ady eds. *The British Economy in the Nineteen-Fifties* (Oxford, 1962) p. 337.
74. Dupree ed. *Lancashire and Whitehall* Vol. II p. 86.
75. See for example, J. Tomlinson 'Productivity Policy' p. 4 and N. Tiratsoo 'The Motor Car Industry' in this volume.
76. Dupree ed. *Lancashire and Whitehall* Vol. II p. 795.

Nine

The motor car industry

NICK TIRATSOO

In September 1954, *New Commonwealth* published a detailed survey of the post-war British car industry and its export trade.[1] Manufacturers, it suggested, had 'dashed out into yawning overseas markets' after 1945 and won a substantial slice of world trade. On the surface, this looked like a great success story, but in reality the position was far less satisfactory. Complaints from customers in Britain's key overseas markets – about their vehicles' lack of size and power, fragile suspension and inadequate dust-proofing – were legion. On investigation, many of these turned out to be 'justified'. What made this all the more serious was the growing re-emergence of foreign competition, and the unflattering comparisons that were now to be heard about the British car and its international competitors like Chevrolet, Volkswagen, Opel and Citroën. The industry, it was concluded, stood at a crossroads and major changes would be needed to secure its healthy future.

This chapter looks at how and why such a situation had arisen. In particular, it will be concerned with Correlli Barnett's recent claim that the real responsibility for what happened rests with the civil servants and politicians of the Coalition and Attlee administrations, since it was this cohort, in the rush for a New Jerusalem, that had shirked its responsibility to develop the kind of cohesive industrial policy for motor cars that alone could have guaranteed long-term health. Barnett's thesis seems plausible, not least because it so coherently distils assumptions and insights that are almost common sense to many of those engaged in the wider, long-standing debate about the reasons for Britain's industrial decline. But is it a fair interpretation of the evidence?[2]

Barnett's argument rests upon a number of interrelated propositions. He suggests, first, that government officials recognised quite clearly at the end of the war that the motor industry was riddled with weaknesses. There were too many companies, and the likelihood, on pre-war experience, of too many models and not enough standardisation of production and parts to ensure low costs. Moreover, export possibilities, again going on previous experience, were likely to be compromised by poor design, limp marketing and an inadequate service and spares organisation. In short, official inquiries painted a picture of an industry 'that could thrive only so long as its main potential competitors remained knocked out by war and car-starved customers were willing to buy anything with four wheels and an engine'.[3]

Barnett then looks at what the government did in response to these findings. He maintains that the necessary solutions were obvious, with an ideal package involding trade-union reform (across all industry, the unions were 'possibly the strongest single factor militating against technical innovation and high productivity'[4]); tax changes and a road-building programme (to stimulate home demand and encourage the emergence of suitable export models[5]); and compulsory amalgamations of firms (to cultivate a few strong manufacturing units with the potential of defeating all foreign competitors[6]). But though the conditions of success were clear, little was done to implement them, because officials and politicians, more concerned with New Jerusalemist goals, simply lacked the appetite for action of this type. The end product was that, over the post-war years, the industry remained frozen in its inefficiency, used by government (to raise export earnings and tax revenue) but not transformed. When foreign competition reappeared, the foolishness of this inaction was fully exposed. The official stance on motor cars just before and just after the end of the war can therefore, be viewed as a perfect illustration of that 'tinkering as industrial policy' which Barnett sees as one of the main reasons for Britain's manufacturing decline.[7]

At first sight, this looks like an impressively coherent argument. But matching it against the evidence produces a less flattering assessment. In fact, all of Barnett's major contentions will be challenged over the following pages. Policy formulation for the car industry at the end of the war, to begin with, was a very much more complex process than Barnett allows, in which official reforming and interventionist impulses were not so much undermined by lack of will-power as frustrated by narrow party political considerations and stubborn vested interests. Nor was the subsequent Labour stance on the industry purely a question of blunt and short-term instrumentalism. Finally, it will also be argued that Barnett's ideal package of measures which should have been taken to transform the industry were, in fact, hardly relevant to its central problems. These points will now be examined in order.

Some official discussion on the future peacetime shape of the motor industry occurred from 1942 onwards,[8] but it was not until the near the end of hostilities, when the War Cabinet Reconstruction Committee Ministerial Subcommittee on Industrial Problems become involved, that debate really intensified. Earlier deliberations had revealed significant differences of opinion between departments over the issue and so it came as little surprise when officials charged with drawing up recommendations to the Ministerial Subcommittee once again found it difficult to reach consensus on policy.[9] It was generally agreed that the motor manufacturers lacked dynamism and would be inclined to take the line of least resistance in the post-war world if left to themselves – they would, it was felt, seek to live off a protected home market and treat exports as a sideline, in the manner of the pre-war years. Most concluded, too, that this would be disastrous, both in terms of the next few years' balance of payments, and in terms of the longer-term viability of the industry. But there was much less common ground when it came to deciding what the government ought to do about this.

One group of officials, discouraged by what they regarded as the limited ambitions of the industry's leading figures and the technical backwardness of the major firms, argued that nothing much could be done, and that the government should concentrate on other branches of the industry (heavy vehicle producers, for instance) with better prospects. Indeed, meddling with the car industry might actually cause harm, it was argued, since it might jeopardise manufacturers' co-operation in supplying fighting vehicles, a vital consideration to those in the Ministry of Supply.[10]

Against this, a more central strand of opinion felt that change was at least possible if the manufacturers could be persuaded that this was in their own economic interests. The industry had long argued that it was badly handicapped by government fiscal policy, because the weight of taxation hindered the growth of the home market (and thus made the realisation of economies of scale impossible) while its type discouraged design of the kind of high-powered, larger vehicles that many foreign drivers wanted. Why not, as one official put it, stop trying 'to make water run uphill' and simply re-design the tax framework?[11]

This kind of solution looked attractive in theory, but was less satisfactory when viewed as a practical alternative. Reducing the total tax burden would be out of the question as far as the Treasury was concerned, while it was hardly compatible with some established notions of social justice. ('I think there would be a general agreement that a great deal of motoring is a luxury. It is a sound canon of taxation that luxuries should take the first burden.')[12] Furthermore, changing the tax basis was more difficult than it appeared because the industry as a whole was very divided as to exactly how this should be done.[13] Finally, there was a suspicion that fiscal matters were not, anyway, at the heart of the problem: even given reform in this area, some doubted that manufacturers really had it in them to export successfully.

To meet this latter point, a third group of officials, centred on the Ministries of Production and Aircraft Production, argued for much more radical solutions. They proposed discussions as to what designs would be most suitable in export markets, and then a full-blooded government campaign to get them built. Use should be made of controls over labour and raw materials and the allocations of 'shadow factories' to encourage and reward compliant firms. No opposition should be tolerated: it was recognised that the motor manufacturers would not like this strategy, but if necessary 'rough treatment' could be used to bring them into line.[14]

Given this diversity of opinion, it was inevitable that the final document presented to the ministers would be somewhat equivocal. The consensus was that leaving the industry alone would not be advisable, and indeed the report went so far as to argue that

> Unless the Government intervened . . . it seems likely that there is little prospect that any manufacturer or group will undertake the large scale manufacture of a car or cars of types likely to produce a substantial expansion of our export trade.

But recommendations about what exactly this implied in terms of policy – what kind of intervention and how it should be achieved – were a lot vaguer, with ministers simply being advised to discuss the matter with the trade, on the basis of a declaration that they required expansion and exports.[15]

In considering this advice, the Ministerial Subcommittee (which included, amongst others, Woolton, Leathers, Anderson, Bevin, Cripps and Dalton) could not avoid recognising that its room for manoeuvre was anyway quite circumscribed. The chancellor had already committed the government to one kind of reforming strategy, by agreeing to implement at some time in the near future a measure of tax reform designed to encourage the production of higher-powered cars.[16] On the other hand, it seemed probable that radical solutions might cause real political trouble, because of the stance being taken by the key employers' organisation, the Society of Motor Manufacturers and Traders (SMMT).[17]

This body had viewed the controls imposed by Whitehall in the early part of the war as appropriate to the national emergency, but it was now arguing that, with victory in sight, the priority should be deregulation and a quick return to the *status quo ante* – unfettered private enterprise production.[18] Moreover, it was quite obvious that the SMMT would go to considerable lengths to ensure that this outcome was in fact achieved. The motor manufacturers and government had of necessity established close relationships during the war, and this allowed the lobbying of key civil servants and ministers.[19] Further influence was being exerted through selected members of both Houses of Parliament.[20] Finally, the manufacturers had also recognised that it was important to carry the battle outside the immediate circles of power and try to win over public opinion, which had given rise to a press and advertising campaign around the slogan 'Take the Brake off the Motor Industry' costing several thousand pounds a month.[21]

Given these various influences, it was inevitable that when the Ministerial Subcommittee did finally come to consider the officials' recommendations, the mood would hardly be towards radicalism. One minister argued the SMMT position in favour of large motor-tax cuts, but this was unacceptable both to his Labour colleagues and, more importantly, the chancellor. In the end, it was agreed, basically, that the whole issue should be shelved pending further inquiry. The need, the ministers concluded, was for 'a strong working-party of officials' who could 'make a thorough and rapid investigation' and then present recommendations 'on steps which should be taken to secure a greatly expanded export trade in all types of motor vehicle'. This was to be set up immediately. Meanwhile, the major manufacturers were to be informed, once again, of the government's wish that exports should be given priority.[22]

Nevertheless, if this formula at least preserved the theoretical possibility of radical solutions to the industry's ills, subsequent actions by ministers in the run-up to the first peacetime election suggested that it was the conservative tide that was running strongest. The country's looming balance-of-payments problems were clearly a great worry, and prompted Dalton to give private guarantees to the manufacturers far beyond anything that had been officially stated:

> As I told you before I am anxious that the motor industry shall export at least half its output, but I should not wish to interfere if that target is reached. We intend that the choice of types of cars and of export markets shall be left to the industry to decide.[23]

Meanwhile, the risks inherent in irritating a leading and vociferous group of employers were weighing heavily on the minds of more than one prominent Conservative. Woolton had been given the responsibility of setting up the working party, but made it known he was dubious about using officials to carry out the review. As an alternative, he recommended an investigation by a 'forceful character with some knowledge of the industry', possibly Air Chief Marshal Sir Wilfred Freeman. Yet even this was too much for Lyttelton, the Minister of Production and President of the Board of Trade in the caretaker government, and in the end the whole initiative was quietly shelved.[24]

What this account demonstrates, it can be concluded, is that Barnett's description of policy debates at the end of the war lacks precision. That the government did eventually adopt a non-interventionist stance on the motor trade is indisputable. But explaining this simply in terms of blanket lack of will and interest amongst administrators surely distorts the actual pattern of events. Barnett has missed not only the real pressure for reform that existed in Whitehall at this time, but also the complexity of forces – particularly the stubborn resistance of the SMMT – which in the end were enough to keep it in check.

What, then, was the character of government–industry relations in the post-war period? Did Labour manage to break the deadlock and introduce reforms? Or are these years when, whatever its applicability before, the Barnett thesis really comes into its own? Did the Attlee government, in other words, intent on building a New Jerusalem, simply use the motor trade to generate, say, export revenue, oblivious to whatever other consequences this short-term instrumentalism might generate?

There is certainly plenty of evidence to support this latter interpretation. It is surely significant, to begin with, that Labour did hardly any thinking about motor-vehicle policy either during the war or after. The industry was not examined by any of the party's reconstruction committees, and though nationalisation was briefly canvassed in 1948, this option was rapidly deemed 'unsuitable' and dropped.[25] In fact, the only document from the left which made any real mention of motors was the TUC's *Interim Report* of 1944. But even here the treatment could not be described as detailed, and was mainly about the recommendation that the trade be put under the supervision of an Industrial Board.[26]

Moreover, it is undeniable that much of the Attlee government's actual policy towards the industry had to do with encouraging exports, however this might be achieved. The official priority was made very clear from the start:

> the present exceptional opportunity for securing overseas markets for motor vehicles should . . . be exploited on an expanding scale. We feel that this must strengthen our long-term position in those markets besides providing a very significant improvement in our balance of payments position now.[27]

Manufacturers therefore found themselves presented with very blunt overall targets – 50 per cent of output to be exported in 1945, rising to 60 per cent in 1946 and 75 per cent in 1948 – and told to get on with it.[28] They were aware, too, that their performance was being monitored and that they would be punished or rewarded, in the currency of raw material supplies, according to what was achieved.[29]

Third, and this again supports Barnett's argument, in comparison with the energy that was spent maximising exports, it is evident that official attempts to institute reform during this period were largely under-developed. The history of the National Advisory Council (NAC), formed in 1946, illustrates the general tenor of events. The NAC was created for a number of reasons, but there was at least some hope in Whitehall that it would act as a catalyst and persuade manufacturers to review issues like product design and standardisation.[30] Indeed the original terms of reference for the Council were left deliberately all-embracing, in that it was

> To provide a means of regular consultation between the Govern-ment and the motor manufacturers on such matters as the location

of industry, exports, imports, research, design and technical
development, production methods and the general progress of the
industry.[31]

Nevertheless, when the organisation was actually set in motion, it quickly
became apparent that there was unlikely to be much of a stir. Motor
manufacturers occupied eight of the Council's fifteen available places,
which prompted the President of the SMMT to crow that it had been
constituted 'so as to work in the closest association with . . . [his]
Society'.[32] Furthermore, the minister in charge (Wilmot, of Supply) was
hardly one to court controversy, emphasising that his objective for the
Council was that it should help further cement already congenial
relations:

> The President [of the SMMT] had referred to the industry and
> government departments as having to live together and having to
> find a comfortable way of doing so. We recognised this, and also
> that the experience and knowledge gained during the war would
> enable us to work together equally well in peace. To foster those
> good relations it was decided to set up [the Council] . . .[33]

In the ensuing years, therefore, the NAC provided 'a channel of
communication' and little else: the different parties tended to rehearse
their positions rather than move towards substantive policy decisions.[34]

Finally, it is also worth pointing out that some important contemporary
sources can be cited arguing Barnett's case. *The Economist*, for example,
long a champion of efficient production, criticised Labour for letting the
motor industry off too lightly in terms of issues like standardisation; the
government, it suggested, needed to be 'a bit more forthright in asserting
the national interest in the policies pursued by the industry'. A
correspondent to *The New Statesman* agreed, pointing out that, in the
rush for exports, other key considerations remained dangerously
underprioritised:

> The Government . . . seems simply to be giving the industry every
> encouragement to make and export as many cars as possible without
> regard to long-term prospects or to type of currency . . . which the
> exports earn. No effort has been made to compel the industry to
> rationalise itself or even to concentrate on the production of fewer
> models.[35]

A good deal of evidence, therefore, can be assembled in support of
Barnett's interpretation of government–industry relations in the post-
war period. Certainly, the impression is that Labour was not very
interested in the car trade as such, but only in what could be got from
the manufacturers in terms of exports. Need anything further be said
about the whole episode?

In fact, the answer to this question is perhaps less clearcut than might be expected. For although Barnett's case does obviously provide some insight into aspects of the post-war situation, a further and more detailed trawl of the evidence suggests that it must also be subject to some important qualification. The point at issue is not whether Labour was export orientated – it clearly was – but rather whether it remained at the same time so indifferent to the case for a suitable industrial policy.

The first remark that is worth making here is about intention and possibilities. Barnett implies, to repeat, that Labour simply was not interested in reforms for the car industry. But this is very much of an over-simplification. For it can be established quite definitely that the government *was* aware of the need for some kind of interventionist strategy, but continued to be partly frustrated over its attainment by, once again, the caucus of manufacturers. This observation can be demonstrated by looking at some of the early interactions between the two sides.

Labour, as has been shown, did not approach the motor industry in 1945 with a readily worked out analysis of its ills, or with a sophisticated vision of how to put things right. But senior ministers had been involved in Coalition ruminations about the trade's future and were aware of all the major problems. The general view was that the motor manufacturers were impossibly selfish and conservative – 'a lot of bloody fools', as Bevin called them[36] – and should therefore not be left to their own devices. The question was whether reforms could be initiated without jeopardising what the country's wider economic position dictated had to be the number one priority – the industry's export performance.

Some members of Attlee's Cabinet felt that such a balancing act might be possible because the manufacturers would be intimidated by the government's huge parliamentary majority, but their illusions did not last long. For it soon became obvious that the industry was very much out of sympathy with not just one, but both of the main official objectives. There was, then, scepticism amongst the manufacturers about concentrating on export markets, because these were felt to be insufficiently reliable and lucrative, and so formalising Dalton's previously suggested 50 per cent target was only achieved after the government had played one of its strongest cards, the threat of controls.[37] But controversy here was nothing compared to that which broke out at even the merest suggestion of government interference in the production process. Thus, when Cripps used the occasion of an SMMT dinner in late 1945 to remind the industry that it ought to think more about what foreign consumers really wanted – 'You have to produce the right car of the appropriate design at the competitive price if you are to sell over the world. We can't force our choice on others . . . We must produce a cheap, tough, good-looking car of decent size' – he was greeted with extreme hostility, both amongst the assembled guests and in the following day's newspapers. The SMMT journal summed up how he was understood to have transgressed:

> Press comment on Sir Stafford's speech has been extensive and not uncritical. In the leading articles of seven or eight national newspapers, Sir Stafford has been criticised for his surprising attempt to explain the problems of design and export selling to a gathering of industrialists and traders, many of whom have made these problems a life study, and who are all surely experts in dealing with them.[38]

Given the continuing existence of these kinds of attitudes, it is perhaps hardly surprising that the government decided to play down the issue of reform, or that potentially interventionist instruments, like the NAC, were effectively neutered from birth.

A second problem with Barnett's thesis concerns his assessment of what the Attlee government was actually doing in relation to the car industry after 1945. Barnett's contention, to repeat, is that Labour had no real industrial strategy and, as has been shown in the preceding paragraphs, there is a good deal of evidence to be marshalled in support of this view. Nevertheless, it can be argued that this is not the end of the story. For although Labour's record at a macro level was desultory, it did rather better with micro-interventions. Specifically, the government provided heavy backing for the one firm which was prepared to adopt progressive policies after 1945, Standard Motors. The rest of this chapter will be devoted to outlining what was involved here, not only because the Standard case-study is of interest in itself, but also because it allows a platform for evaluating the third component of Barnett's argument – his speculations about what *should* have been done about the British car industry in the post-war period.

Standard Motors entered the war as one of the most progressive firms in the 'Big Six', having been turned around during the 1930s by its charismatic managing director, John Black.[39] Because of its good reputation and size, Standard was bound to play an important role in armaments production and so the company quickly found itself being allotted two 'shadow factories' in the vicinity of its main Coventry plant and the prestigious task of assembling Mosquitoes. Yet all this activity did not stop Black thinking about the future, and so from quite early on in the war, he was to be found canvassing opinion about a possible peacetime programme. The post-war world, he argued, would form an enormous sellers' market for British cars, and so his company should explicitly aim itself at the export trade. It would be no good, however, reverting to the policy that had been prevalent in the 1930s, which had involved trying to win sales of several different models. What was needed to ensure low costs and therefore success, was 'concentrated production in huge volume on one single model by the latest methods in one of the shadow factories'.[40]

This vision clearly impressed key government figures, and so when Black approached Dalton in September 1944 for permission to begin the switch-over to civilian production, the minister was quick to give his consent.[41] Moreover, negotiations over the 'shadow factories' proceeded swiftly and satisfactorily. Black was particularly interested in Banner Lane – an enormous works of some 1.2 million sq. ft, which had been built and equipped at a cost of £4.4 million[42] – and had little difficulty in convincing Whitehall that he should be allowed to take it over, at a rent of £33,000 per annum over the first ten-year period.[43] The consequence of all of this was that Standard began 1945 full of confidence: the aim, Black announced, was that the company should produce very much as he had planned, concentrating on a 15 h.p. car, with 5 or 6 seats, which would sweep the export markets.[44]

At this point Harry Ferguson entered the scene. Ferguson was an Ulsterman who had invented a very innovatory tractor system and subsequently had it made, with some success, by Ford in the USA.[45] But Ford and Ferguson were now in some dispute, and so Ferguson had arrived in Britain intent on finding a new manufacturer for his product. After some months, this led him to Black, and to a rapidly drawn-up agreement that Standard should manufacture tractors which Ferguson would then sell.

Black was enthusiastic about the Ferguson venture for a number of reasons. Most obviously, the Ferguson machine was already an established and successful product. Second, the export potential for the tractor seemed considerable, a fact that would almost certainly encourage further government patronage. Finally, it was also known that tractors required less sheet steel in their manufacture than cars – an important consideration given the general prevalence of steel shortages.[46]

Nevertheless, tractor production could not just be started at the drop of a hat, and so Black recognised that he would have to think carefully about what his company's overall strategy should be. In the end, it was decided that, given the capacity of the facilities that were available – Banner Lane and Standard's 'home' factory at Canley – and the potential for economies of scale that were inherent in this type of production,[47] the best option would be to go for the biggest throughputs of the two vehicles that were possible, organised on a virtually uninterrupted three-shift basis. By the autumn of 1945, then, Standard had arrived at a multi-pronged production policy. Manufacture of its pre-war models would be resumed for a period to keep up revenues. Meanwhile, the company's engineers were to be set to work ensuring that there should be maximum interchangeability of components used in the new car and the existing tractor. Finally, and most significantly, it was also decided to make each factory a specialist centre of production – to use Banner Lane for tractors and Canley for cars – and provide enough new equipment to allow both a capacity of 500 units per day, a programme that the company estimated would cost £4.6 million.[48]

Having taken these decisions about manufacturing policy, Black's next move was to consider how best they could be implemented. His board agreed that immediate capital was a priority, and so the company moved to increase its overdraft facilities and promote a rights issue amongst shareholders, the latter step securing some £1.6 million.[49] Meanwhile, an approach was made to the government for dollars to make overseas purchases, and this resulted in Cripps granting quite generous drafts – $0.5 million for machine tools, $5 million for Continental engines (which would be needed for the tractor while Standard developed its own variant) and $3 million for implements to be sold with the tractor.[50] Finally, Black was also active on the question of labour. Several firms in Coventry had ended the war believing that local wage rates would have to be cut, which made for an extremely tense industrial relations climate.[51] Black, however, recognised that his production policy would require an expanded and co-operative work-force, and so he rapidly sought to distinguish his outlook from that of the other employers. Standard, he stressed, was interested in establishing 'confidence, trust and understanding', and so would in future pay a minimum average bonus of 100 per cent on consolidated base rates (the current nationally agreed figure was 27.5 per cent) and at the same time move towards a forty-hour week. To distance his company further from the prevailing mood of confrontation, Black sent a copy of this declaration to the President of the Engineering Union before he had discussed it with other Coventry manufacturers. Reprimanded about this by the Coventry District Engineering Employers' Association, the Standard managing director simply withdrew his company from that organisation.[52]

The achievement of Black's various production targets was always going to take some time because of the necessity of retooling the two factories, and so 1946 and 1947 were both fairly slow years for the company. Design work on the new car, named the Vanguard, proceeded well, and the vehicle was given an enthusiastic reception when it was finally revealed to the press in mid-1947.[53] Tractor production began in September 1946 and at first ran into difficulties. There were shortages of particular grades of steel, and difficulties in developing a suitable type of engine.[54] But by late 1947, this position had been somewhat resolved, and the year's final output – 20,000 units – gave hope that better things were to come.

Events during 1948 further heightened this sense of optimism. The outlook for tractors seemed to be very good because of some big orders

Table 9.1. Output rates of Standard Vanguards and tractors, 1947–51, (Vehicles per day where figures available).

Year	Vanguard	Tractor
1947 4th quarter	—	230
[1948	no figure available]	
1949 1st quarter	230	320
2nd quarter		
3rd quarter		120
4th quarter		85
1950 1st quarter		200
2nd quarter		
3rd quarter		
4th quarter		270
1951 1st quarter	257	
2nd quarter	185	300
3rd quarter		
4th quarter	166	304

Sources: *The Times* 22/12/1947, 2/3/1949; *The Economist* 4/2/1950; *The Statist* 4/10/1950; SMC MSS 226/ST/1/5/1 Meeting 29/3/1951 77 (a), Meeting 17/4/1951 (79) and Meeting 7/11/1951 (106); and SMC MSS 226/ST/3/F/12/1 Copy of Letter Secretary — Sir W. Eady 2/5/1951.

from abroad and a reassurance from Cripps that steel supplies for this product would be prioritised.[55] Moreover the re-equipment of Banner Lane was nearing completion, and output was in fact running at 300 tractors per day by December.[56] Even Ferguson's decision to start up parallel production on his own account in the United States did not seem to be too threatening: the American plant would not be able to meet western hemisphere demand for several years, and anyway there was always Europe, Africa and the east.[57]

Progress with the Vanguard was also proceeding smoothly. The last Standard Eight was finished in July, and thereafter Canley was fully occupied manufacturing the new car, with production reaching 200 units per day by the end of the year.[58] Furthermore, a second capital issue, bringing in £2.4 million, guaranteed the next few years' financing of tools and raw materials for this model.[59]

In addition to all this, Black made something of a breakthrough on the industrial relations front. In the immediate post-war period, Standard had used a payment system with ninety-two separate basic grades besides assorted bonus provisions. This was never judged satisfactory by management because it often provoked argument with the work-force and did not in any way harmonise incentive and effort.[60] Consequently, Black had begun negotiating with the unions to 'draw up a wage system which would be in keeping with the new production system'.[61] The result was an agreement ratified in late 1948 which was judged to be something

of a *coup*. The new system was based upon a very much smaller number
of grades (eight in all), each of which would be guaranteed a weekly
basic rate. In addition, the bonus system was to be entirely revamped:
workers were to be divided into gangs and rewarded according to how
far their actual output measured up to a targeted figure.[62] This pleased
all sides. Standard workers knew that they had both the possibility of
high earnings and the safeguard of a guaranteed minimum. Black, on
the other, could look forward to lower administrative costs ('we shall be
saving a lot of paper, and a lot of people making marks on paper');
better team-work on the shop-floor; and the opportunity, because of the
introduction of the target figure to decide bonuses, of increasing
productivity.[63]

Given all these developments, Standard ended the year with some
fulsome praise from the financial press. *The Statist*, for example, noted
that rationalisation was being practised 'in the most advanced form' by
the company and concluded that Black had succeeded 'in a bold
experiment which only private enterprise could have followed'. *The
Investor's Chronicle* made a similar point, and added: 'Standard, by
putting profit into standardisation, may convince any wavers in the
industry that such a policy pays'.[64]

Over the following three years, Standard did not always find it easy to
live up to these kinds of assessment. The late 1940s were, certainly,
quite favourable in so far as car production was concerned, with sales of
Vanguards increasing from month to month, and major export markets
established in Australia, Canada, Sweden, Belgium and Brazil. Indeed,
the outlook seemed so promising that Standard decided to launch
another model, the smaller Mayflower.[65] On the other hand, the position
with tractor production was far less satisfactory. Difficulties in overseas
markets and currency shortages drastically cut demand in early 1949, so
that output at Banner Lane had to be reduced from 320 units per day in
January, to 120 units per day in June and finally 85 units per day at the
end of the year. The company ended 1949 with the Banner Lane work-
force at three-fifths of its peak size, and a total of tractors produced
(39,611) which was only 71 per cent of the figure achieved the year
before.[66]

Coincidentally, the early 1950s saw the relative strengths of the
tractor and car sectors almost exactly reversed. Vanguard production
had not been interrupted because of raw-material shortages in 1949, but
late the following year, problems over steel were very evident. Moreover,
there was a significant decline in demand for Standard products overseas,
so that a large number of Vanguards, for example, had to be brought
back from Canada unsold.[67] Yet the position with tractors was very
much more favourable. The Ferguson machine, as has been said, needed
less steel in construction than the Vanguard, and anyway the government

was determined to ensure that the tractor sector should remain relatively immune from shortages. Consequently, Standard found itself switching resources and personnel from cars to tractors, and achieving an output figure for the latter in 1951 (73,000 units) which was a post-war record.[68]

What kind of health was Standard in, then, at the beginning of the 1950s? Had the brave experiment of concentrating on a limited number of products been a success? At first sight, Black's vision seems to have been fully vindicated. By 1951, Standard was producing from two very modern factories, each with track systems, that had been equipped at a cost of over £8 million.[69] Both the Vanguard and the Ferguson tractor were well-established products that had generated considerable earnings (indeed, turnover from tractors alone between 1946 and 1951 was estimated at £70.5 million).[70] The consequences of this were enhanced profits – trading and net profits in 1950–1 were, respectively, eight and three times their 1945–6 equivalents – and high dividends – 25 per cent or more every year over the period.[71] Little wonder that for many Standard seemed to be a great success story.

Yet analysing the company's record in more detail suggests that it was, in fact, rather less satisfactory than this would imply. Thus, though both the Vanguard and the tractor did quite well in export markets, there was more than a suspicion that each remained vulnerable to competition. Moreover, as the data in Tables 9.2 and 9.3 demonstrate, Standard's overall financial position was weaker than it appeared. The ratio of net profits to turnover during these years had never been impressive. Significantly, too, looking at the profits that Standard made per vehicle sold reveals that these continued to be very low in relation to the margins achieved by competitors. With access to such information, it is little wonder that, at the beginning of the 1950s, some insiders were predicting that the company might well not have much of an independent future.[72]

In many ways, Standard's difficulties seem puzzling. The company had, of course, adopted a production strategy which many believed, in theory at least, was near optimum, and should be copied by other British companies.[73] Furthermore, government assistance had been considerable: the company, as has been remarked, had been given Banner Lane for a rental of £33,000 per annum, at a time when its replacement cost (excluding machine tools) was probably around £2.3 million,[74] and there had also been help with overseas currency and raw materials. What, therefore, had gone wrong?

Standard's central problem, in a nutshell, was the fact that its expansion policy imposed costs and commitments which the company found it very hard to cover. This can be illustrated by looking at both what expansion meant in terms of obligations and what it generated in terms of actual returns.

Table 9.2. Standard's annual financial performance 1945–51, £s.

	1945	1946	1947	1948	1949	1950	1951
Trading profit	ncf	500,120	657,325	1,648,330	2,617,515	2,885,341	3,918,085
Depreciation (a)	ncf	152,670	346,860	831,042	1,418,340	1,458,156	1,453,532
Net profit (b)	263,056	283,463	198,915	288,176	455,696	585,349	853,069
Dividend							
%	35	35	25	25	25	30	30
amount	108,000	184,800	132,000	198,000	198,000	241,725	323,032
carried forward	138,604	161,449	178,364	193,540	376,236	540,368	935,405

Notes:
i   all figures to year ended 31/8:
ii   (a) = figures include allowance for amortisation of tools etc.;
iii   (b) = i.e. trading profit, less depreciation, tax and directors' fees, plus other income.
Source: calculated from material in SMC MSS 226/ST/2/1/34–40.

Table 9.3. Standard, Ford and Vauxhall profitability, 1950–1952.

year	Standard		Ford		Vauxhall	
	i	ii	i	ii	i	ii
1950	31	8.9	63	17.3	47	13.1
1951	27	7.8	66	16.1	59	12.9
1952	24	6.2	72	14.0	95	16.9

Notes:
(i) trading profit per vehicle sold (£)
(ii) trading profit as a per cent of turnover
Sources: Standard data calculated from material in SMC MSS 226/ST/2/1/34–42; Ford and Vauxhall figures from G. Maxcy and A. Silberston *The Motor Industry* (1959) p. 169.

The most obvious by-product on the debit side that Black's strategy involved was high labour costs: Standard was well known to be top of Coventry's payments league, and certainly gave over a higher proportion of its annual turnover to wages and salaries than most of the other car companies nationally.[75] But expansion created other liabilities too. Standard had decided to repeat, on a rolling programme of investment, which meant that quite large sums (over £1.4 million, for example, in 1949, 1950 and 1951) were needed year by year to cover depreciation.[76] On top of this, Black knew that a high dividend policy was not just an option, more a real necessity.[77] The company might at any time need to draw on its shareholders, yet could never be absolutely sure of their loyalty: Standard's capital was spread widely amongst small investors[78] and anyway motor shares of whatever type were generally considered relatively risky.[79] The consequence was a policy of quite generous provision, with dividends in fact accounting for 47 per cent of net profits over the years 1945 to 1951.[80]

Of course Black at first believed that he would be able to cope with all these outgoings because of the inherent advantages of his overall strategy: he expected productivity gains because of his labour policy, economies of scale as output increased, and good returns in the sellers' markets which apparently existed overseas. To what extent were these objectives attained?

Several authorities have maintained that Standard's labour policy was its real Achilles' heel, because the gang system ceded too much control to shop stewards (they were, allegedly, the organisers of production) and encouraged complacency amongst the work-force.[81] Yet, for this period at least, such a view seems hard to justify, since the balance of advantages that flowed from Black's innovation was so clearly with the company. Certainly, Standard and Ferguson both felt that they had achieved direct productivity gains over these years, and provided figures to prove it.[82] Moreover, management was also aware of several indirect benefits that it had gained. Thus, the company could boast of low rates of labour turnover and lack of problems in quickly increasing establishment, factors that were important given the increasing manpower shortages locally.[83] In addition, Standard had a virtually unblemished industrial relations record, unlike other firms like Jaguar and Humber.[84] Indeed, even the 1949 lay-off at Banner Lane, involving two-fifths of the workers, was achieved peacefully, prompting *The Statist* to observe of Standard's labour policy: 'The system has been severely tested by the difficulties encountered . . . but appears to have stood the test well.'[85]

On the other hand, Black's achievements in relation to both economies of scale and good returns were very much less satisfactory, as a brief further look at the production history of Standard's two major lines will illustrate. The company had originally hoped to produce Vanguards at a rate of 500 units per day, a throughput which would, it was felt, allow a retail price in the region of £400.[86] Yet, as Table 9.1 shows, this output figure was never nearly reached, the maximum daily rate attained being around 250 cars per day in early 1951. The consequence was that, for this product, Standard remained trapped in something of a self-reinforcing, vicious circle: low output meant high costs, which meant high price, which meant low sales, which meant low output and so on. The most obvious outward sign of this was the Vanguard's selling price, which increased out of line with both inflation and the competition, to around £550 in 1951.[87] Some idea of the car's *relative* position against competitors can be gleaned from the figures in Table 9.4.

Standard could in part blame its problems here on factors that were outside its control – foreign governments' currency problems and trade restrictions and the Attlee administration's insistence on export quotas, which made it difficult to build up home sales. On the other hand, the situation was also partly self inflicted. Standard had always considered the Vanguard to be primarily an export product, yet the car's design was shaped, as *The Economist* put it, 'less by market research than by the desirability of using the same engine in it as in the Ferguson tractor'.[88] This inevitably produced growing consumer resistance abroad: foreign buyers had to put up with paint blisters, inadequate suspension and non-existent dust-proofing as long as there was no alternative, but were less inclined to do so when American, German and Italian models began reappearing.[89]

Standard's problems with the Ferguson tractor were of a slightly different kind. The company found, first, that it was saddled with very much greater development costs (around £1.04 million) than had been predicted during the initial discussions about the deal.[90] Black's bigger problems, however, were about price. He had originally quoted Ferguson a figure which included a very small profit for Standard (as little as 2.5 per cent) with the idea that as production increased, and costs fell,

Table 9.4. Vanguard's position relative to competitors 1950 and 1952

	1950: price (£)	1952: kerb weight (cwts)	engine capacity (ccs)	price (£)	pence per pound weight
Vanguard	515	24.25	2088	590	52.2
Ford Consul	415	21.75	1508	470	46.3
Ford Zephyr Six	475	22.75	2262	532	50.2

Source: data in *Autocar* 20/10/1950 and *The Economist* 25/10/1952.

margins would improve.[91] The problem was that this scenario did not develop as planned: output took some time to build up and then had to be cut back drastically in 1949. Yet when Black went back to Ferguson to re-negotiate the price because of this, he found the Ulsterman to be less than receptive. Ferguson's motives are not always easy to reconstruct from the available evidence, but it seems that his long-term aim continued to be the re-establishment of tractor production at a high level in the USA, after his difficulties with Ford (which had become entangled in a complex legal battle) were fully cleared up. The Standard-produced tractor was therefore used as something of a loss leader in markets were there was strong competition (the USA and Canada), in order to keep the Ferguson name and distribution organisation intact.[92] The consequence was that Ferguson continued to be very price conscious – the retail price of the tractor apparently went up by only 5 per cent between 1946 and 1951[93] – and thus, very unwilling to grant Black better margins. Standard, therefore, found itself making money from tractor production but not at nearly the rate which had been expected: as *The Economist* later put it, the Ferguson product provided a 'bread and butter staple', but the butter was 'spread thin'.[94]

Some of Black's problems with the Ferguson tractor were clearly a question of bad luck. However, there was also a degree of poor judgement here. Black should have been more sceptical, for example, about Harry Ferguson's insistence that the target output be 500 tractors per day, since this figure bore no relation to any information about hard orders and was simply based on a rough estimate of the potential market.[95] Moreover, it was evident from the first that the Ulsterman would not be a very reliable or trustworthy business partner. Black's initial understanding with Ferguson, a gentlemen's agreement, was signed in October 1945 with both parties exuberant about their prospects.[96] But the goodwill did not last very long. In late 1945, for example, Black was furious to find Ferguson dishonestly inflating previous output figures of his tractor and producing misleading estimates of its likely future cost, all apparently in an effort to impress the government and potential investors.[97] A few weeks later there was a major row about the tractor engine. Black believed that Ferguson had designed a new engine for their joint product, essential given the legal row about patents that was brewing between Ferguson and Ford. But when the drawings for this engine were revealed, they turned out to be only 'a rough sketch which was not an engineering provision',[98] leading Black to conclude in May 1946: 'I was misled in the first place as to the tractor that we were to make'.[99] Nevertheless, all of this did not prevent Black concluding a formal agreement with Ferguson in August 1946, nor moreover from initialling a document which a leading counsel subsequently judged 'vague, uncertain and incomplete'.[100]

The aim of dwelling at some length on the Standard case was to demonstrate that Labour's stance towards the car industry in the post-war years cannot simply be dismissed as a matter of short-term instrumentalism. In fact, as the example has shown, Labour did try to develop a more rounded strategy, involving an endeavour to 'pick winners' – give backing in various ways to what appeared to be a very progressive firm.

But approaching the Standard story in the way that has been attempted does allow brief comment, in conclusion, on one further related issue – the *quality* of the government's interventions. Standard, it has been argued, was not a complete success. Was this, perhaps, because Labour's efforts on the company's behalf were misdirected or insufficient? Might Labour in fact have done very much better by Standard if it had pursued a very different set of initiatives?

The implication of Barnett's position is that the government certainly ought to have pursued other objectives. As has been shown, he outlines an allegedly ideal package of measures involving trade-union reform, stimulation of demand (via tax reform) and forcible amalgamation of producer units. Yet at least in the Standard case, as has been shown, there is doubt if any of these measures would have been very relevant. The company had no industrial-relations problem, and did not suffer from low absolute levels of demand for its products. Nor would amalgamation with another producer necessarily have provided benefits; Standard had ample capacity, and does not seem to have suffered, so far as can be told, from any particular shortage of capital funds.

But if Labour cannot be criticised on the grounds suggested by Barnett, this does not mean that the government's actions should be seen as necessarily wholly laudable. Standard's weaknesses in this period were essentially to do with its management – they were about design and marketing (factors that were all but ignored) and commercial strategy. Should not Labour have done more to ensure that the management it continued so generously to assist was more up to the task in hand?

Attlee's government was conscious of the general need to improve management standards in Britain and launched several initiatives which were to have longer-term significance.[101] But the achievement of quick, short-term reforms in this area was a totally different question. There was no real precedent for government interference in a private firm's boardroom, no blueprint for how this might be done, and, above all, no political mandate to sanction such an intervention. Given this situation, and in the light of all the other information that has been presented in this chapter, Labour's stance on the car industry in the post-war period should perhaps be seen as a good deal more creditable than historians like Barnett have made it appear.

NOTES

1. D. Scott 'Are British Cars Tough Enough?' *New Commonwealth* 2/9/1954 235–9 and 16/9/1954 289–92.
2. I would like to thank participants at the 1990 Labour and Private Industry Conference and the editors of this volume (particularly Jim Tomlinson) for useful comments on an earlier draft of this chapter; Richard Storey and staff at the Modern Records Centre, University of Warwick, for consistently excellent assistance with sources; and the British Motor Industry Heritage Trust, the Confederation of British Industry and The Engineering Employers Federation for permission to use material in their archives.
3. C. Barnett *The Audit of War* (1986) pp. 274–5.
4. Ibid. p. 274.
5. Ibid. p. 272.
6. Ibid. p. 275.
7. Ibid. esp. pp. 265–75.
8. See for example, The Society of Motor Manufacturers and Traders *Monthly Progress Report* [hereafter *MPR*] Dec 1942 2.
9. Deliberations amongst the civil servants at this time can be followed in Public Record Office, Kew (hereafter PRO) CAB124/626 and WO185/224.
10. See for example, PRO WO185/224 M. 1. (44) 1st Meeting 'Interdepartmental Committee on the Post-War Resettlement of the Motor Industry. Notes of Meeting held . . . on 29/12/1944' p. 3 and Letter K. Hedges – H. Binney 18/11/1944.
11. PRO CAB124/626 Note R. Edwards – J. Jewkes 14/12/1944 and enclosure.
12. PRO CAB124/626 Note by Jewkes 'Post-War Resettlement of the Motor Industry . . .' 28/3/1945 p. 4.
13. W. Plowden *The Motor Car and Politics in Britain* (Harmondsworth, 1973) pp. 315–20.
14. See for example, PRO CAB124/626 Note by Ministry of Production 'Resettlement of the Motor Industry' [nd].
15. PRO CAB87/15 R(1) (45) 9 21/3/1944 War Cabinet Reconstruction Committee. Ministerial Sub-Committee on Industrial Problems. Report by the Official Sub-Committee 'Post-War Resettlement of the Motor Industry' 21/3/1945 p. 7.
16. Plowden op. cit. pp. 317–18.
17. Information on the SMMT can be found in Plowden op. cit. and PEP *Motor Vehicles* (1950) pp. 41–3.
18. See for example, *MPR* April 1944 1–2; June 1944 1–3 and Sept. 1944 3.

19. For one example amongst many of direct lobbying, see PRO CAB124/626 Letter W. Rootes – Lord Woolton 24/3/1944.
20. See for example, *MPR* Jan. 1946 6 and 8.
21. The SMMT spent £35,798 on public relations in 1944, £50,559 in 1945 and £14,513 in 1946, and generally judged its campaigns to be successful: see the SMMT's 43rd Annual Report pp. 4 and 7, 44th Annual Report p. 13 and 45th Annual Report p. 39; and *MPR* April 1945 1–2.
22. PRO CAB87/15 R (1) 45 6th Meeting 5/4/1945 pp. 3–4.
23. PRO WO185/224 Copy of Letter H. Dalton – P. Bennett 1/5/1945.
24. PRO BT64/2898 Corr. Lord Woolton – O. Lyttelton 8/6/1945 and 29/6/1945 and Memo by R. C. Bryant 'The Motor Vehicle Industry. Note by the Board of Trade' 10/11/1945 p. 2.
25. Labour Party Archive, National Museum of Labour History Manchester. Labour Party Sub-Committee on Industries for Nationalisation. Minutes (2) 13/10/1948.
26. TUC *Interim Report on Post-War Reconstruction* (1944) pp. 15–16.
27. PRO BT64/2898 Memo by H. Binney 23/9/1946.
28. Plowden op. cit. p. 321 and p. 325.
29. The most important means of control here was exercised by the Ministry of Supply, which rationed steel according to performance. Most of the relevant papers appear not to have survived, but see PRO SUPP14/331 and 332, files which deal with allocations in 1951 and 1952.
30. PRO BT64/2898 Memo by Bryant 'The Motor Vehicle Industry . . .' op. cit.
31. Ministry of Supply *National Advisory Council for the Motor Manufacturing Industry. Report on Proceedings* (HMSO, 1947) p. 5.
32. *MPR* April 1946 2. The other places on the NAC were taken by two trade unionists, one independent member and four civil servants.
33. *MPR* Dec. 1946 5. Wilmot's sentiments here were very typical of his more general approach, and even his friends recognised that he was a rather weak minister; see e.g. R. Williams-Thompson *Was I Really Necessary?* (1951) pp. 34–7.
34. Relatively few of the NAC's papers survive in the PRO, but some idea of its workings can be gleaned from PEP *Motor Vehicles* op. cit. pp. 45–6. Certainly, the employers seem to have usually seen the body as simply an efficient conduit for presenting their view to the government and, more importantly, the trade unions. Thus, when Sir Peter Bennett (of Vauxhall Motors) reported on the NAC to an FBI Grand Council enquiry on Working Parties, it was this functional aspect that he chose to emphasise. Modern Records Centre, University of Warwick CBI Predecessor Archive MSS 200 F/1/1/188 FBI Grand Council 9/10/1946.
35. *The Economist* 21/6/1947; *The New Statesman* 30/8/1947.
36. LSE Dalton Diary Vol. 30. Entry for 14/4/1944.
37. PRO BT64/2898 M.M. (46) 82nd Meeting. President's Morning Meeting 23/9/1946 and Letter from Sec. SMMT to Members, 11/12/1945.
38. *MPR* Nov.–Dec. 1945 4–5. See, also, on this episode, Plowden op. cit. p. 321.
39. D. Thoms and T. Donnelly *The Motor Car Industry in Coventry since the 1890s* (1985) pp. 96–8.
40. PRO BT106/17 Report by A. D. Carmichael 'Reconstruction-Midland Region No 9' 20/3/1943 p. 2, enclosed with Letter Carmichael – P. A. Warter 19/3/1943.
41. Motor Records Centre, British Motor Industry Heritage Trust, Standard Motor Co. (hereafter SMC) MSS 226/ST/1/1/9 Meeting 20/10/1944, 615.
42. PRO BT208/82 Note [unsigned] 'Standard Motor Co. Ltd. No. 2 Engine Shadow Factory . . .' [nd] and *The Times* 22/3/1945.
43. SMC MSS 226/ST/1/1/9 Meeting 9/3/1945 657.

44. *The Coventry Standard* [hereafter *Standard*] 24/2/1945.
45. On Ferguson, see principally C. Fraser *Harry Ferguson. Inventor and Pioneer* (1972). The advantage of the Ferguson system is well explained in *The Economist* 11/1/1947 (the 'Ferguson mechanism gives hydraulic control from the saddle, and by transferring the weight and drag of the implement, eliminates the need for a heavy tractor').
46. *The Economist* 2/11/1946.
47. PEP *Motor Vehicles* op. cit. p. 129.
48. PRO WO185/224 'Notes on visits paid to Car Manufacturers by Col. R. T. Grantham 19/1/1945'; SMC MSS 226/ST/1/1/10 Meeting 21/3/1946 772 and 773 and Meeting 2/7/1946 789; and *The Investors' Chronicle* 13/11/1948.
49. SMC MSS 226/ST/1/1/9 Meeting 30/8/1945 696; SMC MSS 226/ST/1/1/10 Meeting 5/12/1945 740 etc.; and SMC MSS 226/ST/3/F/12/1 Note [unsigned] 'Share Capital Issues' 21/8/1950.
50. SMC MSS 226/ST/3/F/1/28 Letter Ferguson – Black 2/10/1945; and Fraser op. cit. pp. 166–9.
51. E. D. O'Brien 'The Motor Industry's Problems' *The Banker* Vol. LXXVIII No. 243 April 1946 21; and N. Tiratsoo *Reconstruction, Affluence and Labour Politics: Coventry 1945–60* (1990) p. 17.
52. SMC MSS 226/ST/3/JB/1/27/1/2 Circular by Sir John Black 'Post-War Motor Car Production Wages Policy' 25/5/1945; and Engineering Employers' Federation, Modern Records Centre, University of Warwick MSS 237/3/1/33/340 Memo 'Notes on Meeting with Sir John Black . . . 22/6/1945' and Letter K. Aspland – The Secretary, EAENA, 26/6/1945.
54. PRO SUPP14/865 'Joint Statement by Sir John Black and Mr. Harry Ferguson . . .' 28/10/1947, enc. with Min. by Second Secretary (Supply) 19/1/1948 and SMC MSS 226/ST/3/F/3/2 Note by E. Grinham 17/5/1946.
55. *The Times* 27/1/1948 and *The Statist* 17/1/1948.
56. *The Investors' Chronicle* 13/11/1948.
57. Fraser op. cit. p. 194.
58. J. R. Davy *The Standard Car 1903–1963* (Coventry, 1967) p. 44 and *The Times* 2/3/1949.
59. SMC MSS 226/ST/1/1/10 Meeting 2/3/1948 955 etc. and SMC MSS 226/ST/3/F/12/1 Note [unsigned] of 21/8/1950 op. cit.
60. PRO T229/346 'Case History No 4 (revised draft)' p. 1.
61. Ibid.
62. PRO T229/346 'Case History . . .' op. cit. pp. 2–3; and PRO SUPP14/867 Brochure 'Britain Awakes' [nd].
63. PRO T229/346 'Case History . . .' op. cit. pp. 3–4; and *Standard* 12/6/1948.
64. *The Statist* 30/10/1948 and 20/11/1948; and *The Investors' Chronicle* 13/11/1948.
65. *The Statist* 5/11/1949, 22/7/1950 and 4/11/1950.
66. Table 9.1.; PRO SUPP14/866 Letter B. Belson – W. V. Wood 12/9/1949; and PRO SUPP14/867 Memo 'Harry Ferguson Ltd' [nd].
67. *The Statist* 26/8/1950; PRO SUPP14/331 Note by F. F. D. Ward 19/5/1951; and SMC MSS 226/ST/1/5/1 Meeting 22/8/1951 104 (a).
68. *Standard* 20/4/1951; *The Economist* 5/5/1951; and PRO SUPP14/867 Memo 'Harry Ferguson Ltd' [nd].
69. *Standard* 12/4/1947 (on Canley); SMC MSS 226/ST/3/F/12/1 Copy of Letter Secretary – Sir W. Eady (the Treasury) 2/5/1951 (on Banner Lane); and *The Statist* 4/10/1951 (on the post-war increase in Standard's capital assets).
70. SMC MSS 226/ST/3/F/12/1 Copy of Letter Secretary – Eady op. cit.
71. Table 9.2.
72. See PRO SUPP14/867 Min by F. F. D. Ward 29/3/1954 p. 2.
73. See for example, *Autocar* 18/7/1947.

74. For this estimate of Banner Lane's replacement value in late 1946, see SMC MSS 266/ST/3/F/2/96 Draft Letter Black – Ferguson 12/7/1946.

75. S. Melman *Decision-Making and Productivity* (Oxford, 1958) p. 144; SMC MSS 226/ST/3/JB/1/42/1 Note 'Where the money went in 1947' [nd]; and, for comparison, PRO SUPP 14/394 Diagram 'Ford Motor Company Limited. Disbursement of Total 1947 Income . . .'.

76. Table 9.2 and for example, *The Statist* 26/8/1950.

77. See for example, SMC MSS 226/ST/3/JB/1/47/6–7 Note from Secretary to J. B. 26/5/1948 and SMC MSS 226/ST/1/5/1 Meeting 10/1/1952 123 (d).

78. *The Statist* 22/12/1951 reported Standard's Chairman as saying: 'The number of stockholders on the register of the Standard Company is about 12,000, of which the preponderance hold between £100 and £500 capital'.

79. A point *The Statist* was always making: see for example, the issue of 13/9/1947 ('motor car shares are hardly suitable for the timid investor').

80. Calculated from figures in Table 9.2.

81. Ferguson seems to have ended up believing that Black should have pursued a more robust line with the workforce (see SMC MSS 226/ST/3/F/8/4 'Draft. 2nd February, 1959' p. 1) though this was not reflected in his recorded statements of the late 1940s and early 1950s. For a more general argument that Coventry workers dug 'the pit for their own burial', see P. Thompson 'Playing at being skilled men: factory culture and pride in work skills among Coventry car workers' *Social History* Vol. 13 No. 1 Jan. 1988 45–69.

82. *Standard* 12/6/1948; and PRO SUPP14/87 Brochure 'Britain Awakes' [nd]. See also discussion in Melman op. cit., particularly p. 165.

83. See for example, PRO SUPP14/866 Letter F. C. Limbrey – W. S. Williams 31/3/1949.

84. Tiratsoo op. cit. p. 64.

85. *The Statist* 1/10/1949.

86. *The Investors Chronicle* 13/11/1948; and Davy op. cit. p. 44.

87. SMC MSS 226/ST/1/1/11 Meeting 6/2/1951 1205 gives the Vanguard's 1951 selling price.

88. *The Economist* 7/3/1953.

89. For problems and complaints over the Vanguard, see for example, SMC MSS 226/ST/1/5/1 Meeting 26/7/1951 97; M. Adeney *The Motor Makers* (1989) p. 207; G. Turner *The Leyland Papers* (revised edition, 1973) p. 31; and P. Pagnamenta and R. Overy *All Our Working Lives* (1984) pp. 229–30.

90. SMC MSS 226/ST/3/F/3/2 Note by Grinham op. cit. and SMC MSS 226/ST/3/JB/1/41/1 Note Secretary – Black 6/10/1947.

91. SMC MSS 226/ST/3/F/2/44 Draft Letter Black – H. Ferguson Ltd 16/4/1946.

92. See for example, PRO SUPP14/865 'Note of Meeting . . . in the Treasury on 13/4/1948'.

93. PRO SUPP14/867 Brochure 'Britain Awakes' [nd].

94. *The Economist* 17/1/1959.

95. PRO SUPP14/866 Letter F. C. Limbrey – W. S. Williams 31/1/1949:
it seemed clear enough that the *Ferguson estimates* were really based on potential market rather than actual orders . . . However, at a later stage, estimates were based on orders. It was stated, for instance, that France had a tractor population of 35,000, England had a tractor population of 200,000, but France had 4 times the tillage area of England.

96. SMC MSS 226/ST/1/1/9 Meeting 30/8/1945 696.

97. SMC MSS 226/ST/3/F/2/5 Letter A. R. Smith – C. J. Band 28/12/1945 and SMC MSS 226/ST/3/F/3/6 'Notes by JB 21/5/1946' p. 2.

98. SMC MSS 226/ST/3/F/3/4/2 Memo 'The Agreement between . . . Standard . . . and Ferguson . . .' 18/5/1946 p. 1.

99. SMC MSS 226/ST/3/F/3/6 'Notes by J. B. 21/5/1946' p. 1.
100. SMC MSS 226/ST/3/F/12/1. John Gazdar 'Counsel's Opinion' [nd].
101. Labour's attempts to raise standards amongst British management will be dealt with in N. Tiratsoo and J. Tomlinson *Industrial Efficiency and State Intervention: Labour 1939–1951* (1993).

Ten

The shipbuilding industry[1]

LEWIS JOHNMAN

THE STRUCTURE OF THE INDUSTRY AND ITS POSITION 1940–1945

A 1948 Labour Party report on the shipbuilding industry observed that:
> ... no other major British industry, during the period of its modern history, has suffered periods of depression so prolonged and so severe, so as to almost destroy its resources in money, equipment and craftsmen.[2]

From a position in 1900 of near complete control in the world export market in merchant ships, Britain's share of world tonnage launched had dropped to one-eighth by 1939. Prior to 1914, some 22 per cent of British launchings had been for export, whereas in 1937–8, only 10 per cent of a much reduced output were for foreign order. In 1938 more ships were built abroad for British owners than were on order in the UK for foreign owners. The industry's output between 1929 and 1939 was never more than one-third of its capacity and in some periods over 60 per cent of the insured workers within the industry were unemployed.[3]

In part, the explanation lay in the nature of the UK shipbuilding industry. As late as 1954, the Census of Production listed over 676 establishments engaged in shipbuilding and 104 in marine engineering. After 1945, however, 31 establishments produced some 90 per cent of the tonnage launched and 6 companies with 100 berths accounted for over half the tonnage of mercantile output.[4] The nature of ownership remained in the post-war period a mix of public companies, proprietorship and private limited companies dominated by family ownership. Most firms retained a high degree of independence of operation with any horizontal integration predicated on the protection of market shares and prices, and vertical integration on raw material supplies. The production base tended to operate via a single distributional channel with ships being built in response to a specific order through competitive tendering. The shipbuilding firm was linked to the market place through a specialised product line which was dependent upon management manipulation of the tendering system. The basic work-organisational system was a tripartite, functionally specialised system, where the three main components – estimating, costing and works departments – were

186

hermetically sealed against each other. The role of management was to co-ordinate and balance the flow of work in order to produce a given product at a given cost. Thus the test of work at all levels, given that no unit within the firm was in direct touch with the market and that measures such as the return on capital or derived market share were relatively important, was cost and quality control and the test of the market applied only to the finished ship and the firm as a whole.

The typical shipbuilding firm was very hierarchical in organisation with personal control over major policy decisions and strategy being maintained and exercised. Authority was concentrated at the senior-management level with work functionally specialised and organised in sub-units. Management had three major policy decisions open to it: market shares, improvement of the product and the process of production itself. Most shipbuilding firms sought to stabilise their market positions by forming alliances with buyers and associations with suppliers. This situation rested, to a substantial extent, on the personal relationships, built up over many years, between managing directors and chairmen of building firms and shipping companies. The most important implication of this system was that shipbuilders had little power to manipulate the market. In the upswing, they tended to take on contracts and then considered how best to meet the terms, often taking on market commitments which were beyond the internal capacity of the firm to meet. In the downswing, the firm attempted to gain orders at almost any price in such a way that the cost consequences were detached from the capital structure requirements of the company. In this sense the firm and its market relationships operated as a closed system in that the functional relationship of sub-units within the firm was so close as to make any substantial change in the relationship unlikely.

In the depressed years of the inter-war period individual firms proved incapable of reducing their own capacity.[5] In 1928, the Shipbuilding Conference was established to combat unfair contract conditions, control tendering abuses and research and develop means of assistance. This body was criticised by its own chairman, the Clyde shipbuilder, Sir Maurice Denny in 1940 as 'only a loose price protective association' and he argued that it was 'axiomatic that a conference which exists simply to ensure a profit price to the least efficient member without reference to the necessities of the client is indefensible: it is economically and perhaps ethically wrong'.[6] The conference could do little to influence the real problems of the industry – the fluctuation of demand and output – and nor could the National Shipbuilders Security Limited, formed in 1930 with the avowed aim of buying up and eliminating redundant capacity. By 1939 NSS Ltd had put over 180 berths with an annual capacity of some 1,350,000 gross tons out of capacity leaving an annual capacity of some 2 million gross tons. Despite the loss of over one-third of its capacity, the industry in 1939 was still producing below its capacity.[7]

Industrial relations tended to reflect the market structure of the industry. Most firms retained small-scale, labour-intensive production techniques to avoid high overhead costs during a downswing. In this way the burden of market uncertainty was shifted onto labour through periodic lay-offs. No firm had the desire to increase fixed costs via the use of more capital intensive methods of production. As such the craft basis reflected the way in which work was organised and administered in the shipyards with the basis of specialisation – the squad system – effectively reducing the need for specialised management. The negative aspect of this situation was that high rates of labour turnover tended to heighten concern over job security and led to the defence of controls over jobs and access to them, and accordingly, the unions sought to restrict the number of apprentices, dilution, job flexibility and changing production methods. The role of demarcation in the industry has excited the imaginations of some historians with at least one describing the trade-union position as comprising 'such absurdities worthy of a weird land of nonsense observed by Lemuel Gulliver',[8] but it should be noted that the system had developed symbiotically with the industry and was a defensive mechanism in a situation which suited management practice and which it had done little to attempt to change. Without wishing to minimise the role of demarcation it should be noted that in the period 1950 to 1956 all strikes in the industry averaged a loss of only one man-day per year with an estimated increase in labour costs of approximately 0.5 per cent.[9]

The war caused a substantial revival in the fortunes of the industry and served to bring the government into its running and substantially expose its deficiencies. Between the outbreak of the war and the end of 1944 the tonnage of merchant shipping launched in the UK totalled 5,723,000 gross tons (gt). In 1942 the industry launched some 259 merchant vessels at a total tonnage of 1,302,000gt. Despite this revival in building, the yards failed to launch enough tonnage to balance losses. In 1939, the UK had a gross merchant tonnage of 17.4 million and ended it with some 13.9mgt, a net loss of some 3.5mgt.[10] The industry, however, had missed almost all of the targets set for it by the War Cabinet during the war years, a situation which provoked concern over both the immediate needs of the industry and over its long-term position.[11]

Two major inquiries into the condition of the industry were conducted in 1942.[12] The Barlow Report noted the effects of the inter-war depression on the industry as depressed morale amongst the work-force and inefficient technology. The report recommended the dilution of labour to attempt to overcome bottlenecks in riveting, plating, welding and

Table 10.1   British war-time merchant shipbuilding 1939–1944

	Vessels	Tons ('000)
1939	60	240
1940	182	809
1941	234	1157
1942	259	1302
1943	236	1202
1944	269	1073

Source: *Shipbuilder and Marine Engineer* June 1945.

electrical work, the modernisation of equipment, new piece-work agreements and a detailed yard-by-yard analysis of labour in order to achieve a more efficient deployment.[13] The Bentham Report criticised the management of the industry and recommended the standardisation of ships and components and the concentration of the production of certain vessels in certain yards. The report also recommended new yard layouts, prefabrication, improved cranage, more welding points and better fitting-out berths. Most machinery in the yards was 'left over from the last war or previously' and the report concluded that large numbers of standard and specialised tools were needed.[14]

In an attempt to counter the situation revealed by the Barlow and Bentham Reports the government established the Shipyard Development Committee. Under the auspices of this body some £6 million was invested in new plant (of which the government contributed £1.5 million which was equivalent to 75 per cent of the programme relating to merchant shipbuilding) and contributed to new tools, cranes and welding equipment in the industry. Despite this, substantial difficulties remained over the introduction of new production methods in what were essentially small production units in marine engineering. There were also serious difficulties over welding, mainly inadequate electrical power supplies. The number of welding points in shipyards rose from 1,000 in April 1942 to 3,065 in 1944, and the number of persons employed as welders from 730 to 1737, but as was noted 'the provision of new labour did not keep pace with the extension of plant'.[15] There were, however, fairly strict limits on how far such a programme of re-equipment and reorganisation could be pushed in the war where the demand was for production at all costs.

Consideration of the longer-term, post-war situation in the industry began in 1942. Talks were held between the two ministries which had control of the industry – the Admiralty and the Ministry of War Transport – and shipbuilders, to discuss the post-war situation and unanimity was reached on a number of issues. First, that the market fluctuated far too wildly to secure the stability of the industry and therefore some form of planning was necessary. Second, that there should be some form of co-ordination between merchant and naval construction with naval orders being placed when merchant orders slackened off. Third, that controls over materials and labour and the licensing system should be retained, at least in the transition period. Fourth, that the essential starting point from which the future of the industry should be considered was to agree on the absolute minimum size of the industry and to plan on that basis; and finally, it was agreed that the government would have a long-term co-ordinating role to play in the future of the industry.[16]

The two ministers responsible for control of the industry, the First Lord of the Admiralty, A. V. Alexander and the Minister of War Transport, Lord Leathers, both believed that some form of government control of the industry in the post-war period was essential, as Alexander put it, to avoid the 'chaotic conditions' of the past.[17] Both men agreed that the inter-war experience of the industry had bred highly conservative attitudes which were inimical to efficiency.[18] Their thinking on this issue was focused by a scheme for regulating orders from the Joint Committee of Shipbuilders and Shipowners (JCSS). This advocated industrial self-government with a joint board of the shipbuilding and shipping industries being responsible for issuing licences and builders undertaking to accept no order without a permit. As J. R. Hobhouse, the Joint Chairman of the General Council of the Shipbuilding Conference, admitted, the intention of the scheme was to exclude the government from the industry:

> The position is this . . . [we] are . . . fairly convinced that we shall do the job better than the Government will do it . . . I will not conceal from you that we would very much like to be free of Government control and I think . . . we should take the view that we ought to fight to get rid of Government control.[19]

To which Leathers and Alexander replied that some form of regulatory control would continue to be exercised by the government.

In response to the JCSS initiative, Alexander and Leathers proposed an alternative scheme. This was based on the belief that the recent history of the industry proved that it was incapable of solving its own problems and that government assistance was essential.[20] They argued that government policy towards the steel and coal industries would inevitably react on the price of raw materials and that some form of co-ordination was essential in this area, and also, that the full employment aspirations of any future government required the retention of government control in an industry which had suffered one of the highest rates of unemployment between the wars. They did not believe that rigid control would be necessary beyond the transition period nor that a full-scale inquiry into the industry and its efficiency was required. What they envisaged was an independent, informed body which could anticipate any difficulties which the industry might face and alert the government to them. Accordingly, they proposed a shipbuilding advisory board as an intermediary between the government and the industry.[21] The recommendations were accepted by the government and the Shipbuilding Committee was established in November 1944.[22]

The Shipbuilding Committee exercised its functions for the final months of 1944 and throughout 1945. A system of permits to shipowners to negotiate for new ships was instituted as a means of regulating priorities between owners or between types of ship or yard. Priority was given to vessels where keels were to be layed down within eighteen months of the application. Permits were valid only for a limited period, were considered quarterly and issued in excess of capacity to allow for a proportion not maturing into orders. The licensing system remained in force whereby the Admiralty would issue a licence to enable materials to be ordered once it had received a permit. The aim of the permit–licence procedure was to enable the government to keep control of the industry should the wish to order prove to be in excess of the industry's capacity, or if the flow of orders was such that it was likely to produce an imbalance in the industry.[23] In the event, neither of these fears was realised. By July 1945 the issuing of permits to neutral owners was approved and by the end of the year it was decided to discontinue the permit system as it was no longer necessary to regulate priorities between owners. The Committee's final recommendations were that every effort should be made to restore the mercantile marine to its pre-war figure of 18mgt and that the level of employment in the shipbuilding and repairing industries should be prevented from falling below 90,000. It also concluded that by 1955 world tonnage would stand at not less than 70mgt, UK tonnage would be 18mgt, and that in the same ten-year period the total output of merchant ships from British yards would be 12.5mgt.[24]

1945–1951: SHIPBUILDERS AND THE LABOUR GOVERNMENT

By early 1946 the issue facing the Labour government was what form of control should be exercised over the industry. Despite the clear declarations that they favoured a full return to private enterprise, the industry seemed sanguine with respect to a Labour government. The main trade journal *The Shipbuilder and Marine Engineer* ventured the opinion that:

> While the change of government will, perhaps, affect the shipbuilding industry less than other major industries, such as coal and transport, there may be a continuation of some existing controls, and possibly some eventual direction of the industry, so far as broad policy is concerned, through joint representation of Government, employers and workers.[25]

No serious objection had been raised over the Shipbuilding Committee's

work or its views as to the future of the industry. As A. V. Alexander
pointed out, the scope of the Shipbuilding Committee 'was intentionally
limited to specific points arising during the transition period' and that
what was now required was a more permanent body which could plan
the longer-term future of the industry.[26]

The Lord President's Committee thought that a shipbuilding advisory
committee on similar lines to the Shipbuilding Committee should be
established, and that:

> there is every advantage in announcing this body and getting it to
> work quickly so as to leave no cause for uncertainty in the industry
> and at the same time to implement the warning already given in
> your announcement on nationalisation that the industry, although
> not down for nationalisation, will be expected to have full regard to
> the public interest . . . an independent Chairman . . . in the
> circumstances . . . seems inevitable, but the appointment may be a
> precedent for other industries which are not, or not at present, to
> be nationalised . . .[27]

Nita Watts, of the Economic Section, also felt that an advisory committee
would be of 'considerable assistance' but warned that the Lord President's
Committee should make it clear that the government was not committed
either to the target level of output or to maintaining a minimum level of
employment, arguing that these had to be 'subject to revision to confirm
the overall economic plan' and with 'later indications of the prospects
for the industry'. She stated that the prospect of flexible economic
planning had been 'compromised to a certain extent' by pledges to
maintain a certain minumum level of employment in the building industry
and that to do the same in shipbuilding 'would introduce another
undesirable element of rigidity into the future economic system'.[28]
Despite this view, it was also pointed out that, 'the trends visible so far
conform directly to what the Committee forecast', that restoring tonnage
to pre-war levels would take until 1950 and that at some time prior to
that date the government would be in a position to judge whether an
increased level could be justified.[29]

The Shipbuilding Advisory Committee (SAC) was duly established
and began its deliberations in June 1946.[30] At this early stage in the
Committee's existence the problem of material supplies emerged, with
Sir Amos Ayre complaining that steel supplies were inadequate and
urging that shipbuilding should be given the same priority as the export
trade.[31] By the date of the Committee's fifth meeting in November, the
steel position had not perceptibly eased, a range of other shortages and
bottlenecks, including timber, were being complained of, as was a
shortage of skilled labour, particularly in the finishing trades.[32] This
picture was confirmed by the trade press with the *Shipbuilder and
Marine Engineer* reporting steel and labour shortages on both the Clyde

and the North East Coast throughout the year. The journal noted that the prices of British-built ships were between 70 per cent to 100 per cent above those of 1938. The price of steel plates had risen from £10 10s.6d. to £16 16s. 6d.; labour costs had risen some 75 per cent, and the price of completed accessories was up by 199 per cent.[33] On Clydeside, a decline in coal output had restricted the output of steelworks with local steel stocks exhausted by November. In the sector as a whole, heavy steel prices had increased by 5/- per ton in September; pig iron prices by 2/- per ton and the prices of certain finished products had also risen.[34] As well as material costs there were also complaints concerning the shortage of skilled labour in the finishing trades, all of which was blamed on competition from the housing programme.[35]

Despite noting that there was 'little likelihood that prices will fall' and that 'the tendency may well be in the opposite direction'[36] the mood amongst shipbuilders remained reasonably buoyant 'because of the urgency of the need for new tonnage, the present high level of building costs has perhaps played a secondary part in recent orders, early delivery dates most of all being keenly sought'.[37] The quarterly production figures showed that the volume of work on hand was the largest since 1922, and it was envisaged that the level would be maintained throughout 1947, although worrying signs were noted. Robin Rowell, the Chairman of Hawthorn–Leslie, took the view that 'it was disturbing . . . that virtually no deep sea ships of importance were being equipped to burn coal',[38] and there was also anxiety over the future of those yards which had formerly depended upon the production of tramp tonnage as their staple output.[39]

Indeed, there was a general feeling that the market trend was away from specialised, coal-fired tramp production and towards standardised, diesel-propelled, tanker production as the staple of the industry, with all the implications which this entailed for production methods and yard layouts. This allowed British shipbuilders to worry about and decry foreign competition at the same time. American methods of producing standardised ships in pre-fabricated sections, for example, had 'never . . . seriously disturbed or dismayed' British shipbuilders because 'their confidence born of assurance in the technical skills and craftsmanship, was never more justified than it is today by the present healthy state of the industry'.[40] Although German and European capacity was regarded as being 'out of the picture for many years to come',[41] when the SAC received a progress report on the dismantling of German capacity,[42] it reacted strongly with Murray Stephen declaring that the situation: 'confirmed the industry's worst fears in regard to demolition . . . as . . . practically nothing had been done to dismantle the German yards'.[43] Sir Amos Ayre stated that 'if the United Kingdom were to maintain its pre-eminence Germany could not be allowed to enter into competition' and the Committee took the view that representation should be made to the First Lord that 'it was of first importance for the British shipbuilding industry . . . that the steps for the demolition of the German yards should be carried out'.[44]

These two problems – shortage of material and the potential revival of foreign competition – continued to exercise the minds of shipbuilders and the SAC throughout 1947; and, consequently, began to concentrate the mind of government on the industry's problems. By the end of 1946 the SAC observed that output was some 200,000gt below the estimate for the year and that 'the shortage of materials might account for the difference'.[45] The two issues conjoined in a row over Italian shipbuilding which, as Sir Amos Ayre complained, was quoting prices less than the value of material used in the ships. The worry was that British steel exports were being used in the Italian industry at the same time as British producers were complaining of shortages. The SAC considered – and rejected – the reintroduction of the wartime system of export licensing but fearing that 'competition from Italian ship-builders might become serious', as it had been in the period between the two wars, 'recommended that steps be taken to prevent steel and other materials being exported to Italy'.[46] Sir Amos Ayre believed that foreign competition was 'emerging in a severe degree'[47] and that despite the strength of British order books 'we may not be very far off the time when competition of a very keen order will be experienced'.[48] Throughout the early months of the year the trade press was inundated with complaints concerning shortages of materials. Sir Murray Stephen complained that neither labour nor yard layout was the major problem in the industry but supplies of materials.[49] This was a theme echoed by Sir Robert Micklem, the Chairman of Vickers–Armstrong, and J. Ramsay Gebbie, the Chairman of the Wear Shipbuilders Association,[50] although the complaint was given an added political twist by the Anchor Line Chairman, Phillip Runciman, who widened the attack arguing that 'any decision to nationalise shipping would end it . . . and . . . might end the British Empire too',[51] and Sir Claude D. Gibb, who complained of 'a huge superstructure of planners being superimposed on the producing force'.[52]

Shortages of materials also began to affect costs and delivery dates. The industry received a singular shock when the Blythswood yard at Scotstoun lost a Norwegian tanker order to Sweden because of rising costs and inability to guarantee the delivery date.[53] By May, the SAC was noting that book orders stood at 3,500,000gt of new construction, of which planned annual production was 1,700,000gt, but that the estimated steel allocation would only allow construction of some 800,000gt per annum. The committee argued that the consequences of steel shortage would be: serious unemployment, late delivery dates leading to the cancellation and loss of orders particularly on the foreign account, a loss of exports, invisible exports and earnings, and a delay in the restoration of the domestic mercantile marine. The committee urged that ministers should bring the matter before the Prime Minister and Cabinet with a view to gaining a greater allocation of steel.[54]

The situation continued to deteriorate throughout the year. In May all shipbuilding regions complained of serious shortages of: steel, timber, paint, electrical components and machinery parts.[55] A. J. Mair, the Managing Director of Laing's and R. C. Thompson, the Managing Director of Joseph L. Thompson's, both of Sunderland, stated that British costs were well above those of Sweden. J. C. Nisbet, the Managing Director of the Tanfield Steamship Company of Newcastle, complained that 'shipbuilding costs were 200% above the pre war level' and Thompson further averred that 'we cannot give any forward delivery . . . so we cannot book further orders'.[56] J. Ramsay Gebbie noted that inadequate raw-material supplies to the company of which he was the managing director, Doxford's, meant that they were producing only 5.5 ships per annum instead of 10, despite the fact that the firm's order books were full for three years ahead.[57]

In this litany of complaint, shipbuilders and owners again focused their ire on the government. Sir Frederick Rebbeck, the Chairman of Harland and Wolff, complained that shipbuilders' programmes had been jeopardised by shortages which 'a Government priding itself apparently on planning, has signally failed to rectify'.[58] Sir James Lithgow, opined that the government was competing with industry for materials and labour, that 90 per cent of workers were 'letting the nation down'[59] and attacked the government as 'intellectual snobs and sentimental idealists' who lived on the prosperity of others.[60] This theme was taken up by H. M. Macmillan, the Chairman of the Blythswood Shipbuilding Company, who attributed rising costs to 'the vain men put into authority over us . . . who . . . had subjected the country to all sorts of nostrums which must – sooner or later – prove disastrous'.[61] Robin Rowell also complained of the 'stultefying effect of controls . . . and shortage of materials'[62] and Sir Maurice Denny summed up the general tone with reference to the Bible: 'The Israelites grumbled that they were expected to make bricks without straw, but they had only one shortage, they did not know how lucky they were'.[63]

The situation was presented to the SAC in a more formal manner, through a paper by Sir Amos Ayre, which argued that the targets for shipbuilding between June 1945 and June 1947 had been badly missed. The planned figure had been 1.50mgt whilst the actual figure amounted to 0.97mgt. The continuing state of shortage meant that the target figure for the year ending June 1948 of 1.7mgt might well amount to 1.1mgt and the calculated shortfall up to June 1948 was 0.97mgt. This shortfall had only been overcome by the addition to the UK register of some 1.88mgt in tonnage from the USA and via reparations. Ayre remained confident that material shortages were a short-term problem which would soon be solved and predicted that the desired level of the post-war fleet – 18mgt – would be achieved by June 1950. If this were to prove correct, he argued that there would be some fall in employment after June 1949, by which date it was possible that some new naval work would need to be commenced.[64]

By the close of the year, the Ministry of Transport was noting the 'growing conviction' in the ministry and at the Admiralty that a concrete plan needed to be developed for the industry. The memo stated that deliveries of all classes of merchant vessels were generally going back from nine to twelve months and sometimes longer. This was in part due to raw-material and steel shortage and partly to poor labour output. The paper took the line that the time being taken to build was now 'abnormal' and that this was the reason for high costs. By the end of 1948, it was possible that there would be a vast accumulation of orders and a progressively slower rate of production with costs rising accordingly, and as the memo made clear, 'we seem to be arriving at a point at which we ought to consider effective means of concentrating our capacity on the types of merchant ships which we need most or on building for the most desirable of our foreign clients'. It was observed that there was no system of priorities in the industry apart from raw-material allocation and the licensing system, although this was held to be useless as licences were issued automatically, as was stated: 'Anyone can place orders, but who can get satisfactory deliveries?' The memorandum favoured the reintroduction of the permit system which, by limiting the validity and only issuing licences in respect of keels which were to be built fairly soon, would keep orders on a reasonably short head, although the disadvantages of the scheme were seen as political objections from owners and builders.[65]

Despite the continuous complaints of the industry concerning steel shortages, figures released in 1948 showed it had fared reasonably well. Deliveries of steel had substantially exceeded allocations in 1947 and the position in 1946 had been similar. Despite this the new steel allocation for 1948 was attacked as 'deplorable' with all areas reporting rising costs, rising unemployment, further delays and falling orders.[66] In March, the Ellerman Line cancelled orders for six vessels because of costs and delivery dates[67] and the SAC responded by terming the situation as 'serious' and pointed out that the present allocation approximated to only 1mgt of new ships per annum, whereas during the war, with 60 per cent of the industry engaged on warship work, the merchant sector had still managed an output of 1mgt and had even exceeded this figure. The shortage of steel was causing long delays in

Table 10.2. Steel allocations and deliveries to the shipbuilding industry 1947.

	Allocations (Tons)	Deliveries (Tons)
1st quarter	204,100	215,468
2nd quarter	144,380	231,700
3rd quarter	191,110	220,103
4th quarter	190,620	248,681

Source: PRO BT199/4 Note by the Admiralty and Ministry of Transport February 1948.

the delivery of ships, with nine firms reporting that they were up to three months late, twenty-seven were six months late, seventeen were nine months late and thirteen anything from one year to eighteen months late. It was argued that this could 'bring about a critical condition in relation to foreign orders now on hand' and that 'many shipowners might cancel their contracts if faced with such a great delay in completion of their ships'. The total value of orders on hand was valued at £300 million, of which approximately £100 million was for export, and the feeling was that if this were to be lost then such a loss would be permanent and would simply represent an increase in competition from foreign builders.[68] The SAC position was supported by the Shipowners' Association and the Chamber of Shipping which petitioned the government to do something with respect to delivery dates and costs.[69]

The SAC was further agitated in the course of 1948 by a Board of Trade directive which targeted hard currency areas as the preferred destination for exports.[70] The implication of this for the industry was that the licensing system would be tightened up and the automatic issuing of licences halted. Vessels under 1,600 gross tons would not be affected but for larger vessels preference was given to tankers and dry-cargo vessels for British owners. Second preference was given to tankers for soft currency areas and third preference given to the USA, Canada, the Dollar Account area and the Argentine, where licences would be automatic provided full payment was made in the currency of the country concerned or in convertible sterling. Last preference was given to dry-cargo ships for soft-currency areas where licences would be difficult to obtain. Although this appeared surprising, given the relatively low priority given to the dollar area, it was a reflection of the huge capacity of the American yards and the prevailing nature of demand in British yards. The SAC, however, felt that this directive unnecessarily discriminated against those foreign owners who traditionally built in Britain and whose business would be transferred elsewhere and consequently appealed for a flexible application of the Board of Trade directive.[71]

The Labour Party was sufficiently worried about the condition of the shipbuilding industry in 1948 for the research department to produce a ninety-one-page analysis of the industry and its problems.[72] The report outlined the main problems of the industry as being: the bespoke nature of demand and the consequent fluctuations in building, the lack of any marketing strategy, geographical concentration and consequent problems of unemployment in periods of slump, demarcation consequent on fluctuations in employment and poor labour relations. The report proposed that a plan for the industry should have as its aim 'the securing of industrial efficiency and, as far as is possible, the maintenance of full employment'. Any plan had to produce a total annual capacity proportionate to the needs of the British merchant fleet and the export market, achieve a smooth flow of launchings to utilise maximum capacity, maintain stable employment and 'achieve . . . the highest standard of technical efficiency'. It was on this final issue that the report felt that financial assistance might well be necessary.[73] The report agreed with the consensus view of shipbuilders that 'the slump comes as surely as night follows day'[74] and advocated a detailed scheme which would eliminate redundant capacity in such a way that the remaining yards had sufficient work and avoid what had occurred between the wars. The shipbuilders themselves had failed to do this in the inter-war period:

> partly because they were largely occupied with the financial aspects of the case . . . paid . . . too little attention to questions of efficiency and unemployment . . . and . . . partly because firms could not be persuaded to abandon their individualistic attitude and forget their own particular interests in the interest of the industry as a whole. It would seem, today, that some form of nationalisation might best achieve that unification of the industry which is vital for the success of any attempt to draw up a plan for the industry as a whole . . . a scheme which embraces the entire industry is essential if any lasting prosperity is to be achieved.[75]

The report argued that new methods of construction, such as welding and prefabrication, required a complete reconstruction of the yards and that this could be best achieved via government finance and assistance.[76] Alternatives to nationalisation were considered but it was felt there was 'no . . . good reason . . . why the State should act as nurse maid to private enterprise when it is in trouble. It seems inevitable that a prosperous shipbuilding industry will require heavy expenditure and it is very doubtful whether the industry is willing and or able to undertake this'.[77] By the end of 1948 the party's research department was advocating nationalisation and the party was considering nationalisation of the industry for inclusion in its next manifesto.

Some of the issues which had worried both the party and the

government were aired in the Report by the Shipbuilding Costs Committee.[78] This inquiry was established in 1946 to examine the reasons for the rise in costs in British shipbuilding since the war. Its main conclusions were that the industry, as an assembly industry, bore the end cost of the complete equipment used in the building of a ship. The standardisation of certain details in construction was already extensive and there was no demand for standard types as the vast majority of UK building was for special trades. There had been a steady and continuous rise in the cost of all classes of ships since 1945 and that this was due in the main to a rise in raw material and component prices and increased wages, a position which had been badly exacerbated by shortages of materials. The committee argued that variations in cost could be reduced to a minimum if a range of conditions were met: there should be a steady demand for ships, steel and other materials should be freely obtainable on normal delivery terms at stable prices, the practice of subcontracting for supplies under fixed contract prices should be restored and the industry should be free of labour troubles.[79]

The original intention of the inquiry had been that the Minister of Transport should have a series of talks with shipowners over costs, but Sir Cyril Hurcomb, the Shipbuilding Committee Chairman, had discouraged, indeed 'did his best to prevent the Minister from taking a very active part in the matter' on the grounds that the issue was of private concern between shipowners and builders.[80]

> The shipbuilders then did their utmost to influence the terms of reference of the Committee as to make it ineffectual in dealing with the two principle matters with which the Minister was most concerned, namely, why were shipbuilding costs so much higher than pre-war and what was the level of costs to make it possible for our shipbuilders to compete with the foreigner? In the end, it was agreed that the Committee would have nothing to do with the total price of ships, but would confine their consideration to why costs vary from one yard to another in this country. They were precluded from taking into account shipbuilder's profits and the Ministry was very careful to stand aside from their activities and to avoid being drawn in as witnesses for the Committee.[81]

The end result had been 'a very non-controversial report' which provided 'no useful recommendations on which action could be taken'.[82] The committee, dominated by shipbuilders, and taking evidence from shipbuilders, concluded that there was nothing wrong with the geographical layout of the yards, nor with the management, financial strength or rate of modernisation of the industry. The Ministry of Transport summed up the report:

> there is nothing wrong with the industry that increased supplies of materials, fixed quotations from the sub-contractors and increased

output from labour will not cure. The pronouncements are stated as conclusions but the Committee make little or no attempt to illustrate the evidence from which they draw their conclusions . . . the Report offers little help in determining whether shipbuilding costs are right or wrong or whether the industry is in need of overhaul or not. It neither calls for nor suggests further action.[83]

So useless was the report in the ministry's view that 'the best thing to do . . . was to . . . find some way of burying it'.[84]

The SAC and the trade press, however, continued to complain about the revival of foreign competition. Concern was voiced over this issue with the SAC noting the revival of Scandinavian building and the fact that prices were lower in Sweden, Denmark and Norway.[85] The main worry, however, was the revival of German and Japanese shipbuilding,[86] a fact which the trade press also bemoaned. Sir Murray Stephen took four days in the *Glasgow Herald* to rail against German shipbuilding,[87] and Robin Rowell also lamented the situation in *Lloyd's List Annual Review*.[88] Speaking at a launching on the Clyde, Stephen declared that 'there . . . were . . . plenty of shipyards in the world without those of Germany, to supply the needs of world shipping and there is no reason why they should be allowed to put us in danger again',[89] and addressing the Glasgow Rotary Club in April, termed German and Japanese competition as 'unfair'.[90]

The issue of foreign competition came to a head in 1951 when the government accepted a proposal by the Dutch government that shipbuilding should be liberalised. What this meant was that the system of permits and licensing would end and that henceforth no permission needed to be sought for the building of a ship in, or from, any country to which the liberalisation measures applied. The decision split the SAC, with the shipbuilding representatives arguing that liberalisation would open up British shipbuilding to unfair competition, but the shipowners arguing that they were anxious to 'receive the benefit of current world prices'.[91] This provoked a renewed round of complaints from ship-builders. Sir John Boyd noted that in the second quarter of 1951 the total tonnage commenced by Germany and Japan exceeded that begun in the UK and that they 'were very quickly resuming their former places as competitors of the UK'.[92] The trade press also renewed its criticisms. *Shipbuilding and Shipping Record* argued that the aim of the Japanese government was the removal of all trade restrictions and controls on shipping and shipbuilders; and added that the cost differential between British and Japanese yards was now down to 6 per cent.[93] In response to this the SAC resolved to 'request H M Government to ensure that the interests of the British shipbuilding are safeguarded in this respect'.[94]

Following the appearance of the Labour Party research department report, the government had to decide whether or not to nationalise the industry. Pressure for nationalisation was eased as a report to the Production Committee showed the industry with over 4 mgt on its order books and estimated completions in 1949, 1950 and 1951 of 1.1, 1.15 and 1.2mgt respectively. On this basis the report argued that the immediate position of the industry was reasonably secure; that any extension of control would simply deter shipowners from ordering, and that whilst high costs and late delivery dates remained problems, it was 'of the utmost importance . . . not to come to the assistance of the industry too early and thereby interfere with the powerful incentive to reduce the prices of new ships . . .'[95] Serious foreign competition was expected in the longer term but there was no reason why UK output between 1952 and 1960 should not reach 1mgt annually by which stage naval building could be taking up any slack which appeared in merchant building.[96] Furthermore, a working party on the industry reported to the Cabinet in May 1950 that various means of assistance to the industry – closer co-operation between builders and owners, alternative work in the shipyards, taxation relief and scrap and build – had been considered but were rejected as inadequate.[97]

In May 1950, the Cabinet also had before it a paper by the President of the Board of Trade on 'The State and Private Industry'[98] where Harold Wilson described the relations between the government and private industry as 'a vacuum in our thinking'. He advocated Development Councils as 'an acceptable alternative to nationalisation' in the belief that this would bring 'some degree of settlement to particular sections of industry . . . and . . . sharpen industry's appreciation of its public responsibilities'.[99] Wilson specifically called for the production of standard ships and argued that 'the shipbuilding industry represents the biggest menace to our full-employment policy'.[100] These suggestions were not well received by the shipbuilders and the announcement in *Labour Believes in Britain* that a Development Council would be established for shipbuilding provoked predictable anger. George Barr commented that: 'it would be a tragedy for British shipbuilding if State ownership was accepted as a solution to its future problems . . . it would mean doom for a great industry'.[101] Lord Rotherwick, chairman of the Greenock Dockyard Company, attacked nationalisation as 'a vast patronage business . . . filled by the Government with their own socialist followers, who are generally inefficient',[102] and, Sir Murray Stephen stated that, if nationalised, the industry 'would lose a large part of its work at one stroke'.[103] *Shipbuilder and Marine Engineer* declared on the eve of the 1950 general election that 'it would be advantageous if the present opposition were to gain seats' in the shipbuilding areas so that the 'voice of private industry' could be heard.[104]

Harold Wilson had expressly argued for the idea of the mixed economy on the grounds that it was, 'correct for us to turn the attack we are now

getting on our nationalised industries back on to the appropriate sections
of private industry',[105] but the position with regard to shipbuilding
remained unclear. As an internal Labour Party paper stated, the expected
slump 'which formed the basis of many of the arguments both for and
against public ownership has not materialised', order books were full,
and 'as yet no steps have been taken publicly to set up a Development
Council for the industry'.[106] This remained the position when the party
lost the 1951 general election. The ultimate irony came when *Shipbuilder
and Marine Engineer* reported on a booklet by the Northern Area of the
Conservative Association which outlined Conservative policy towards
the industry:

> This advocates some form of control, to ensure a distribution of
> orders that would maintain steady employment, a reduction in
> taxation to permit shipbuilding profits to be adequately 'ploughed
> back'; and financial encouragement to shipowners to permit the
> replacement of fleets over a period of 20 years. The document has
> met with the approval of shipowners and shipbuilders, although the
> advocacy of control has not escaped criticism.[107]

In other words, the industry was willing to accept measures of state
intervention from a Conservative government which it had been
unwilling to accept from a Labour government.

CONCLUSIONS

The relationship between the Labour government and the shipbuilding
industry fits neatly into what Arnold Rogow has termed a system of
'business in government'.[108] Rogow has noted that the 1945–51
governments' industrial planning machinery was essentially a carry-over
from the war and that whilst this was understandable it presented the
government with grave problems. In essence it meant that private
industrialists and businessmen were charged with planning and
controlling their own industries. As *The Economist* commented: 'The
great defect of collectivism . . . is not that the bureaucrats will control
industry; it is that they will *not* control it but cede their duty to the
private monopolists'.[109] As has been amply demonstrated in the foregoing
sections what almost all shipbuilders sought was a complete end to any
form of government intervention in the shipbuilding industry. The
Shipbuilding Advisory Committee, therefore, limited its activity to
complaining about what builders saw as the major problems of the
industry – costs and foreign competition – without ever widening the
scope of its considerations. These criticisms in themselves were always
centred in politics – rising prices, be they for steel, coal, labour, timber
or components, material and/or labour shortages and the re-emergence
of German and Japanese shipbuilding – were the sole fault of the Labour

government and its ideological convictions and had nothing to do with endogenous or exogenous factors.

This situation left the government with serious problems as to what should be done with respect to the industry. In this sense the SAC was less than useless, concentrating its energies on the maximisation of output – and by extension profits[110] – to the exclusion of all else. The industry was schizoid with respect to the future. It recognised that foreign competition was based on new production methods, particularly pre-fabrication and welding, which were in turn related to new types of vessel, where the change in the nature of demand, away from coal-fired tramp tonnage or specialised vessels, towards diesel-fired standardised tonnage (particularly tankers and dry-cargo vessels) was apparent. Yet, as the inquiry into shipbuilding costs revealed, the shipbuilders refuted the suggestion that there was anything wrong with the industry. It was no accident that once the period of replacement building – where the priority was for vessels almost without reference to cost – was over; and the industry liberalised internationally, that the bespoke nature of demand in the UK broke down and the industry began to feel the full impact of competition. With the British yards reluctant to change to more capital-intensive methods of production, and the industry's dominant figures unwilling to face any weakening of personal control, the industry was locked into a vicious cycle of its own making.

There is little doubt that had Labour won the 1951 election a Development Cpuncil would have been established for the industry. The question of whether this, or full-scale nationalisation, would have made any difference to the short-, medium- or long-term performance of the industry must be rhetorical. The quandary for the Labour government was what a democratically elected socialist party, committed to industrial planning, was to do with an industry which resolutely opposed everything which the government wished to do with the industry? Certainly there seemed to be little future in either industrial self-government, or the 'business in government' system; as Thomas Balogh commented:

> controls are almost indistinguishable from cartels. Controls which might encourage efficiency go by the board. 'Volunteerism' – the self-control of vested interests by voluntary compacts – which is . . . a muddled concept is encouraged. What can the result be but sluggish vegetation . . .[111]

As a demonstration of the efficacy of private industry, shipbuilding was a disaster.

APPENDIX 10.1

The aim of this appendix is to provide some detail on the pre-1940 careers of those individuals involved in the control of the industry via

the Shipbuilding Committee and the Shipbuilding Advisory Committee.
If the various criticisms cited in the conclusion of this essay concerning
industrial self government and the business in government system are
correct it also seems incumbent to point out that such a system was of an
earlier origin. One of the most interesting aspects of the industry was the
longevity of the personnel. A substantial number of those individuals
who were responsible for control during and after the Second World
War had been involved in the business in government system of the First
World War and the self government and rationalisation process of the
inter-war period. Whether this represented tapping the best available
expertise with respect to the industry or was an encouragement, in
Balogh's phrase, to 'sluggish vegetation' is an open question but it does
seem unlikely that men with the clear political stamp of Cunningham
and Lithgow would ever be sympathetic to state intervention, particularly
from a Labour government.

The appendix provides details of the pre-war and wartime careers of
the membership of the Shipbuilding Committee.

The Shipbuilding Committee, 1944–1945

Chairman

Sir Cyril Hurcomb	Ministry of Shipping, 1915–18; Permanent Secretary, Ministry of Transport, 1927–37; Director General, Ministry of Shipping, 1939–41 and Director General, Ministry of War Transport, 1941–7.

Representing the First Lord of the Admiralty

Sir James Lithgow	Chairman of Lithgow's Group; Director of Shipbuilding Production, 1917; President of the Clyde Shipbuilders Association, 1908; the Shipbuilder's Employers' Federation, 1922; The British Employers' Federation, 1924 and the Federation of British Industries, 1930–2. Member of the Board of the Admiralty and Controller of Merchant Shipbuilding and Repairs, 1940–6.
E. A. Seal	Board of the Admiralty since 1925; PPS to the First Lord, 1938–40; PPS to the Prime Minister, 1940–1; Deputy Secretary of the Admiralty, 1941–3 and Under Secretary of the Admiralty, 1943–5.

Representing the Minister of War Production

Sir Vernon Thompson	Chairman and Managing Director of the Union Castle Steam-Ship Company Ltd; Ministry of Shipping, 1918–21; Chairman of the Tramp Shipping Subsidy Committee and Tramp Shipping Administrative Committee, 1935–7; President of the Chamber of Shipping, 1936–7; Member of the Committee of Lloyds Register of Shipping from 1927; Principal Shipping Adviser and Controller of Commercial Shipping, Ministry of Shipping and War Transport, 1939–46.
G. C. Duggan	Ministry of War Transport.

Representing the Shipbuilders

Sir Amos Ayre	Chairman of the Burntisland Shipbuilding Company until 1936; District Director Shipbuilding (Scotland) at the Admiralty, 1914–18; President National Confederation of Employers Organisation, 1934; Chairman until 1939 of the Board of Trade Advisory Committee on Merchant Shipping and Director of Merchant Shipbuilding at the Admiralty, 1940–6.
Murray Stephen	Managing Director of Stephen's and Co.; Board of National Shipbuilder's Security Ltd, 1931–9; President of the Clyde Shipbuilder's Association, 1937; the Shipbuilding Employer's Federation, 1938–9 and the Shipbuilding Conference, 1941–8.

Representing the Shipowners

Sir John Hobhouse	Director of the Ocean Steamship Company of Liverpool, Partner in Alfred Holt and Co., and Director of the Royal Insurance Company; Deputy Regional Commissioner for the North West, 1939–40; Chief Shipping Representative for the North West in the Ministry of War Transport, 1941–5; Chairman of the Liverpool Steam Ship Owners' Association, 1941–2 and the General Council of British Shipping,

	1942–3; sat on both the Shipbuilding Committee and the Shipbuilding Advisory Committee during the period of office of the 1945–51 Labour government.
W. G. Ropner	Director of Ropner's; Deputy Director of Ship Management Division and Head of the Convoy Section, Ministry of Shipping, 1939–45; President of the Chamber of Shipping and Chairman of the General Council of British Shipping, 1950.

Representing the Shipyard Operatives

Mark Hodgson	Technical Advisor to the Admiralty, 1916–18; General Secretary, the United Society of Boilermakers, 1936–48; President of the Confederation of Ship-building and Engineering Unions, 1943–5 and 1947–8; Member of the National Production Advisory Council for Industry, 1945–65 and Chairman of the Northern Regional Board for Industry, 1945–65.
J. W. Stephenson	

The Shipbuilding Advisory Committee, 1946–1951

Chairman

Sir Graham Cunningham	Chief Executive and Controller General of Munitions Production at the Ministry of Supply, 1941–6 and member of the Economic Planning Board from 1947. Although nominally 'independent' Cunningham was on the Council of the right-wing industrial ginger-group Aims of Industry and as such could hardly be expected to be very sympathetic to the broad thrust of Labour's industrial policy. See Labour Party Archive, GS/IND/2/vii.

Representing the Shipbuilders

Sir Amos Ayre	See Shipbuilding Committee above.
Sir Murray Stephen	See Shipbuilding Committee above.
Sir John Boyd	Vice President of the Shipbuilding Employer's Federation, 1931–6 and

	member of the Admiralty Central Committee on the Essential Work Order, 1941–5.
George Borrie	Barclay Curle and Co.; Senior Vice President of the Shipbuilding Employer's Federation.
Thomas Morrison	President of the Shipbuilding Employer's Federation.

Representing the Shipowners

| Sir John Hobhouse | See Shipbuilding Committee above. |
| Sir Guy Ropner | See Shipbuilding Committee above. |

Representing the Trades Unions

Sir Mark Hodgson	See Shipbuilding Committee above.
Gavin Martin	General Secretary of the Confederation of Shipbuilding and Engineering Unions.
H. N. Harrison	President of the National Union of General and Municipal Workers.
Stanley Jones	National Union of Seamen.

Representing the Admiralty

Vice Admiral C. S. Daniel
C. B. Coxwell

Representing the Ministry of War Transport
R. H. Keenlyside
J. M. Glen

NOTES

1. Material from this paper was first presented at 'The 1945–51 Labour Government and Private Industry Conference', in September 1990, held under the auspices of the Business History Unit at the London School of Economics. I should like to thank the conference organisers, Helen Mercer, Neil Rollings and Jim Tomlinson and the conference participants for comments. Thanks also to Nick Tiratsoo and especially to Patricia Vass who rendered an incoherent text manageable. All errors remain my own.
2. Labour Party Archives, National Labour History Museum, Manchester (hereafter LPA) R.D./146 'Shipbuilding' September 1948 1.
3. Ibid. p. 1; see also J. R. Parkinson 'Shipbuilding' in D. H. Aldcroft and N. K. Buxton eds. *British Industry Between The Wars* (1982 edn) pp. 79–102.
4. J. R. Parkinson *The Economics of Shipbuilding in the United Kingdom* (Cambridge, 1960) pp. 22–6.
5. A. Slaven, 'Management and Shipbuilding, 1890–1938: Structure and Strategy in the Shipbuilding Firm on the Clyde' in A. Slaven and D. H. Aldcroft eds. *Business, Banking and Urban History* (Edinburgh, 1982) pp. 35–53. The analysis of the structure of the industry draws heavily from this work.

6. 'Sir Maurice Denny' in A. Slaven and S. Checkland eds. *The Scottish Dictionary of Business Biography* (Aberdeen, 1986) pp. 212–14.
7. LPA, R.D./146, 'Shipbuilding' p. 12.
8. C. Barnett *The Audit of War* (1987 edn) pp. 121–2.
9. Parkinson op. cit. p. 165.
10. M. M. Postan *British War Production* (1952) Table 29, pp. 295 and 300–3.
11. Ibid.
12. Public Record Office, Kew (hereafter PRO) ADM1/11892 Labour in Naval and Mercantile Shipyards (Barlow Report) July 1942 and PRO BT28/319 Report to the Machine Tool Controller on the Equipment of Shipyards and Marine Engineering Shops (Bentham Report) September 1942.
13. PRO ADM1/11892 'Barlow Report' July 1942.
14. PRO BT28/319 'Bentham Report' September 1942.
15. PRO ADM1/12506 'Report of the Shipyard Development Committee' August 1943.
16. PRO MT9/3648 'Notes of an informal discussion between representatives of the shipbuilding and shiprepairing industries, the Admiralty and the Ministry of War Transport, on post war problems' 12/10/1942.
17. PRO CAB24/207 Memo by the First Lord of the Admiralty (A. V. Alexander) 'Shipbuilding Industry: Relationship with Government after the War' April 1944.
18. PRO ADM1/17037 Memo by the Minister of War Transport (Lord Leathers) 'Shipbuilding'. See also the memo by the Under-Secretary of the Post War Shipbuilding Committee (E. A. Seal) advocating continued control of the industry by the Admiralty 13/5/1944.
19. PRO MT9/3956 'Notes of a meeting held at the Admiralty to discuss the Government's scheme for the Shipbuilding Industry' 16/11/1944.
20. The joint proposal began as separate schemes advanced by Alexander and Leathers. See PRO CAB87/7 Memo by the First Lord of the Admiralty (Alexander) 'The Shipbuilding Industry 17/3/1944 and ADM1/17037 Memo by the Minister of War Transport (Leathers) 'Shipbuilding' 3/5/1944. These proposals were subsequently modified; see PRO MT9/3956 Report by E. A. Seal on 'The Post War Shipbuilding Committee' 12/5/1944; PRO ADM1/17037 Note by E. A. Seal on 'Lord Leathers' memorandum' 13/5/1944; PRO MT79/3956 Discussion of 'Report by the Post War Shipbuilding Committee' 15/6/1944; PRO CAB124/207 unsigned memo on 'The Shipbuilding Industry' July 1944; Memo by J. Jewkes on 'The Shipbuilding Industry' 10/7/1944 and Memo by C. H. Wilson on 'The Shipbuilding Industry' 8/7/1944. In August 1944, Alexander wrote to Leathers, that: 'it is becoming urgently necessary for the Government to take a decision in this matter . . . as . . . it is no use leaving the shipbuilding industry to drag on as it was left after the last war' and advocating a joint stance; PRO MT79/3956 Letter from Alexander to Leathers 29/8/1944; see also PRO ADM1/17037, Note by the Minister of War Transport and the First Lord of the Admiralty, 'Post War Prospects of British Shipbuilding', September 1944.
21. PRO MT9/3848 Note by the Minister of War Transport and the First Lord of the Admiralty, 'Post War Prospects of British Shipbuilding' September 1944.
22. PRO MT9/3956 'Shipbuilding Comittee' 29/11/1944. See Appendix 10.1.
23. PRO ADM1/19104 Memo initialled J. L. 'Shipbuilding' 12/11/1945.
24. PRO MT73/2 'Final Report of the Shipbuilding Committee' March 1946.
25. *Shipbuilder and Marine Engineer*, September 1945.
26. PRO ADM1/19104 Letter from A. V. Alexander to A. Barnes 'Prospects of Shipbuilding in the UK' 21/11/1945.
27. PRO CAB124/208 Memo initialled TMN 'Shipbuilding Industry' 16/1/1946.
28. PRO CAB124/208 Memo by N. Watts 'The Shipbuilding Industry' 22/2/1946.
29. PRO CAB124/208 Memo initialled TMN 'Shipbuilding Industry' 16/1/1946.
30. PRO BT199/1 'The Shipbuilding Advisory Committee' June 1946. See

Appendix 10.1.

31. PRO BT199/1 'Shipbuilding Advisory Committee' Second Meeting July 1946.
32. PRO BT199/1 'Shipbuilding Advisory Committee' Fifth Meeting November 1946.
33. *Shipbuilder and Marine Engineer*, March 1946.
34. *Shipbuilder and Marine Engineer*, March, August, September and November 1946.
35. *Shipbuilder and Marine Engineer*, June 1946.
36. *Shipbuilder and Marine Engineer*, January 1946.
37. *Shipbuilder and Marine Engineer*, February 1946.
38. Quoted in *Shipbuilder and Marine Engineer*, November 1946.
39. *Shipbuilder and Marine Engineer*, January 1946.
40. *Shipbuilder and Marine Engineer*, April 1946.
41. *Shipbuilder and Marine Engineer*, January 1946.
42. PRO LAB8/1086 Memo by C. B. Coxwell 'German Shipbuilding' October 1946.
43. PRO BT199/1 'Shipbuilding Advisory Committee' Fourth Meeting October 1946.
44. Ibid.
45. PRO BT199/1 'Shipbuilding Advisory Committee', Fifth Meeting November 1946.
46. PRO BT199/1 'Shipbuilding Advisory Committee' Sixth Meeting January 1947.
47. *The Glasgow Herald* 18/1/1947.
48. *The Journal of Commerce* 20/11/1946.
49. *Shipbuilder and Marine Engineer*, January 1947.
50. *Shipbuilder and Marine Engineer*, March 1947.
51. *Shipbuilder and Marine Engineer*, April 1947.
52. *Shipbuilder and Marine Engineer*, January 1947.
53. *Shipbuilder and Marine Engineer*, February 1947.
54. PRO BT199/1 'Shipbuilding Advisory Committee' Eighth Meeting May 1947.
55. *Shipbuilder and Marine Engineer*, May 1947.
56. Ibid.
57. *Shipbuilder and Marine Engineer*, June 1947.
58. *Shipbuilder and Marine Engineer*, July 1947.
59. *Shipbuilder and Marine Engineer*, September 1947.
60. *Shipbuilder and Marine Engineer*, October 1947.
61. *Shipbuilder and Marine Engineer*, October 1947.
62. *Shipbuilder and Marine Engineer*, November 1947.
63. *Shipbuilder and Marine Engineer*, December 1947.
64. PRO BT199/4 Memo by Sir Amos Ayre 'Estimated Order of Possible Restoration of UK Mercantile Marine to 18.5m tons', 31/10/1947; see also PRO BT199/1 'Shipbuilding Advisory Committee' Tenth Meeting November 1947.
65. PRO MT73/96 Note by J. Nance 'On the desirability of re-introducing the permit system or a modification of that system', 6/12/1947.
66. *Shipbuilder and Marine Engineer*, January, February and March 1948.
67. *Shipbuilder and Marine Engineer*, February 1948.
68. PRO BT199/1 'Shipbuilding Advisory Committee' Eleventh Meeting February 1948.
69. PRO CAB124/522 'Correspondence from the Shipowners' Associations on the post war shipping position' February 1948.
70. PRO MT73/96 Statement by Harold Wilson 'Hard and Soft Currencies' 19/1/1948.
71. PRO BT199/1 'Shipbuilding Advisory Committee' Fourteenth Meeting September 1948.
72. LPA R.D./146 'Shipbuilding' September 1948.

73. Ibid. p. 52.
74. Sir R. Johnson, Chairman of Cammell Laird and Co. quoted – ibid. p. 53.
75. LPA R.D./146 'Shipbuilding' p. 54.
76. Ibid. pp. 53–5.
77. Ibid. pp. 56–7.
78. PRO MT73/9 'Report of the Shipbuilding Costs Committee' July 1949.
79. Ibid.
80. PRO MT73/9 Letter from M. Custance (Ministry of Transport) to N. A. Guttery (Admiralty) 2/12/1949.
81. Ibid.
82. Ibid.
83. PRO MT73/9 Memo by M. Custance 19/7/1949.
84. PRO MT73/9 Letter from M. Custance to N. A. Guttery 2/12/1949.
85. PRO BT199/1 'Shipbuilding Advisory Committee' Sixteenth and Seventeenth Meetings March and May 1949.
86. Ibid.
87. Sir Murray Stephen 'Revival of Shipbuilding in German Yards' *Glasgow Herald* 13, 14, 17 and 18 October 1949.
88. H. B. Robin Rowell 'Shipbuilding: A Challenging Position', *Lloyds List Annual Review*, 30/12/1949.
89. Quoted in *Shipbuilder and Marine Engineer*, January 1949.
90. Quoted in *Shipbuilder and Marine Engineer*, April 1949.
91. PRO BT199/1 'Shipbuilding Advisory Committee' Twenty Fourth Meeting March 1951.
92. PRO BT199/1 'Shipbuilding Advisory Committee' Twenty Fifth Meeting August 1951.
93. *Shipbuilding and Shipping Record*, 23/11/1950, pp. 497–8.
94. PRO BT199/1 'Shipbuilding Advisory Committee', Twenty Fourth Meeting March 1951.
95. PRO MT73/178 Memo by the First Lord of the Admiralty and Minister of Transport 'The Future of the Shipbuilding and Shiprepairing Industries' 1/7/1949.
96. Ibid.
97. PRO CAB134/646 'Report of the Working Party on the future Level of Shipbuilding and Shiprepairing Industries' May 1950.
98. PRO PREM8/1183 Memo by the President of the Board of Trade (H. Wilson) 'The State and Private Industry' 4/5/1950.
99. PRO PREM8/1183 'Personal covering note to the memorandum' May 1950.
100. PRO PREM8/1183 op. cit. p. 12.
101. *Shipbuilder and Marine Engineer*, August 1949.
102. *Shipbuilder and Marine Engineer*, October 1949.
103. *Shipbuilder and Marine Engineer*, December 1949.
104. *Shipbuilder and Marine Engineer*, February 1950.
105. PRO PREM8/1183 'Personal covering note to the memorandum' May 1950.
106. LPA GS/IMO/10/ii R/27 'Conference Resolution on Shipbuilding' January 1951.
107. *Shipbuilder and Marine Engineer*, October 1951.
108. A. A. Rogow 'Relations between the Labour Government and Industry' *Journal of Politics* Vol. 16 No. 1 1954.
109. Quoted in ibid. p. 12.
110. No attempt has been here made to calculate profit levels for the industry. The complaint that it was crippled by taxation and short of capital is, however, rather undercut by some sketchy evidence on final dividend payments. John Brown's paid final dividends, free of tax, of 10 per cent each year between 1942 and 1945. R. W. and Hawthorne Leslie paid 15 per cent, less tax, between 1941 and 1945 and for 1946–7 announced record

profits and a dividend of 21 per cent. Swan Hunter and Wigham Richardson paid 12 per cent tax free for 1944–5 and 16 per cent for 1946–7. Denny's in 1945 paid 17.25 per cent less tax. Yarrow's in 1944, 15 per cent tax free; Cammell Laird in 1946 15.5 per cent; Burntisland 15 per cent less tax in 1946 and Stephen's for the two years 1945–7 18 per cent less tax in both years. See *Shipbuilder and Marine Engineer*, January, April, June and December 1945 and June, July, October and November 1947.

111. Quoted in Rogow op. cit. pp. 22–3.

Eleven

The film industry

NICHOLAS PRONAY

The incoming Labour government of 1945 took over responsibility for an industry which had had an appalling record for over twenty years. Having made a flying start in 1896 and built up a large home market and not inconsiderable exports, it all but collapsed when it came into open competition with the American film industry after the First World War. By the end of 1924, the last of the major British film studios had gone out of business, not a single full-length feature film was in the course of production, and more than nine out of ten films seen by British people in British cinemas were no longer British but predominantly American.

Faced with these facts Parliament passed the 1927 Cinematograph Films Act which compelled cinema owners to show a certain number of British feature films each year, thus restricting the number of imported films which could be shown, and defined 'British films' in terms of the nationality status of the creative personnel employed and of the location of the production studio. The Act was introduced with great reluctance by the Conservative government of Stanley Baldwin as it breached the commitment to free trade. The reasons were not principally economic but political. As it had been put in Parliament already in 1918, the fledgling medium of film was seen by the ruling circles as 'this modern, up-to-date educational engine . . . perhaps the most valuable means of propaganda'.[1]

This perception of film which led to the Cinematographic Films Act of 1927 remained the justification for continuing and indeed extending state intervention in the film industry throughout the Conservative period to such an extent that by the time Labour came into office film was a 'private-sector industry' only in a limited sense. Politically, a degree of ideological, political and 'moral' content – control through the British Board of Film Censors, unthinkable for the press or publishing, was built up and overt and covert sponsorship for the production of ideologically suitable films was also practised.[2] Economically, protection through the quota was extended in 1938, the MacDonald and Baldwin governments exerted pressure for directing private capital into favoured studios, especially Alexander Korda's London Films producing prestige epics,[3] and when over £3 million had been lost and further 'encouraged' private investment dried up, the establishment of a film-bank came to be under active consideration during the Chamberlain administration. This combination of political and economic concerns and measures can be said to have made the film industry an early example (for better and worse) of the mixture of public- and private-initiative approach well before it became Labour policy.

During the wartime Coalition government the immediate responsibility for the film industry passed to Hugh Dalton, as President of the Board of Trade. In 1943 the Palache Committee, commissioned by Dalton to make recommendations for post-war policy concerning the film industry widened this perception further:

> A cinematograph film represents something more than a commodity to be bartered against others. Already the screen has great influence both politically and culturally over the minds of the people. Its potentialities are vast, as a vehicle for the expression of national life, ideals and tradition, a dramatic and artistic medium and as an instrument of propaganda.[4]

Much the same perception as the politician's and the civil servants' coloured the views of the progressive left and the intellectuals. In 1947 Ivor Montagu encapsulated the views of these influential voices during the Labour period:

> Is it conceivable that if the cinema had been invented even as late as broadcasting – cinema with its infinite possibilities for national education, national expression, international get-to-know-each-other – it would ever have been allowed to get into the largely foreign and exclusively profit-interested stranglehold that grips it now?[5]

It had been hoped that by compelling cinemas to give over a proportion of their programme time to British films a secure market-share would be created for British studios. This would attract, with perhaps some initial pressure, private investment in British film production enabling British film-producers to improve the standards and market appeal of their films. Eventually a British film industry would develop which could:

a) compete with Hollywood in market appeal,

b) project 'British' (establishment) values and ethos at home,

c) provide prestige films for British cultural propaganda in the empire and abroad.

It was, however, the incompatibility between these aims which made the British film industry a perennial lame duck. Using the evidence of box-office returns, surveys and the observations of contemporaries, social historians of British film have shown that the British working-class cinemagoers, the largest part of the cinema-audience, preferred the Hollywood 'dream factory' product because they found their *personal* aspirations more reflected in it, despite, as Peter Stead put it, the 'strange accents set in exotic surroundings', than in those produced in

Britain.[6] It would have been perfectly possible to aim for building up a British film industry with wide market appeal to provide employment and contribute to rather than drain the exchequer – provided it was left free to produce Hollywood clones in terms of the cultural and social ethos which the films 'projected'. It would have been possible, in addition, to have a small but viable 'niche' film industry producing films with 'British themes', provided they drew on British *popular* culture, the traditions principally of the music hall, the seaside theatres and working men's clubs – as the success of the George Formby and Gracie Fields musicals, the Ealing comedies, the Hammer horrors and the *Carry On* films showed. To meet the needs of 'cultural propaganda' by producing high-budget prestige films, costume dramas of suitable incidents of British history, film versions of British literary classics and high-brow film-as-art productions, would have required facing up to the necessity for direct state subsidies for such films, just as for other cultural propaganda activities, such as the British Council. Other countries, such as France, operated such policies in peacetime and to an extent this was practised also in Britain during the Second World War, in both cases with a measure of success.[7] The problem to which no answer had been found through the Quota Acts down to 1945 was how to kill two birds with one stone: establish an industry which produced films which were popular and was thus commercially viable *and* one which projected the values and ethos of the cultural and political establishments of Britain.

There was also another unresolved contradiction in the policies which had been applied since 1927. There were in fact not one but two industries with conflicting interests. On the one hand, Britain had a highly developed and successful *cinema* industry. By 1939, over 4,500 cinemas had been built and the habit of going to the cinema once a week or more often had been established amongst 40 per cent of the population: the largest ratio of seats and customers per head of population in the world. By 1945 the *cinema* industry brought in £40.8 million in tax revenue and employed some 80,000 people[8] – albeit, as people preferred Hollywood films, at the cost of adding 4 per cent on average to the deficit of British trade with the United States.[9] On the other hand, there was the *film* industry, with under 10,000 employees and little economic significance. Any drastic step for cutting off the importation of American films in order to build up home production could have spelled ruin for the part of the industry which was successful and revenue generating. The policies of the 1930s had not, in fact, faced up to having to deal with two industries with conflicting needs.

In coming into power the Labour government had thus inherited from the Conservatives a muddled and largely ineffective policy for dealing with the problems of the film industry. Paradoxically, however, it also inherited a well-established, bipartisan policy of extensive state intervention. From its own side the Labour government had inherited the belief, common amongst a coalition of broadly left-oriented people with varied concerns about film, that the root of the problem lay in 'monopoly capitalist conditions' prevailing in the industry.[10] This group included most of those who could be termed the 'labour intelligentsia' and came to include (at least as far as rhetoric was concerned) both Sir Stafford Cripps and Harold Wilson, the two central figures in the Labour government's policies towards the film industry.

To understand the twists and turns of Labour policy we must first therefore look at the arguments about 'monopolistic tendencies'. The maximum claim which could be made for the extent of the concentration was that the Rank and Associated British Picture Corporation (ABPC) circuits accounted for 25 per cent of cinemas and 30 per cent of cinema seats *between* them, and this only in 1943 when a number of the small one-man cinemas were closed owing to the war. The Palache Report stated that, 'We understand the phrase "Development of Monopoly" in the President's letter to refer to tendencies which appear to threaten the future prospects of an independent and unfettered British Film Industry. By independent we have in mind both freedom from foreign domination and freedom from dominating British control.'[11] In 1950 when the number of cinemas stood at 4,660, the Rank Corporation controlled 570 or 12.23 per cent and ABPC, 450 or 9.65 per cent. In terms of simple numbers a situation where two *competing* companies own respectively around 13 per cent and 10 per cent of the outlets can scarcely qualify as monopoly conditions for producers. Nor were these two companies large fishes in a tank of minnows. By 1950 there were some 120 companies which owned more than 10 cinemas. The Essoldo circuit based in Newcastle, one of the largest, owned over 100. As far as the market side of the argument was concerned, there was much to be said for the comment of E. T. Carr in 1944, that 'While there are 3,800 independent cinemas in Britain, any talk about monopoly is absurd'.[12]

On the production side the argument is stronger, or at least was at the time when Labour came into power. In 1943 Rank owned 56 per cent of available studio capacity and ABPC 16 per cent. A substantial proportion of studios had, however, been requisitioned for war purposes. In 1948, by which time they had been released again, the Gater Report, commissioned to establish the case for the building of state-owned studios for the use of 'independent' film producers, found that there was no shortage of studio space at all and that Rank and ABPC had been only too willing to rent out surplus studio space to any independent film producer able to make use of it, and at terms which could not be regarded as unreasonable.[13] In fact both ABPC and Rank, in particular, tended to act as umbrellas and facility houses for those independent film production companies which could raise the finance for a film.

Why then could 'monopoly' be the central perception around which Labour's thinking revolved? There were some particular features of the film industry which at their face value lend some plausibility to the argument. The major circuits owned many of the city-centre cinemas, in London especially so. Of the eleven 'shop window' West End cinemas seven were owned by Rank and about the same proportion of their equivalents in the largest towns around the country. Typically these were also the biggest cinemas, as well as the poshest, though that was in itself of little significance because the overwhelming majority of cinema seats were to be found in the small to medium local houses to which the working-class patrons went. The point was that films premiered in them attracted press attention and publicity and thus *other* cinema owners would also want them for their own local clientele. The extensive advertising which the two main circuits could carry out, together with the simultaneous release of the films in their prestige cinemas locally, would have a similar effect. A film which failed to be bought by either of the major circuits for showing in the *minority* of cinemas it actually owned would thus also have less chance of being reviewed and less chance of being taken up by the independently owned *majority* of the cinemas. Even if it were, it would be certainly a less desirable property in terms of the rental paid for it. Hence its chances of making a profit were less. The number of new, full feature-length films registered with the Board of Trade in 1950, a good but not the best year, was 382 (of which 74 were British).[14] Taking a ratio of about 10:1 as between the number of cinemas and films, it could therefore be argued that a market share of about twice that ratio could have a decisive effect on the fate of each of the films, and especially of the much smaller number of British films.

These factors should, however, be put in context. The number of feature-length films shown in Britain during the fifteen years between 1935 and 1950 averaged 427, of which around 75 per cent on average were American. In the 1945 to 1950 period the proportion of non-British full feature films averaged 68 per cent, most of them of course American.[15] The same 'problem' would therefore have applied to American films distributed in Britain, yet there were no similar complaints from Hollywood. Furthermore, with over four times the number of cinemas in other hands, each of the supposed 'monopolists' had to do their very best to select films which were liked by the audience for otherwise they would have gone to cinemas which chose more successfully.[16]

The real problem was that Rank and ABPC were 'combines', vertically integrated companies, acting as distributors (including distributors for some of the major Hollywood companies) and exhibitors as well as being major film production companies, whereas none of the other cinema owners, including those of the larger cinema chains, were, in any comparable sense, vertically integrated combines. Vertical integration allowed them to play every trick in the book to favour their own productions and it gave them a substantial measure of control over the by far largest and most valuable part of the cinemas' film supply, American films. This was also the case in the United States where the five major studios were also into distribution and cinema-owning, also in fact owning only about the same low percentage of cinemas (17 per cent) overall but also with the same tendency for owning the majority of the city-centre prestige, first-run cinemas.[17] Vertical integration in the US film industry raised the same debate about impairing the ability of people of getting what they wanted in their cinemas rather than what suited the studios by freezing out alternative kinds of films and film-makers, also called 'independents'. There was in Britain a serious additional abuse made possible by vertical integration, the conflict of interest within the combines between being *British* film producers and exhibitors *and* distributors of *American* films. It could be better for their corporate profit to show and distribute more American films than to produce more British films, especially because there was also a significant, though not dominant element of American shareholding in both Rank and ABPC.

It was therefore ironic in the circumstances, that it should have been the United States' Department of Commerce and not the Labour government's Board of Trade which took decisive action in the summer of 1949, broke up vertical integration and forced the Hollywood moguls to get out of cinema-owning altogether. This was doubly ironic in view of all that the British left as well as Labour politicians had been saying before and since Dalton had commissioned the Palache Report in 1943 about the evils of 'monopolistic tendencies' as much as in view of the belief on the British left about the US government being subservient to 'monopoly capitalism'. Harold Wilson wrote that very September when the US Order of Separation came into force about how 'we cannot allow national film policy economically, morally or artistically to be dictated by these two Oriental potentates. The power of the circuits must be broken . . .'[18] Unlike his counterpart at the head of the US Department of Commerce, Wilson felt that 'busting up' the combines would be too radical a step constitutionally, too great an interference with private enterprise and the rights of shraeholders.

The truth was, however, that in Britain the steam behind the hunt for 'monopolistic tendencies' as the root cause of all evil in the film industry came in fact from the *success* of the combines, on the whole, to supply the majority of the cinemagoers with what they actually liked in their capacity as exhibitors–distributors–importers and as producers from at least seriously trying to make films which appealed to 'Mr and Mrs

Ninepennies'. The real aim of the agitation against the 'monopolistic combines' was not in fact that owners of individual cinemas and small local chains should have a more genuinely free choice to choose films which their clientele wanted to see. It was rather to be able to use the power, more accurately the influence, of vertically integrated combines with major circuits for making 'the people' watch the kind of films which their paternalistic betters thought 'they' ought to be watching; the kind of films they liked themselves and which would be uplifting for the people. They also believed that the 'ordinary public' could be educated into liking them eventually, if only the combines could be made to show widely these 'superior kind of films' and to wean them off the 'Hollywood rubbish', which the people had only come to like because they had been made accustomed to them by the trade in the first place. The roots of this campaign against the circuits and the combines went back to the 1930s and to the failure of the British documentary film movement to reach a wider audience.

Early in the development of the documentary movement, in the first half of the 1930s, cinema owners did try out the documentary as an alternative to the short films, such as cartoons or travelogues, which then made up the cinema programme, but it fell flat. Whereas these 'creative treatments of actuality with a social purpose', earnest and artistic presentations of grim social conditions, were a hit with the intelligentsia and were generally well received by educated middle-class audiences, it soon emerged that the last thing the great majority of working-class people wanted was to be reminded of the conditions and difficulties they wished to escape from when they went to the cinema.[19] As it was they who bought by far the largest proportion of cinema tickets, the consequent exclusion of documentary films by the cinemas and the reluctance of the major studios to invest in the production of documentaries and feature films of the quasi-documentary 'realist' recipe enraged the documentarists as well as the intelligentsia which would have liked to be able to see such films. Naturally, in the mood of the 1930s, it was taken as a consequence of and evidence of a conspiracy between philistinism and capitalism. The hope for the creation of a specifically British and realist film-school was pinned therefore on the 'independent' film-makers. That is, on individual producers, or small largely *ad hoc* companies, who raised money for particular projects from distributors, or banks against a promise from a distributor and hired a studio, crews and actors for the making of the film. The problem with vertically integrated combines, from this perspective, was that the independent producer would have to compete with them at several levels at once. As distributors, the 'combine' would naturally weigh an application for providing the capital (or distribution guarantee which was the same thing) for an independent project against the films which they were producing in their capacity as film-makers; as production companies they would weigh the hire of their studio to the independent producer against their own production needs – and as major exhibitors the independent producer's film would compete for a place in their programme against the films which they either produced or imported themselves. The cause of the 'independents' thus became an emotive issue of supporting Davids against corporate Goliath, fighting for 'quality', social conscience and the artist and striking out against the profit motive, the box-office mentality, capitalism and philistinism.

Various leading members of the future Labour government had been publicly associated during the 1930s and in wartime with the documentarists in their campaigns through pamphlets and in the press against 'monopoly' and had spoken for the cause of a socially aware, realist British cinema to be created by the 'independents'. On their part, the documentarists took every opportunity to propagandise for Labour through their films, especially during the later years of the war.[20] There was a widespread expectation therefore amongst them as well as the intelligentsia and the cultural elite that Labour would boldly deal with the problems left by Tory tinkering as part of the promised social reconstruction. Had not the 1945 manifesto, after all, talked about 'The "hard faced men" and their political friends . . . [who] . . . controlled . . . largely the press and the cinema . . . the means whereby people learned about the world outside . . .'.[2]

That expectation was an unfortunate legacy, for in truth there had been no prior planning within the Labour Party. In fact the Parliamentary Labour Party's Trade and Industry Group had only come round to appointing a films subcommittee in the autumn of 1945. The situation was the worse because the officials of the Board of Trade who had been dealing with the film industry had long been doubtful about just how much independent talent there actually was and how much of it had been prevented from making films, at least reasonably marketable films, by the combines. After he had been in the Board of Trade for some time during the war Dalton came to share the same doubts and grew to regard the combines as the only viable part of the British film industry. So did his assistant, the young Hugh Gaitskell. Having at first asked for the Palache Report with a brief which invited radical proposals for curbing the combines and supporting the independents and having in the interim introduced some temporary measures in that direction, Dalton moved towards a different approach. It was, however, not Dalton but Sir Stafford Cripps, who had been more involved with and had lent his name (and money at times[21]) to the more left wing of the documentarists seeking a radical change in the film industry, who became President of the Board of Trade in 1945. On coming into office Cripps could have drawn on some plans already prepared in the Board of Trade under Dalton. These were along the Dalton–Gaitskell lines of looking at films as just another consumer industry; favoured a few large companies, by necessity the existing combines, as alone having the economic muscle for large-scale production programmes; and because it was simpler for government to deal with a few companies than with a multitude. Cripps was not in tune with this policy approach, but without a coherent and prepared plan of his own.

The position therefore when Labour took office was that it was quite unready to tackle the multi-faceted and complicated issues involved. Film policy had to be evolved once in power, to be made on the hoof, in fact, amidst not just the largest programme of change undertaken by any government in modern times but as it turned out to be also in a period of almost constant financial and economic crises.

After implementing some temporary measures and making some very vague speeches in the autumn and winter of 1945–6 the government thus pleaded lack of parliamentary time and postponed producing its own policy until the Cinematograph Films Act was due for renewal in the 1947–8 parliamentary session. This meant that it would not be until three years from the time Labour took over that whatever policy was decided could be implemented. Even if time had been on the side of the government this would have entailed a great loss of momentum. Should time not be on the side of the government it presented a hostage to fortune.

The first policy-plan to emerge, in the summer of 1946, was by the Parliamentary Labour Party's Trade and Industry Group's Films Subcommittee, produced after a thorough, nine-months-long study.[22] The members proposed that the Rank and ABPC circuits should be reduced to under 350 cinemas each; two new state-owned circuits of about the same size should be created and the size, quality and location of cinemas be equalised between these four large circuits; the two state-owned circuits should be independent of each other and should compete with each other as well as the commercial circuits; they would be expected to make a return at the prevailing rate of interest on their assets, but beyond that their brief was to educate public taste by widening the range of films shown and to provide an alternative market for independent British producers. The two state-owned circuits should also be entitled to set up their own renting organisation and enter into production in the same way as Rank and ABPC. Effectively, there should be four vertically integrated combines: two within the public sector serving the public interest matching the two in the private sector working for the market *per se*. As for protection from Hollywood, the Subcommittee proposed that the quota system should be changed to a import footage tax. 'We are most anxious that . . . the best type of foreign film should be available in the country, not only for the entertainment of the cinemagoer but also as a stimulus to the British film industry'.[23] A footage tax would much less affect the good, high-budget American films but would keep out the low-budget poor type of film.

This was a coherent, well-thought-out, in some ways rather clever, policy-plan designed to achieve both the political–cultural and the entertainment–fiscal revenue objectives, within a truly mixed-economy framework. It might have worked and the subsequent history of British film might then have been less depressing than it has turned out to be. The Labour members of parliament who had spent much time on familiarising themselves with the complicated affairs of the film industry had been, however, wasting their time. As so often, once in power Labour ministers turned to their civil servants rather than to their party for policies.

Any ideas in the course of drafting the new Cinematograph Film Act for a radical restructuring with a mixed-economy type of public sector–private sector involvement – even to the minimal extent of making a state-owned studio available for them to hire or a state-supported 'film-bank' to loan–finance independent producers, which had in fact been under active consideration during the last Conservative administration – were sunk by Dalton's blanket refusal to provide any public funds at all for independent producers. It was thus not surprising that the new Act introduced at the beginning of the 1947–8 session was little more than an extension of the muddled and incoherent policies represented by the 1927 Act and its 1938 revision – except for a few rather ill-thought-out mildly dirigiste additions passing as Labour policy. The Act had four principal provisions. First, the reconfirmation of the principle of a quota of British films which cinemas were obliged to show – with power now given to the Board of Trade to fix from time to time by statutory instrument what the percentage would be rather than as before being determined by Parliament as part of the Act. Second, that in addition to cinemas being required merely to show a certain number of British films per year, they were now also compelled to show them during normal programme-times (rather than to an empty house out of hours as had been done on occasions). Third, that the Board of Trade would have power to stop the purchase of additional cinemas by the combines thus to check the supposed 'tendency to monopoly' (a policy which had in fact been operating by voluntary agreement since 1943). Fourth, the Board of Trade would also have power, ultimately, to compel the combines to show up to six British films produced by 'independent' companies, provided a Selection Committee, presided over by a representative of the Board of Trade, deemed them to be worthy of showing. This was supposed to ensure that films of 'cultural' values were not consigned to oblivion by the crassly box-office standards by which the Rank and ABC combines were assumed to select films.

The right to stop further purchases of cinemas and the tribunal for aggrieved independent producers against the combines as cinema owners were the only additions of significance to the policies which had been operating since before the war. The original intention of placing an additional quota on the two combines obliging them to show a fixed number of independent productions was dropped in the face of opposition in the Lords resulting from effective lobbying by the combines. The 'Selection Committee' was an inoperable idea. No sane producer would have chosen to advertise that his film had been judged unfit for exhibition by *both* main circuits and that the one now showing it does do not only by order of the Board of Trade but because it had lost out in the ballot, quite literally, as to which of them should have the privilege, this being the remarkable method laid down for determining which circuit was to show a film approved by the Selection Committee! The only film which came to be shown under this bizarre procedure during the decade while the Act was in operation was a whimsical film with a rather political theme which the combines had rejected – because they thought it might go down badly with Labour![24]

The Act which emerged from two years of delay for 'planning' was thus a tiny, tame and utterly un-radical mouse of a measure which did nothing to address, least of all within some recognisably Labour framework, the future of the British film industry. In any case, it had been effectively rendered out of date before discussion of it in Parliament had even started by the decision of the government to take a truly radical step just before the start of the parliamentary session. This was the imposition on 6 August of a 75 per cent *ad valorem* duty on imported films.

The full story of this débâcle had been told elsewhere.[25] In a nutshell, a mere eight months later the government found itself obliged ignominiously to climb down before Hollywood and remove the duty, with the face-saving grace, if such it was, that American studios should invest a proportion of their income from the British market in Britain. It was presented as a concession but in fact was a major defeat in its own right, since they could invest it in making films in Britain, films which would not count towards their quota! The government was forced into capitulation by the imposition of a boycott by American studios, backed up by some pressure from Washington. The results on the film industry and Labour's policies towards it were widespread in their effects and uniformly disastrous. When the Americans announced the boycott, Rank and its counterparts were asked to step up film production to fill the screens. It was hoped that this would also improve long-term prospects since the duty would have increased the price of Hollywood films and thus would further open up the market for British films. When, however, a mere eight months later the duty had to be rescinded and the films accumulated in Hollywood flooded in, the public flocked to see what they had missed. The films which British studios had rushed out or were rushing to complete, and some of which were even worse than usual for the rush, were practically wiped off the screens for many months.

That was not all. The immediate purpose of the imposition of the duty had been, of course, to save dollars and a publicity drive on the theme of patriotic necessity was launched with 'Food or Flicks', 'Bacon before Bogart' and similar slogans. In fact with Hollywood reacting by a boycott within two days the only alternative to closing most of the cinemas as the supply of some 70 per cent of their fare disappeared overnight, was the recirculation of Hollywood films already in the country. Old Hollywood films thus went on a glorious second run and (not being subject to the new import duty) earned millions *more* dollars for the USA than would have been the case otherwise.

It would be nice to believe that it was at least an honourable mistake, a desperate measure taken in the heat of the moment by a government in justifiable panic over the imminent collapse of the pound during the summer of 1947. But as Professor Jarvie has shown, it had in fact been under discussion on and off for over two years. Board of Trade officials had been instructed in the spring of 1946 to be extremely careful not to breathe a word about it so as not to jeopardise the negotiations for a massive US loan to help Britain through the aftermath of the war. Such a demonstration of perfidious Albion did not help with cordial relations when the deception came out. Detailed discussions then took place throughout April 1947 with the decision to go ahead taken on 5 May. It was fully realised that should the Americans respond with a boycott there would be chaos in British cinemas. With amazing arrogance and ignorance of Americans, it was felt, however, that Hollywood would neither dare nor be able to fight to the finish when it came to it. The studios were hard up for cash, would not stick together in any case and given British firmness, after a lot of protesting, they would make the best of a bad job. There was to be no prior consultation. The Americans were just to be told.

When within forty-eight hours of the imposition of the duty the American Motion Picture Export Association announced that its members (all eight major studios) would halt all shipments to the UK, there was no contingency plan to deal with the consequences of this colossal misjudgement. No preparations had been made for building up British film production beforehand, not even prior consultation with British studios.

A second example of being out of touch with realities came a few months after the duty was rescinded and the Americans had lifted the boycott. In June 1948 the newly appointed President of the Board of Trade – Harold Wilson taking over from Sir Stafford Cripps following a cabinet reshuffle two months after the imposition of the duty – raised the quota to 45 per cent under the powers conferred on him by the newly passed Act. This was felt by the Americans, with justification, to be a breach of the spirit if not the letter of the conditions of the agreement for ending their boycott and they threatened to reimpose it. That was avoided only because of the farcical reason that there had not in fact been enough British films produced to fill their quota. Through various exemptions and other devices the 45 per cent in practice only worked out at 37 per cent for the year, and that only with some backlog of British productions from the previous year in the pipeline. In the following year it was lowered to an official 40 per cent which again fell short in practice, and then was quietly dropped to 30 per cent afterwards. For all practical purposes things were back to where they had stood in 1936.

The result for the film industry was a desperate situation lasting for at least well over a year. In the summer following the lifting of the boycott confidence was at such a low ebb that finance was almost impossible to find and there was no alternative to extensive cuts in production plans across the industry and to staff being laid off – many of them would never be able to return. The 75 per cent *ad valorem* duty of 1947 was thus that unusual achievement, a complete disaster. No dollars were saved, on the contrary, and the British film industry had been brought to its knees. Rank reported a loss for the year of over £4 million as the result (or so it claimed though there is some doubt about how much it would have lost in any case) and Sir Alexander Korda (whose company was being built up with government support alongside Rank to beat the Americans in America at their own big-budget/star-vehicle game) teetered on the edge of bankruptcy, and to avoid which needed the immediate injection of £1 million from the Treasury and the promise of more to come.

The boycott and its consequences were an educational experience for the politicians, especially for Harold Wilson whose first job was to negotiate the government out of the pit of the *ad valorem* duty dug by his elders. These negotiations coincided with the passage of the Act through Parliament. It is not surprising either that the policy represented by the Act was felt to be out of date already, or that the new President of the Board of Trade should make sorting out the film industry his personal project. The absence of any positively interventionist measures from the 1948 Cinematograph Act had not represented Sir Stafford Cripps's own views but rather the flat refusal of Dalton as chancellor to provide funds. Cripps's own instincts had been for taking a much more positive approach, to introduce a film-bank for providing alternative capitalisation for independent producers at the least and he might well have contemplated going even further down the road recommended by the radicals, such as Paul Rotha, as well as the Labour Party's Films Subcommittee. When, shortly after Wilson took over from Cripps at the Board of Trade, Cripps was moved again this time into the Exchequer, Wilson could set out on his own course for reconstructing the film industry knowing that whilst there was little money for anything at this moment of austerity, there would at least be a sympathetic chancellor, rather than one opposed on principle to any direct financial involvement of the state in the film industry.

Thus even while the Act was proceeding through the House, Wilson set about establishing a new National Film Production Council to bring all sides, including the combines and the unions, together to devise ways for increasing efficiency and growth. He personally presided over its inaugural meeting in April 1948. The Council agreed that the first thing needed was comprehensive information about the costs and earnings of recent productions. The last thing the combines wanted to disclose, however, was the truth about their finances. As the Campbell Report for the Bank of England had observed some years earlier the prevailing 'standard of commercial morality' was one of the principal reasons for the problems of the industry.[26] Financial mismanagement, bordering on the scandalous at times, was a way of life. It is hardly surprising therefore that the information was not forthcoming; that the Council did not meet for six months and even then it had been agreed that its members should not be asked in future to provide such information. It proved useless for any practical purpose. Next, Wilson set up three public inquiries as a basis for the policies to be adopted. One inquiry's brief was to establish whether there was need for the state to build additional studio facilities for the independent producers and whether they should be owned and run by the government. Chaired by Sir Henry Gater, it concluded, as we have seen, that there was no shortage of studio space in the industry as a whole but also that if it was still felt necessary to create and run a separate studio for the independents, this should be conditional on the independents forming themselves into a co-operative.[27]

Another inquiry was to try and establish the truth about production costs, the first attempt at which had proved abortive in the context of the National Film Production Council. Although this time the excuse for not providing information because of the presence of the unions which would affect wage negotiations was not employable, the companies just as effectively avoided giving the information sought. It became clear that the Board of Trade's own statistics were just as inadequate. All

Wilson got was another round of the anecdotal and incidental data which had bedevilled all previous attempts at formulating a realistic policy.[28]

The third inquiry (eventually chaired by Professor Arnold Plant), was to examine the distribution and exhibition side of the industry. This report took a very long time to arrive and turned out to be a mixture of a great deal of precise information and complete lack of information in critical areas, especially where the booking and accounting practices of distributors were concerned. It disclosed some of the murkiness resulting from vertical integration but it drew the opposite conclusion from the American courts dealing almost simultaneously with the same issues. These came to the conclusion there must be divorcement because neither regulations banning particular dirty tricks currently practised nor a code with a quasi-voluntary regulatory trade body to operate it would work since the abuse was inherent in the system of vertical integration. The Plant Committee rejected divorcement in favour of just those approaches. The committee was nevertheless pessimistic about how far the trade could be relied on to reform and police itself. An independent authority was therefore proposed, but without extensive powers, acting rather as a co-ordinator and arbitrator, relying on the moral authority of its members and on the possibility that if it was not obeyed the government might in future replace it with something less palatable to the trade. The Committee also rejected the other suggested hard alternative to divorcement that the state should itself enter into the production and exhibition of films.[29]

The setting up of such inquiries gave the appearance of a thorough and systematic approach based on hard evidence, the kind of approach which a planned society's government would adopt. Before, however, any of these committees could report, in fact before two of them even started their work, Wilson jumped to his own conclusion that what was really needed was a framework for channelling capital from the City into those sectors of the film industry which the government deemed in need of capitalisation. This was to be done on the same model already adopted in other industries, through either the Finance Corporation for Industry or the Industrial and Commercial Finance Corporation. Both were funded and operated jointly by the Bank of England and the major banks. Whether they could best be regarded as a demonstration of the readiness of the City to play its part in a partnership with government, in the creation of a planned and rational economy where private capital behaved in a socially responsible manner investing funds in industries which needed building up rather than in whatever gave maximum return, or as a danegeld paid by the banks to keep the Labour government off nationalising them, it was understood that a certain element of risk of losses in supporting government-favoured projects was part of the game. Neither of the corporations was, however, prepared to touch with a barge-pole the shady world of film finance, about which the banks knew a lot more than the Board of Trade could ever find out, not even when Wilson persuaded the Treasury to offer guaranteeing half of any losses.

With some independents, and above all Alexander Korda's company, getting close to bankruptcy, ostensibly because of the consequences of the American boycott, and both finance corporations still adamantly refusing to co-operate, Wilson took another jump. In July 1948, with the ink on the Cinematograph Act barely dry and before his inquiries for examining the case for and the proper form of a state-funded film-bank had been completed, with Sir Stafford Cripps's personal backing, Wilson announced that a film fund was to be established with £5 million from the Treasury. This required legislation, however by exploiting a loophole in the Finance Acts a company was set up to which the Treasury 'loaned' £2.5 million. In September Korda was handed £1 million with a promise of another £2 millions in the future. A Bill, for legalising the transaction, was squeezed into the parliamentary timetable for 1948–9, emerging as the Cinematograph Film Production (Special Loans) Act. The stated purpose of the Act was to make 'temporary provision for the lending of money to be employed in financing the production or distribution of cinematograph films'. The body created to do this was the National Film Finance Corporation.

The National Film Finance Corporation represented a major departure from the past. It was Wilson's baby and he remained very proud of it. 'I announced the establishment of the NFFC, which continued for some 40 years before being replaced by a new body which I chaired for several years'.[30] It was also, like its creator, however, a curious amalgam of purposes and policies. The Act stated that it was to lend money only to *distributors* not to producers; normally to provide only end money, an additional sum to what the commercial distributor(s) had already agreed to invest or would be willing to invest if a loan were forthcoming; it should assist the whole independent sector. On the other hand the Act explicitly stated that it should not be involved in the choice of individual subjects or projects and should not be or act as a public body which would have to be subject to parliamentary questions on individual decisions relating to particular film-projects. In short, it was simply to be a finance house, a banker primarily to the independent film producers, a point reinforced by stipulating that its members should have business experience.

In practice, however, it was committed to lending £3 million to British Lion, that is to the distribution *arm* of Alexander Korda which was a major *production* company, in no way an independent distributor taking a chance on financing the production of an independent's film. Korda through his British Lion and London Film Productions was principally producing massively expensive prestige films designed to fly the cultural flag in the USA and Europe – most of which turned out to be of the 'high critical acclaim but a flop at the box office' variety.[31] This sum was massively above the production cost of the independent type of film, or even of a series of them as the average, total, independent production budget was in the £50,000 to £200,000 range, and it at once accounted for 60 per cent of its total lending capital. How, then, could the NFFC be expected to be able to provide finance for the independent sector as a whole which had at least a dozen companies of the established and serious kind and many more up-and-coming ones? If it was to be a finance house whose members were to have 'financial, industrial or commercial' experience first and foremost and not a policy-making organisation involved in the choice of subjects and policy issues, then why was Lord Reith, of all people, made its chairman? He was no banker, had no experience as a financier or as a film producer or of anything commercial in its nature. On the other hand he was a policy-maker *par excellence*, the founder of the BBC, a former Cabinet minister and a manager of public corporations by instinct, habit and experience. He described in his autobiography how he regarded his own qualifications when looking for a suitable job in 1945 as 'Special, probably unique experience of public corporations'.[32] He was also the high priest of public-service ideals and purity as against commercialised media. How was the man supposed to fit the job, the purposes and *modus operandi* of the NFFC as defined by the Act?

With 60 per cent of its capital already committed to Korda and some further 'loans' made to other favoured production companies with but a legalistic curtsey to the supposed central idea of lending only to *financiers* of film productions, it is scarcely surprising that in February 1950, within six months of taking up his post as chairman of the NFFC, Lord Reith should have been writing to Harold Wilson stressing that 'there must soon be a clear, long term policy to which it (NFFC) will work'. He was manifestly himself unclear what policy Wilson had actually wanted him to carry out. He referred to 'the independent producers – whom to save was perhaps the first cause of the Corporation's establishment' and to 'financing producers' with hardly a mention of distributors. Reith had no doubt, however, what the overall policy issues which he needed to address were, and they were certainly not the 'production or distribution of films on a commercially successful basis' as explicitly stated in the Act:

> issues at stake . . . The most compelling are of the moral order –
> evidenced in the influence which the industry can exercise over so
> considerable a proportion of the population – interests, outlook

and behaviour, in the projection of England and the English way of life to the Dominions and foreign countries; in the enhancement of the prestige and worth of England.[33]

Even though he had only been involved with the film-scene for some nine months it was clear to Reith that the NFFC was, in the form in which it had been set up, but a stop-gap and the government would need to make it part of a much better-thought-through long-term policy. He identified the need for a new distribution framework at home and abroad, possibly the establishment of two state-controlled distribution companies respectively for home and overseas; powers of supervision for the NFFC over the independent producers to whom it lent public money, if not directly then at least to be able to satisfy itself that the company was provided with business advice and supervision; capacity to own studios; power to form groups of producers rather than trying to deal with individuals or companies, and he identified, as did Rotha and others earlier, the crying long-term need for training film personnel.[34]

The reports of Wilson's committees of inquiry came in gradually following the establishment of the NFFC. They lent support to the case for a more broadly based policy and for some properly constituted authority with power to carry it out. They also indicated the centrality of the need for sorting out the distribution system for films and of the relationship between producers, exhibitors and distributors, though differed in the recommendations as to what should be done.

Nothing was done, however, during 1949–50 to address these major issues while British film production was failing at an alarming rate. Employment in the industry fell from 7,253 in 1948 to 4,104 in 1950[35] and all the major film companies claimed that they were facing massive losses. So unpromising, it was claimed, had film production become, that bank and other sources for raising finance were drying up. The next stage in Labour policy towards the film industry thus came to be another unplanned measure rushed into operation by quasi-parliamentary means – the introduction of direct subsidies. From a combination of a reduction in the Entertainment Tax levied on cinema admissions and increases in the prices of certain categories of cinema seats and the so-called Eady Levy on the exhibitors, the total sum going into the film production industry as a whole was boosted by some £3 million, of which about £1.5 million went to producers of British films. It was introduced in the summer of 1950 as a temporary crisis measure and was regularised in Labour's last budget. The capital provided for the NFFC was also raised from £5 million to £6 million.

In January 1951 the final stage in the story of Labour and the film industry was announced. This was the Group Production Scheme, arrived at after some nine months of arguments over the proposals which Reith had been putting forward in increasing detail since February 1950. Characteristically again, the government, effectively Harold Wilson, avoided tackling the two central problems of distribution and training and created instead another curious amalgam. There were to be three groups into which combines and independents, including both existing and up-and-coming production companies or producers were to be organised. Group One was to be built around the Rank combine working from Rank's Pinewood studio complex. The studio would be taken over by a new holding and management company, British Film Makers Ltd in which the NFFC held the controlling interest. The company's tasks would be, in Reith's words, to:

> control expenditure at all stages . . . approve script and budget . . . undertake, on behalf of all producers in the group the commercial negotiations which are usually an anxiety and distraction to the producer. It will arrange studio rentals, distribution terms, bank loans, completion guarantees etc.; it will provide certain common services. All this makes for efficiency and economy; for more artistic freedom for the producer; for the team spirit which is as desirable in this business as elsewhere.[36]

The resulting films would be owned by the holding and management company while distribution rights would be assigned to General Film Distributors, Rank's distribution company, which would in return guarantee 70 per cent of the production budget, with the NFFC providing the rest.

Group Two would be formed on the same lines with ABPC and work from its Elstree Studios. It would be run jointly by an NFFC representative and an ABPC representative.

As for Group Three, Reith wrote:

> The third company, 'C', will be different. The financial difficulties and risks of first features make it hard for the young and unknown producer. But his opportunities can be increased by production, in an inexpensive studio and on location, of feature films of moderate cost.[37]

It was to bring together young, unknown or up-and-coming producers who would find it difficult to get backing from distributors. It was to make low-budget feature films, up to £50,000 as a rule. Whether they were to be shown as B Features or First Features was one of the loose ends which later led to bitter recriminations.[38] The brief was, however, clear that they were to be 'different' in style and approach, though exactly how was another loose end.[39] In the reams of correspondence and memoranda leading up to the formation of Group Three much was said about these films being in the British realist tradition; references were made to wartime feature documentaries such as *Western Approaches*, to Italian neo-realist films such as *Bicycle Thieves* and to combining the artistic and political aspirations implicit in this genre with the cost-benefits of realist films, being supposedly shot on location rather than in expensive studios and using real people or character actors instead of expensive 'stars'.[40] Group Three's brief did, however, state two aims specifically. 1) Group Three was to produce feature films for the commercial cinemas which were to compete for their place in the programmes on their attractiveness to the average cinemagoer, and not documentary or educational or art films for film-society audiences. 2) Group Three was also to be a kind of training studio for young feature-film producers, directors and others, people who might have come from the government's own documentary film establishment, the Crown Film Unit, or from other documentary film companies and who wished to move into the commercial feature-film industry.

Unlike the others, Group Three was to be run as a company set up directly by the NFFC with its own Board of Directors, under the Chairmanship of Sir Michael Balcon of Ealing Studios. Its productions were to be financed by 50 per cent of the budget provided by the NFFC which was to recoup it only after the commercial provider of the other half had recouped the whole of its investment.

Group Three was, perhaps, the most curious of these amalgams of incompatible aims and policies. If the idea was to produce films which were different and in some ways of higher cultural values than the typical B feature, then educating the public taste would necessarily have to be involved. That would have needed a well-thought-through and watertight distribution policy and arrangements to ensure exhibition in the right places, at the right times and in the right programme context. Instead there was, if anything, an even less tight distribution arrangement for Group Three than for the other groups. Associated British Film Distributors, the ABPC combine's distribution company, was supposed to distribute Group Three films – in competition with its own productions and imports – yet without any clear and binding agreements about the scheduling of the films.

If the purpose of the exercise was to make *feature* films for the commercial cinema, then how could they have chosen John Grierson, of all people, to be in charge? Grierson had never made a feature film in his life, not even a feature documentary. Nor had he ever worked in the commercial cinema. Grierson was in fact the founder of the documentary movement, the guru of non-commercialism in film-making and the castigator in the most abrasive and memorably stinging terms of the box-office mentality, the commercial cinema, its moguls and ethos. And if the idea was to provide training, then to do that in a way where the products of the trainees had to compete on a commercial basis with the products of Hollywood and the combines was simply absurd. Grierson was a gifted and challenging teacher of film-theory and its applications.

He would have made an excellent director of that national film-school which the government should have established, like the French government did, costing a fraction of the money wasted on Group Three in the end. From its inception Group Three carried within it the recipe for becoming that 'disaster' which Harry Watt, the great documentary and realist film maker sadly called it in retrospect.

The incoming Conservative government left these last-minute arrangements of the Labour government in place virtually unchanged. Thus Labour's policies had a chance to be tested in practice despite leaving office. Korda's British Lion went into receivership in 1954 and over £2 million of public money vanished with it.[41] Group Two only managed to produce five films before it collapsed. Group One collapsed after two years after having produced a mere fourteen films. Group Three closed down three years later, after bitter recriminations all round, having produced twenty-two films and lost close to £500,000 in the process.[42] It produced only one film which was 'different' in the sense in which it was hoped its films should be, *The Brave Don't Cry*, about a Scottish mining disaster. The majority of its films were panned by even those critics committed to the 'realist' ideal as uninspired, second-rate, run-of-the-mill productions, in no way superior to what the commercial cinema studios could produce. The audiences voted with their feet. There was much acrimony over the distribution arrangements and their role in its failure to capture an audience.[43] It made little if any contribution to training up new production talent.[44] Even Grierson had to admit that it had failed to do anything at all about the most pressing, perennial need of the British film industry, bringing forth good screen writers.[45]

In overall economic terms – despite all the public money pumped in directly as well as indirectly through the massive loss of tax revenue from the millions written off the profits of Rank and Korda, of the banks and finance houses and from the employees who lost their jobs – British film production at the end of the Attlee government was 18 per cent *less* than it had been in 1939, seventy-four films (first-feature length) as against ninety. The number of British production studios had shrunk from twenty-six in 1945, to nine in 1951, and all this in a period when the cinema audience increased from 19.75 million to 26.84 million per week.[46]

As far as the much vaunted Labour aim of countering the 'monopolistic tendencies' in the film industry is concerned, nothing had actually happened.[47] In 1951 the same two vertically integrated combines were still in being, operating in effect just as they had been in 1945. The only positive result, if it is to be taken as such, was that in 1951 both combines managed again to break even and show a small profit in 1952. As far as the other much talked about cultural–ideological aim of reducing

Americanisation and of the penetration of American capital was
concerned, the record is worse. By the time Labour left office American
distributors had come to handle 68 per cent of all films shown in Britain
in 1951, a larger proportion than in 1945. Thanks to the débâcle of the
75 per cent *ad valorem* duty, there was also in fact much greater
penetration by American capital into the British film (production)
industry than had been in 1945. By 1950 MGM, Warner Bros and Walt
Disney were all busy producing films in Britain, including some of the
most 'Americanised' versions of British history Hollywood ever produced.
Perhaps the saddest comment on the results of what Peter Stead
described as a period of 'endless meetings and reports [which] had
produced no great political initiative and no new economic formula' was
that audience surveys showed that in many categories the term 'British
picture' was thought of as 'a disparaging term, even a warning'. His
overall view that 'the politicians had been unimaginative, perhaps even
treacherous' might, however, be going too far.[48]

There is one final, perhaps thought-provoking, question to be raised
about what can only be described as a profoundly depressing story. It
certainly was the story of the Labour *government's* film policies, or lack
of a policy, but how far is it fair to describe them as *'Labour'* policies?
The proposals of the Parliamentary Labour Party's Trade and Industry
Group's Films Subcommittee were echoed in broadly similar and no less
moderate and sensible policy proposals for a mixed-economy approach
to the cinema industry from the union side of 'Labour', especially from
the Association of Cinematograph Technicians. What a pity that neither
Cripps nor the young, intellectual lions of the government, such as
Harold Wilson and Hugh Gaitskell, who were in charge of this area
could deign to listen to the people who were not only the backbone of
the party and of the movement in whose name they ruled, but who also
knew the business they were talking about. These 'labour' policies might
not have saved the British film industry in the long run, perhaps nothing
could have, though they could hardly have proved less successful.

Alternatively of course, the government could have taken the free-
enterprise route, broken up the vertically integrated combines,
encouraged from the start American companies to set up shop in Britain
and force greater efficiency and proper cost-accountancy into the British
film industry all around by real competition. The products might not
have satisfied the political and cultural concerns, as some of those
produced under Labour certainly did, though direct commissioning
could have achieved that end at far less cost, but it would have resulted
in a prosperous *industry* which employed British labour at the technical
and creative levels and contributed to the exchequer instead of being a
drain on it. By following neither route, all that the government's policies,
as distinct from 'labour' policies, had actually done was to allow Rank

234

Nicholas Pronay

and Korda and some lesser fellow moguls to continue running one of the murkiest examples of the unacceptable face of capitalism – as distinct from private enterprise operating in a properly conducted free market – propped up with public money.

NOTES

1. N. Pronay 'The Political Censorship of Films in Britain Between the Wars' in N. Pronay and D. W. Spring eds. *Propaganda, Politics and Film 1918–45* (1982) p. 128.
2. T. J. Hollins 'The Conservative Party and Film Propaganda Between The Wars' *English Historical Review* Vol. 96 1981 359–69.
3. K. Kulik *Alexander Korda, The Man Who Could Work Miracles* (1975). See also S. Street 'Alexander Korda, Prudential Assurance and British Film Finance in the late 1930's' *Historical Journal of Film, Radio and Television* Vol. 6 1986.
4. M. Dickinson and S. Street *Cinema and State: The Film Industry and the British Government 1927–84* (1985) p. 145.
5. Ibid. p. 170.
6. P. Stead 'The People and the Pictures. The British Working Class and Film in the 1930s' in N. Pronay and D. W. Spring op. cit. p. 89.
7. For French film policy, and also for the policies adopted by other European countries see I. Christie *State and Cinema in Europe: A Survey of Aid Provision* (1981).
8. P. Perilli 'Statistical Survey of the British Film Industry' in J. Curran and V. Porter eds. *British Cinema History* (1983). This invaluable publication draws together the scattered data from the annual Board of Trade publications into a series of tables.
9. I. Jarvie 'British Trade Policy *versus* Hollywood, 1947–1948: "food before flicks"?', *Historical Journal of Film, Radio and Television* Vol. 6 No. 1 1986 20 and see Table II p. 22.
10. F. Klingender and S. L. Legg *Money Behind the Screen* (1936); Association of Cine-Technicians *Film Business is Big Business* (1939); R. Bond *Monopoly: The Future of British Films* (1946); F. Mullally *Films – An Alternative to Mr. Rank* (1946).
11. *Tendencies to Monopoly in the Cinematograph Industry: Report of the Committee Appointed by the Cinematograph Films Council* (HMSO, 1944). (Palache Report) p. 2.
12. Dickinson and Street op. cit. p. 146. E. T. Carr had long managerial experience of the distribution and exhibition side of the industry. For some further data and an elaboration of these arguments for 'monopolistic tendencies' see Paul Rotha's confidential report of 1945, prepared for Sir Stafford Cripps at his request, which was subsequently published as 'The Government and the Film Industry' in P. Rotha *Rotha on the Film* (1958).
13. *Report of the Film Studio Committee* (HMSO, 1948).
14. Perilli op. cit.
15. Ibid.
16. In fact the Rank organisation in particular employed some of the most advanced and sophisticated audience research methods of the time for selecting films. Their records, now deposited in the British Film Institute, provide impressive evidence of that, as well as a most valuable record of the tastes of British audiences.
17. R. Sklaar *Movie Made America, A Cultural History of American Movies* (1975) pp. 272–4.
18. PRO BT64/4515 in Dickinson and Street op. cit. p. 219.
19. For an examination of audience reactions to documentary films and a review of the acrimonious cross-accusations between the documentarists and the

cinema owners see P. Swann *The British Documentary Movement, 1926–1946* (Cambridge 1989). For a discussion of working-class attitudes to both the British documentary and 'realist' productions see P. Stead *Film and the Working Class: Feature Film in British and American Society* (1989). For the results of the wartime efforts to educate public taste through effectively making the showing of documentaries compulsory and by supporting the production and exhibition of feature films with a 'realist' and socially serious approach through the Ministry of Information, see, N. Pronay and J. Crofts 'British Film Censorship and Propaganda Policy during the Second World War' in J. Curran and V. Porter op. cit. and J. Poole 'British Cinema Attendance in War Time: Audience Preference at the Majestic, Macclesfield, 1939–1946', *Historical Journal of Film, Radio and Television* Vol. 7 No. 1 1987. Poole concludes that realist, socially and culturally serious British feature films did not succeed in attracting the working-class audience: that such films had the lowest appeal.

20. N. Pronay '"The Land of Promise": the Projection of Peace Aims in Britain' in K. R. M. Short ed. *Film and Radio Propaganda in World War II* (1983).
21. P. Rotha *Documentary Diary* (1973) ch. 'The Peace Film'.
22. Parliamentary Labour Party (1946) *Trade and Industry Group; Report of Films Sub-Committee: Proposals for Improvement in the British Film Industry* British Film Institute Library. R. 3253.33, p. 3.
23. Ibid. p. 3.
24. The film was *Chance of a Lifetime* making a rather obscure case for workers' control, directed by Bernard Miles and produced by *Pilgrim*, the company owned by Sir Stafford Cripps's personal protégé, Del Guidice. For the way Cripps was using Treasury money for keeping the wolf from 'dear Del's company's door, which produced high-brow films which Cripps, unlike the majority of cinemagoers, loved, see H. Wilson *Memoirs 1916–64* (1986) pp. 104–5.
25. I. Jarvie op. cit. whose account outdates that in Dickinson and Street op. cit. and which is followed throughout here. For the disastrous effects on British film studios see also R. Murphy 'Rank's Attempt at the American Market, 1944–49' in Curran and Porter op. cit.
26. Dickinson and Street op. cit. p. 136.
27. *Film Studio Committee* (1948).
28. *Report of the Working Party on Film Production Costs* (HMSO, 1949).
29. *Cinematography Films, Distribution and Exhibition of Cinematograph Films, Report of the Committee of Enquiry* (HMSO, 1949).
30. H. Wilson op. cit. p. 104.
31. Typical examples of the Korda films, which acutely demonstrate the conflict between the propaganda need to produce national and cultural flagship films and of having a viable film industry as a branch of the entertainment–consumer industry, were: 1947 – *An Ideal Husband* complete with Paulette Goddard as the star, real emerald jewellery and miles of vastly expensive Technicolour, dubbed by one critic as 'Wilde and Woolly'; 1948 – *Anna Karenina* which managed to cost £700,000 in *black and white* and *Bonnie Prince Charlie* in colour, both of which lost vast sums; 1949 – *The Last Days of Dolwyn* and *The Small Back Room* cultural classics but money losers; 1950 – *The Elusive Pimpernel* and *Gone To Earth* both produced for the American prestige market but proved unmitigated disasters and in 1951 *The Tales of Hoffman*, high art but a very expensive loss. As against these, there was *The Third Man* (1949) and *Seven Days to Noon* (1950) which gained both critical acclaim, including some Academy Awards, and recouped, in the case of *The Third Man* with a good profit, their costs. For the building up of London Film Production as the British answer to Hollywood's best ('producing the Rolls Royce and not the Ford') a cinematic part of the America-beating drive which produced the Brabazon and other 'white elephants' and on the drawing in some of the best independent talent, as well

as the extravagance and great power pretensions which accompanied it, see Kulik op. cit. ch. 18 'The revival of London Films' and ch. 19 'British Lion and the £3,000,000 Loan'.

32. J. C. W. Reith *Into the Wind* (1949) p. 525. Wilson told Reith, when being asked to accept the chairmanship that 'it was much bigger potentially than what the Act indicates'. C. Stuart *The Reith Diaries* (1975) p. 364.
33. PRO BT64/4519 in Dickinson and Street, op. cit. p. 216.
34. S. E. Popple 'Group 3: An Examination of the Impact of State Intervention upon the Independent and Documentary Cinema, and its Relationship with the Commercial Sector' (unpublished MA, University of Leeds, 1988) pp. 31–2.
35. Perilli op. cit.
36. PRO BT64/4522 in Popple op. cit. p. 51.
37. PRO BT64/4522 in Popple ibid. p. 51.
38. R. D. MacCann 'Subsidy for the Screen: Grierson and Group 3, 1951–55', *Sight and Sound* Vol. 46 No. 3 1977.
39. 'There is or should be in this scheme (Group 3) more than the usual element of adventure. We should have every hope that the omelettes will appear, but plenty of eggs will probably be broken in the process' – noted R. C. G. Somerwell, the Head of the Films Division of the BOT, on Reith's proposals for the Group 3 scheme. PRO BT64/4521 in Popple, op. cit. p. 39.
40. Sir Wilfred Eady, Secretary of the Treasury, in his memorandum *The Film Industry* of 31 May 1950. PRO T228/273 in Popple op. cit. p. 33.
41. Not of course Korda himself, nor effectively British Lion or London Film Productions. With some £2.2 million of the NFFC's money owing, he was allowed in effect to refloat both with investments from American sources, as well as to retain his personal wealth, including his collection of paintings, later sold for nearly half a million pounds.
42. Figures in MacCann op. cit.
43. E. Sussex *The Rise and Fall of British Documentary* (Berkeley 1975), presents the reflections of the documentarists including Grierson's self justification which claims that no money was lost. M. Balcon *Michael Balcon Presents . . . A Lifetime of Films* (1969) presents the views of the Chairman of the Board of Directors for Group Three. Two of the documentarists, Paul Rotha and Harry Watt, directly blamed Grierson for the quality of the films. Watt wrote: 'Group 3 was a disaster . . . the films were notably old fashioned, snobbish and second rate.' H. Watt *Don't Look at the Camera* (1974) p. 191.
44. Popple op. cit. examined the careers of Group Three directors and other staff, and found the claims made by the documentarists about training up new talents unjustified. He also provides a summary of critical reactions to the films.
45. Sussex op. cit. pp. 191–2.
46. Perilli op. cit.
47. The same applied, of course, in respect of the press about which with much publicity the Royal Commission on the Press was set up to investigate 'the growth of monopolistic tendencies in the control of the press'. No real case for 'monopoly' in the press was established.
48. P. Stead op. cit. pp. 157–8.

Index

research and development, 92, 98–100, 102–5, 107–8, 152, 168; *see also* science

research establishments, 104–5, 157; *see also* under individual establishments

Restrictive Trade Practices Act 1956, 65

retailing, 59–62

Richard Thomas and Co. Ltd, 83

Richardsons, 88

Rogow, A. A., 1–3, 202

Rolls Royce, 100

Ropner, W. G., 206

Rostas, L., 44, 82

Rotha, Paul, 225, 229

Rotherwick, Lord, 201

Rowell, Robin, 193, 195, 200

Royal Air Force, 95, 98, 102

Royal Commission on the Taxation of Profits and Income, 127, 129, 132

Royal Dockyards, 92

Royal Ordnance Factories, 100, 105–6

Runciman, Philip, 194

Sandys, Duncan, 97

saving, 120

Schuster, Sir George, 147–50, 154

science, 5–6, 98, 101–5, 111, 152; *see also* research and development

Scotland, 81, 232

Seal, E. A., 204

Second World War, 1, 7, 17, 21, 38–43, 57, 59, 63, 74, 82, 91–5, 110–12, 117–18, 120, 132, 139–43, 159, 163–7, 188–91, 204, 214, 219–20

Services, 79, 94, 96, 101, 105–6, 110–11; *see also* defence and rearmament

shipbuilding, licensing of, 190–1, 196–7, 200; shipbuilding industry, 5–6, 8, 93, 96, Ch. 10 *passim*; marine engineering, 186, 189; merchant shipping, 186, 188–91, 196, 198; ship-repairing, 191; Joint Committee of Shipbuilders and Shipowners, 190; *see also* under names of individual companies

Shipbuilding Advisory Council (SAC), 192–7, 200, 202–4, 206–7

Shipbuilding Committee, 191–2, 199, 204–6

Shipbuilding Conference, 187; General Council of the Shipbuilding Conference, 190

Shipbuilding Costs Committee, 199

shipowners, 190–1, 194, 196–7, 199–202, 205–7; Joint Committee of Shipbuilders and Shipowners, 190

Shipowners' Association, 197

Shipyard Development Committee, 189

Shirley Institute, 157; *see also* research establishments

Skinningrove, 81, 83, 85

Society of British Aircraft Constructors (SBAC), 109

Society of Motor Manufacturers and Traders (SMMT), 8, 165–6, 168–70

South Durham and Cargo Fleet Group, 81, 83–6

Standard Motors, 109, 170–80

standardisation, 41, 162, 168, 171, 174, 189, 193, 199, 201, 203

Steel Co. of Scotland, 83

Steering Committee on Post-war Employment, 65

Stephen, Sir Murray, 193–4, 200–1, 205–6

Stewarts and Lloyds, 80, 83, 88

Strachey, John, 22

Strauss, George, 19, 96–7

Streat, Raymond, 140–7, 150–8

Supplies and Services (Defence Purposes) Act 1951, 26

Supplies and Services (Extended Purposes) Act 1947, 18

Supplies and Services (Transitional Powers) Act 1945, 18, 21–2

Sweden, 194–5, 200

Tanfield Steamship Co., 195

Target, 42

tariffs, 63, 83

taxation, 5–6, 8, 49, Ch. 7 *passim*, 163–5, 180, 201–2, 214, 220–4, 233; capital gains tax, 124, 129–30, 132–3; capital levy, 119; death duties, 119–20, 124, 132; entertainments tax, 229; incentives, 118–21; income tax, 117, 121, 123, 125; indirect, 121; National Defence Contribution, 117, 123; profits, 47, 117–32; purchase tax, 121, 138; Royal Commission on the Taxation of Profits and Income, 127, 129, 132; Special Contribution, 119–20; *see also* depreciation allowances

textile industry, 75, 78–80, 93; *see also* cotton and woollen industry

Thompson, R. C., 195

Thompson, Sir Vernon, 205

Thorneycroft, Peter, 56, 68

timber, 192, 195, 202

tobacco, 93, 121

trade associations, 2, 8, 28–9, 39, 41, 48–50, 56–60, 62–4, 67–8, 108–9, 139–40, 146, 152, 154, 159, 187; *see also* under individual trade associations

trade unions, 40, 42–3, 92, 100, 107, 125, 127, 131, 137, 139, 146–9, 151–2, 154,